Playing
Through

Also by Curtis Gillespie

FICTION
The Progress of an Object in Motion

NON-FICTION
Someone Like That

Playing Through

A Year of Life and Links
Along the Scottish Coast

CURTIS GILLESPIE

Scribner

First published in Great Britain by Scribner in 2002
An imprint of Simon & Schuster UK Ltd
A Viacom company

1 3 5 7 9 10 8 6 4 2

Simon & Schuster UK Ltd
Africa House
64–78 Kingsway
London WC2B 6AH

Simon & Schuster Australia
Sydney

www.simonsays.co.uk

A CIP catalogue for this book is available from the British Library.

ISBN: 0-7432-0925-7

Golf clubs Illustration by Liane Payne

Typeset in Garamond by M Rules
Printed and bound in Great Britain
by The Bath Press, Bath

For my mother, Pat,
and my siblings, Bruce, Keith, Conor, Janine and Matthew

Part One

you deadhead a memory and two more appear
longer and deeper and more alive than the last

'All Our Wonders Unavenged'
Don Domanski

1

In my mind, the story always begins in my bedroom, in 1987, in a flat at 2 Alfred Place, St Andrews, when I awoke to find my narrow, messy bed had not its usual one occupant, but two. Moving slowly and quietly, I propped myself up on one elbow to have a peek. She wasn't much to look at, really; over-tall, gaunt, cold to the touch, and with a stiff page of mustard-coloured hair. Not that I found her unattractive. Quite the opposite, and to prove my devotion I nuzzled up close, whispered sweetly into her ear, wondering huskily how we'd managed to come together under such unlikely circumstances. I placed my hand on her javelinesque waist, stroked along the racoon-like black and white stripes of her skin. Haughty and distant – the way she'd been from the start, in truth – she chose to say nothing. *Go ahead, be fickle*, I thought, running a hand through my messy, longish hair. *You're the same as the other seventeen.* I rolled over and away from her, scanned my bedside table for my clock, found it, and discovered I was late for lunch, let alone breakfast. I also found, beside the clock, a small sheaf of paper – perhaps thirty sheets – and a handful of envelopes. The notepaper was light blue in colour, highly elegant, of a sophisticated grain. There looked to be an emblem confidently embossed at the top of each sheet of stationery. Picking up a single page, I saw the words *Royal and Ancient Golf Club* curled above the scalp of a heraldic logo, and *St Andrews* beneath the chin. It seemed golf had been involved in acquiring this paper (as well as my bedmate). A match, possibly, the day before between the University of St Andrews Varsity Golf Team, on which I played, and the Royal and Ancient Golf Club of St Andrews, known to the world as the R&A.

I looked down at the paper again. I had no idea how I'd ended up with the stationery, and it seemed a good bet the answer wasn't going to enhance my reputation in the better circles about town. Swinging my feet out of bed, the damp chill of March on the east coast of Scotland – which being indoors did not parry in the least – speared at my legs and torso. I reached for a T-shirt, put it on, and glanced back into my bed. My naked, steely companion ignored me. She was as stiff and uncommunicative as a long steel pole; this did not come as a surprise, since she was, in fact, a long steel pole. Flinging back the bedsheets, I removed the pole and leaned it against the wall, at which point its coarse page of plastic yellow hair uncurled to reveal a home address. A large black 1 beside a large black 8. This flagpole had been torn – presumably by me – from its home, the green on the final hole of the hallowed Old Course. It's a big field, really, the 18th hole, but a field rumpled with humps and mounds and swales, and the massive weight of its own history, and which concludes at the green fronted by the Valley of Sin. This is perhaps the most recognisable, most consecrated, spot in all golf. I considered the flagstick leaning in such a slatternly way against the wall, and felt my blood thinning, felt the need to sit down. I might as well have snuck into the Galleria dell'Academia in Florence and snapped the privates off Michelangelo's *David*.

Something moved in the dregs of my memory, and I tried to tease out a coherent string of events. Too much alcohol had been involved, it was clear. I thought hard, concentrated even, but in the same way you get tyres and shopping trolleys when you dredge a lake looking for a body, so the night before emerged from the deep in muddy clumps of apparently unrelated imagery, each of which drew a cringe: walking down South Street and seeing my short, curly-haired friend Simon grabbing some poor dog by the testicles, and saying, 'Oy, oy, 'ow's that then?' My taller, spotty, red-headed friend George, who also played on the golf team, attempting, and failing, to clear a car park full of cars in the heaving of some sort of spear (my bedmate, perhaps). The team's best golfer, Mike, banging on the door of the local curry house deep into the night because he was so desperate for a vindaloo. Me, belching softly, loosening the knot of a tie while slumped geriatrically in a deep leather chair. This must have been a dinner at the Royal and Ancient after the match. Few other occasions could incite the wearing of a tie.

I got dressed, brushed the malt-flavoured algae off my teeth and tongue, and went downstairs to use the phone. Jane, then one of my flatmates and still a dear friend, regarded me with immediate amusement. I sat down beside her. A fellow golfer, and a member of the Ladies' Team, Jane was not averse to a drink every now and then, and so I reasoned that if anyone was inclined to be sympathetic, it ought to be her. I was mistaken. She brushed a strand of black hair away from her eyes. 'Got what you deserved, looks like to me.'

'I woke up with the flagstick from the eighteenth green of the Old Course in bed with me.'

Jane actually kicked her heels in the air as she snorted with laughter. 'Oh, that's brilliant!' she exclaimed. 'That's too rich. You are a marked man, my friend.'

'I don't think anyone saw.' I rested in my palms the pulsating bowling ball that was my head. 'What time did I get in? Do you know?'

In the years following her graduation, Jane went on to work very reputably in the world of high finance, and even at school she was nothing if not a confident and accurate dispenser of information. 'I got in at about two. Your door was still open, the room empty. Nick and Sue were already asleep. I read for thirty minutes, fell asleep fifteen minutes after that. No sign of you to that point, I'm afraid.'

'I have to phone George or Gareth, maybe Mike.' I looked at my watch. 'Two. They'll be up.'

'No, they won't,' laughed Jane. 'They're bigger piss-ups than you! Anyway, I'm off. Tee time at half-two . . . on the Old Course. You'd better get that flag back in the green by the time I come through eighteen. I want to know where I'm aiming.' She waited for me to raise my miserable head before peeling off another ripple of laughter. She had very good teeth, I noticed with some bitterness.

Gareth's phone was busy – his roommates, I reasoned – so I sought out Mike next. As the Number One player on the team, and the only one with any real talent, Mike was looked upon with some awe by the rest of us. A long-hitting left-hander, Mike is now a high-ranking executive with IMG, the company that represents Tiger Woods. His phone was busy. He was still asleep, of that I was sure. He'd been one of the most serious drinkers the night before, and for a man as skinny as he was then, he could drink all night.

George was my next best bet. As a long-time consumer of considerable amounts of ale, George had the ability to attain a certain level of inebriation very quickly and then maintain that level throughout the night, no matter how much he drank. In this way, he often claimed, he could be a sociable and relatively articulate evening's companion, all while getting utterly and comprehensively 'pished'. I knew this to be the truth. I'd come to the University of St Andrews in 1986 to do a doctorate in history, and hadn't known a soul upon arriving. My second week there, I tried out for, and made, the Varsity Golf Team, which was where I'd met George and Gareth. They were two of the most amiable people I'd ever met, and two of the biggest drinkers. The phone continued to ring, which was no surprise, since I was not really expecting George to answer. As I was about to replace the phone on its cradle, a startled 'Hello?!' sprang from the other end.

'George?'

'Yeah.'

'You're up.'

'Yeah . . . well, it's two in the afternoon.'

'You don't sound hungover.'

'. . . yeah . . . who's this anyway?'

'Curtis.'

There was a short stretch of emptiness coming from the other end of the line, and for a moment I thought we'd been disconnected, but a low chuckle soon began gurgling from my earpiece. 'Fuck me sideways,' he muttered. 'You were fabulous, mate.'

'I hardly remember a thing.'

'Not me. I remember it all. Every last ugly, bloody minute of it all.'

I wondered why he didn't sound hungover. 'I remember Simon grabbing a dog by the testicles. And I remember you chucking something across the parking lot. I think it might have been the flagstick from the eighteenth green of the Old Course.'

George released his trademark high-pitched cackle. 'You're the one that nicked it, boyo. Right off the green. Sprinted through the

Valley of Sin practically fucking brandishing it. It was fucking brilliant.'

A queasy feeling began to drip from the lining of my stomach. I grilled George further about my behaviour and the behaviour of the group in general. I also mentioned the notepaper to him. He did not know how I'd come into possession of it, but when I asked him who I'd played in the matches earlier in the day, the name he uttered unlocked the sequence of events.

'Robert Burns.'

He was not referring to the famous Bard of Scotland, but a Royal and Ancient member who'd been my opponent earlier in the day. A genial man and a capable golfer, he'd cleaned my clock on the course and then plied me relentlessly with drink before, during and after dinner. He had also offered me a tour through the stunning rooms of the Royal and Ancient clubhouse. The R&A, like many of the elite golf clubs in Scotland, is a bastion of money, misogyny and snobbery, but these are merely global criticisms. On a local footing, I liked Mr Burns and was frankly overawed by the history and utter absolute golfness of the building itself. It was then, and is even more today, a symbol throughout the world of where golf had come from (and, less wonderfully, about who gets to make the rules). I'd eagerly agreed to the tour. We'd made our leisurely way through room after room crammed full of leather chairs, tables crowded with books and newspapers, bookshelves ten feet high overflowing with every imaginable text on golf, and oil portraits everywhere of the greats of the game's history. The primary sensory impressions were the clubby comfort of oak-panelled walls, the squeak of leather chairs and the scent of hair oil on elderly male scalps. The central lounge looked straight out on to the 1st tee and 18th green of the Old Course, the game's Mecca. It was a kind of journey through the heart of golf and I was entranced.

Mr Burns had loaded me up with an abundance of club para-phernalia – pamphlets, brochures, even a small history of the club – but at one point on our tour, he ducked into the washroom, and while I waited in the hall for him to emerge I noticed, on a small oak stand, a large stack of writing paper and envelopes with the blue richly textured R&A logo embossed across the top. The only thought I had time for was that my father would be thrilled to have a letter composed on the official notepaper of the Royal and Ancient Golf Club of St Andrews. Just as I slipped a few pages and a couple of envelopes into my other papers, Mr Burns abruptly emerged from the washroom and saw me staring at the paper goods.

'Ah, yes, the club notepaper,' he said, waving a dismissive hand at the stack. 'Take all you like.'

It would have been suspicious to say no, so, purple with shame, I crammed a few more pages in amongst the raft of material he'd given me, down where I'd stashed the paper I'd nicked.

'You can write a letter to someone,' he said, smiling broadly.

'My father would love a letter from here,' I said, 'on this letter-head. He'll get a kick out of that.'

'Golfs, does he?'

'He doesn't play much any more, but he'd love to visit here. We've talked about coming over on a trip some day.'

'He golfs and he's never been here?'

I shook my head.

'That's criminal. You must rectify that.'

'I hope to.'

'You bring him along. We'll all have a game.'

We shook hands and I left Mr Burns. The rest of the golf team were just putting on their jackets when I met up with them in the foyer. We mingled for a moment, and then I claimed an urgent need for the washroom. I excused myself momentarily, found my way back to the scene of my crime, and returned my ill-gotten notepaper to the immaculate stack, keeping what Mr Burns had given me. When I rejoined the golf team, we exited the R&A, and carried on to the Jigger Inn. We met up with some other friends who were not part of the golf team, and then we all went forward to the Whey Pat Tavern, and from there . . .

I rang off from George. Back upstairs in my room, I took my notepaper in hand. It was so beautiful, existing merely as a single sheet of paper. It seemed like a piece of artwork in itself. Already I was imagining the pleasure it would be to sit down and write to my father on this paper. I would tell him about the golf courses. I would tell him about the state of my own game, which was then excellent (though it has not reached those heights since). I would describe the old stone buildings, and the pubs, and the gnarled caddies who populated those pubs. There was so much to talk about, though it wasn't until I'd nearly finished the letter that I realised the one thing I'd not discussed at all was my studies or my supervisor. I do not remember whether I consciously decided to omit a report on my studies, but I had a reason for avoiding it.

Two weeks after my night out with Mr Burns and the golf team, and just a week after I'd written to my father on the R&A letterhead, I travelled to Oxford to visit a friend from Edmonton who was also doing a doctorate in history. She was to give a presentation on her studies, the topic of which I've lost in the mists of time and inattention. Afterwards, during a discussion in the bar, her supervisor seemed to take an intense interest in my topic, which was to marry biography and intellectual history. I was going to focus on a man named James Oswald, a Scot, who'd been

Commissioner of the Treasury in the early years of the reign of George III, but who, more importantly, had been a confidant and intellectual sparring-partner of both the philosopher David Hume and the economist Adam Smith, the two towering figures of the Scottish Enlightenment. After my friend's talk that evening, Professor Grouse asked me if I might come round to his office the next day, so that he could hear more on what I planned to do with a figure as interesting and woefully understudied as Oswald. I was flattered and nervous: flattered because he appeared to be taking me seriously; nervous because I was not yet confident that I knew enough about Oswald to discuss him in the chambers of an Oxford don.

The next day, Grouse and I chatted amiably around the topic for a quarter of an hour or so. I mentioned a huge archive of unstudied material in Devon that I'd seen before Christmas. He nodded, apparently impressed, and then cut straight to the point he wanted to make. 'Look,' he said. 'I think this is a superb topic, and I'd be happy to supervise it myself, down here. What would you think about that? What would you make of transferring to Oxford?'

I was momentarily stunned, unable to take in information of this type. *Oxford.* Yes, perhaps it betrayed a certain vestigial colonial awe in my make-up, but to me the names Oxford and Cambridge still carried a totemic power. They were just words, but it's foolish to admit that words don't matter. Attending Oxford over St Andrews was never going to make me a better or worse academic or teacher, yet I was immediately stung by the temptation.

'We can make it happen rather easily,' said Grouse offhandedly. 'We only need to make certain that it's acceptable to two people, those two people being you and your supervisor, which is Professor Crabnook, isn't it?' He paused briefly. 'Interesting chap, Crabnook.'

The clarity of my brilliant future turned ever-so-slightly milky. Yes, Crabnook. In St Andrews. I knew him well enough now to understand, intuitively, without even thinking it, that he was going to be a problem. He could be helpful and cheerful one day, and then insulting and dismissive the next. I never knew whether he considered me worthy of his time or the time of the graduate History Department, or whether he even considered me of sufficient intelligence to be attending university at all. He was, and still is, a respected academic. His work on Scottish history is well-read and well-respected, and he remains one of the world's foremost scholars on the Jacobite uprisings of '15 and '45. Yet as soon as Grouse stipulated that his consent was required, my guts contracted.

'Let me talk to him first,' I said to Grouse. 'I can't honestly say how he'll react. But, yes, in theory I'd like to do my doctorate here.'

'Good,' said Grouse, smiling as he stood. He held out a hand, which I took. 'I'll work on the assumption that you'll be my student here starting next autumn. Leave the paperwork to me. I'll leave the rest with you and wait for word as to when I'm to proceed.'

I stepped out of Grouse's office believing the heavens had opened for me alone, that some deity had elected me to receive the greatest possible fortune. How could it be, I wondered. How could I possibly deserve this?

Of course, I didn't deserve it. This was obviously the case, because it didn't happen. How could I have known that Grouse would be unable to hold himself to his word? And that an ambush awaited me back in St Andrews?

X

There was nothing so terribly odd about a note from Professor Crabnook in my mailbox at the History Department. He wasn't the most attentive adviser I could have imagined, but he did attempt to contact me occasionally, though as often as not it involved wanting to get out and play a game of golf. Part of me always suspected that the only reason he ever talked to or about me was because I happened to play on the Varsity Golf Team. But his note, which I picked up just a day or two after arriving back from Oxford, was free of information, save that he wished to see me in his office the next day after lunch. This suited me, since I thought it would be better to discuss Oxford sooner rather than later.

I arrived at the door of his office the next day. It wasn't unusual to hear him muttering about one thing or another behind the door, and this was the case today. The first time I'd been confronted with this noise, back in October, I assumed he'd been hectoring a student, and waited for twenty minutes before realising it was a monologue, a kind of self-stimulating filibuster. For all I knew, he might not have even known he was audible. I knocked firmly.

The door snapped open and there he was, with his greying wire-brush hair and flat eye-sockets, which contained eyeballs that tended to gaze in different directions. The world has an image of the eccentric British academic: the rumpled corduroy blazer, the solipsistic behaviour, the scattershot personal hygiene. There are reasons this image retains its currency beyond the cliché, and I had one of them before me. Or rather, I was before one of them.

'Gillespie,' he said. 'Sit down.'

I sat as directed, and was prepared to open right away with Dr Grouse and Oxford, but Crabnook immediately began to question me about my topic, about my preparation to do a doctorate, about my commitment to scholarship in general. 'Are you really sure you want this?' he said aggressively, jabbing a finger at his bookshelves and the walls of his office, to indicate, I supposed, the academic life.

'Yes,' I said, hearing a quaver in my voice. 'Of course.'

He walked around from behind his desk and sat on the edge of it, so that he was both close to, and above me. I thought I could smell his body odour, a sharpish stink reminiscent of day-old peeled onion skins. 'I don't think you do. And you're not going to get it from me. I won't have students running around behind my back. I won't have it. And I won't have substandard students associated with my name. It isn't going to happen. Do you think I'll just bring students here from all over the world, do all that work, do people all kinds of favours, and then just let them scamper down to Oxford? Not on your bloody life.'

'Dr Crabnook . . . How?'

He raised a hand, palm outward. 'Grouse phoned me.'

'What?'

'Ah, yes, didn't quite work out the way you'd planned, did it? Well, he said he thought about it and thought he ought to phone me first as a professional courtesy.'

'He told me he'd let me talk to you first.'

'His actions indicate otherwise.'

I looked at the floor and when I brought my gaze back up, Crabnook had returned to his seat behind the desk. 'Of course, I told him I wouldn't release you, and that you weren't worthy of St Andrews, let alone Oxford, not that one's superior to the other, mind you. In any case, I believe he's changed his opinion about you and your topic.'

'That's not true.'

'That's my opinion, which is what matters. I don't think you'll be finishing your doctorate here, either . . . Let me see . . .' He paused and pretended to shuffle through some papers on his desk, though it was transparently a moment he was taking to gauge my reaction, which was to say nothing and glance out of the window. It was a stunning day, calm, sunny, wonderfully warm for March. In the letter I'd written to my father just the week before I'd mentioned to him how you could almost see the R&A from the History buildings, they were that close. It ought to have been a devastating moment, and I suppose I wasn't too comfortable, but my heart was not racing, my ears were not flushing scarlet.

'Right, yes,' Crabnook continued softly, as if talking to himself. 'You asked me before Christmas, didn't you, if you could transfer the Oswald archive up here? So you could work here, instead of out in the field?' He paused and then directed as withering a glare as he could muster, which wasn't much, given that his eyes looked in different directions. 'It's as I've thought pretty much right from the first. You're just not cut out for it. Anyway, just so the year isn't a waste for you, I'm quite certain that we can get an M.Phil. out of this for you. A Masters you call it. That would be something anyway.' He stopped and stared at me. His lack of height and the weird flatness of his eye sockets, combined with the slightly eggy texture of his eyeballs and the failing light inside the room, made him appear almost alien, otherworldly. I put a hand to my forehead, and it was just two cold pieces of skin meeting. I stood up.

'Let me know,' he said, as I went to his door, 'whether you want to do this M.Phil. thing or not.' He paused and loudly cleared his throat. 'I won't be supervising you, of course.'

I spoke with the head of the department, the esteemed J. P. Kenyon, who was quite sympathetic in private, but pronounced himself unable to act on the matter in any formal way, except to see about effecting a transfer. There was no way to stay at St Andrews, because in that small department there was no historian other than Crabnook with any knowledge of the period I was studying. The problem with trying to transfer, as Kenyon saw it, was that there was really nowhere for me to go. When I called Grouse in Oxford a couple days after my session with Crabnook, he claimed to be upset about the whole thing, though his consternation did not translate into any sort of action. He couldn't follow through now, because to do so would be to completely alienate a fellow scholar, namely Crabnook. He was not going to be known, he said, as a 'student poacher' and would not proceed without Crabnook's approval, which was manifestly not forthcoming.

Sympathy was spread over the affair like Cornish double cream across a scone, but no one raised a formal hand against Crabnook. His pride, both personal and academic, had been injured, and in the process I'd aroused what I perceived as his instinctual Scots antipathy towards the English. With me, he was choosing to make a point. And in the realm of adviser/student relations the British system mirrors that of the island's still tangible class system. There are those who have power, and those who do not.

I chose not to do the M.Phil. because I did not want to study in a place where I knew I would soon be leaving. And in any case, an M.Phil. was, in academic circles, universally recognised as a failed Ph.D., or at least the consolation prize of someone unable to complete a doctorate. I didn't want that on my record. Yet nor could I just leave town. It was only March. I was supposed to be in school until the late spring, and to go home now simply because there was nowhere else to go would have been doubly humiliating. And so I stayed in St Andrews. I went to Macgregor's Café on Market Street every day where I sat with my pen and pad of A4 paper, and began to work on the series of short stories that would eventually become my first book. Revenge, failure, humiliation and self-pity are useful tools for the writer, and though it would still be many years before I published my first short story, it was in Crabnook's office that I unhooked academic bait from my line and started casting instead for my true love: writing. I stayed in St Andrews until June and though I formally remained a member of the History Department, I wrote fiction the entire time (most of which has mercifully met the bin). It felt right to stay. After the initial shock wore off, it felt even as if I was being directed by a force that knew my own heart better than I did. I stayed, happy to do so, happy to be free to do what I'd always wanted to do, which was write. Besides, there was still golf to be played.

Yet there was a deeper truth behind the dramas and personalities: despite the actions of Professor Crabnook – who, on top of everything else, was a spectacularly and uniquely incompetent golfer despite decades of effort and regular play – the truth is that it ultimately was not his fault that I failed at history, though I did blame him. (Not that I ever learned to blame myself, either; accepting responsibility for a failure of that magnitude was beyond the scope of my admittedly biased self-interpretation.) In truth, Crabnook merely hastened the inevitable. The bridge that collapsed ran between myself and history; or if not history itself, then in the dust and cobwebs of that which comprises real historical enterprise, namely, primary research. I have always found it odd, in retrospect, that I didn't warm to primary research, since I am at heart an empiricist. This is what drew me to history in the first place. Any combination of persuasive writing and meticulous research always impressed me to the core, so that historians like Simon Schama (before he became a pop culture star), John Brewer, Carl Berger, Robert Darnton, David Cannadine, Linda Colley, and Donald Creighton were my draw. My good friend Philip Lawson (who has since passed away, much too young, from cancer) was a brilliant British Empire historian who steeped me in bedrock values about the craft of history, the most fundamental being that induction and empiricism were at the heart of any proper historical enterprise. In other words, conclusions could only be based on the available evidence. It's a wonderfully steady rudder in the heavy seas of history, though the waves of postmodern theory that have crashed through academia in the last fifteen years have made such a utilitarian instrument seem dull, almost quaint.

Nevertheless, it was inside this intellectual vehicle that I sped away to St Andrews to pursue a Ph.D., to write about Oswald and his relationships with Adam Smith and David Hume. The early years of the reign of George III fascinated me, and I had decided – as if all it took was a decision – that I was going to be a historian to remember, one who would cast new light on the relationship between the Scottish intellectual elite and the bamboo palace that was the British Empire. I was going to do it by combining elegant prose with faultless primary research. I left Canada carrying within me the belief that a solid, well-made chair never outlives its utility, no matter how many other pieces of postmodern furniture first captivate the eye.

Except that I didn't write much and detested primary research.

That's not quite the way it happened, of course. It would be better to say that I found primary research did not move me. Phil had told me before leaving Edmonton that I would know I was hooked the day I opened up that first box of old documents, swept away the dust, and held the passage of time in my very own hands. He was right that I would *know*, but he guessed wrong – and so did I – about *what it was* that I would know. The moment was emotional, not intellectual, and though it was terrible and shocking, it was also more sedate than you might think a life moment ought to be. Still, there is a clarity to this memory, the kind of clarity that people usually reserve for instances of severe personal humiliation or self-flagellation.

I should also add that this road-to-Damascus discovery did not even take place in Scotland, but in the heart of rural Devon. James Oswald's closest remaining relative was (and still may be for all I know) the Lady Daphne Butterfield, of Hillweather House, Devon. She had in her possession all of Oswald's personal papers, and made them available to me at not inconsiderable inconvenience to herself. Just before Christmas, she agreed to allow me into her home, where for a week she fed me, drove me around the countryside, kept me company, shared her family's history with me, and generally acted with such great good nature and hospitality that even today I regret not doing justice to the study of her heritage.

It was on the second day of my stay at Hillweather House that it happened. Lady Butterfield had set up a work area for me in the study of the east wing of the house. Her prim and greying Ladyship now lived on her own in Hillweather House, and she'd shut down part of the east wing and virtually the entire upper floors, since it was pointless to keep them open. Her children lived in various places throughout England, and her husband, Lord Butterfield, to whom she referred in only the most oblique and cheerless of phrasings, apparently resided in Morocco or Algeria. She provided little information about him, only to say that he still 'lived in England' but that he spent a great deal of time conducting 'business' in North Africa. She informed me that as it was approaching Christmas, there was every possibility he might show up at the house for the upcoming holiday season. It all seemed highly coded, and yet somehow emblematically English. And when I say 'house' it must be clear that I mean a structure with a square footage greater than the sum total of all the places I'd lived in my life to that point. Hillweather House was a sprawling eighteenth-century manor home, fronted by lush holly-green fields sloping gracefully towards the burbling silver stream that tacked its way back and forth along the valley floor. As I began to work my way through the papers of James Oswald, sheep grazed in a perfect visual cliché outside the window, and towards the latter part of my week there, a fox hunt actually made its baying, bloodthirsty way across the field on the opposite side of the valley. Such were the privileged surroundings of Lady Butterfield.

Before me, on a separate table from my work space, was a large safebox-style crate, with a brass latch Lady Butterfield had opened for me. Inside was a treasure trove of documents. Letters, note-books, diaries, sketches, accounting papers. The smell was intensely historical: dry, brittle, dusty, a little like long-faded sandalwood. The pages were the colour of parchment, mottled beige, stiff to the touch. This crate was a portal, a direct entry into the past. I did a brief visual inspection of what I could immediately see and touch, and then pulled out a letter. It was addressed to Oswald. 'My dear James,' it began. I immediately glanced to the bottom of the one-page letter to identify the sender. 'Regards, Your Friend, David Hume.'

In my hands was a letter from David Hume to James Oswald. I was holding an irreplaceable original document – one piece in a lifelong correspondence: here was Hume, the greatest Scottish philosopher, writing a letter to his good friend and billiards partner, James Oswald, Commissioner of the Treasury. Hume's handwriting was clear, the note was informal and friendly in tone, the topics of no real consequence, except to arrange a date to discuss matters of apparently greater importance. Yet there it was, my thesis in a nutshell. The influence of Oswald on the Empire and on the Scottish Enlightenment as put forward by David Hume and Adam Smith. Here in my hand was a letter involving two of the three principals, and it was 250 years old. It was, in my academic world order, priceless.

I read it through once more, made a notation on an index card, put the letter to one side and reached into the crate for the next piece of paper.

It wasn't until that evening, after a long day's work slogging through a mountain of documents, that I realised what had happened. I'd been so busy throughout the day – organising reams of material into camps, doing up index cards for each piece I found before reading it, taking notes of things that I knew would be important later on – that I'd hardly stopped to think about how this torrent of information and impressions had affected me. Laying in bed that night, I remembered Phil's words, his impassioned assertion that the moment would come when I'd be hooked, when the dusty pages in my hands would be rearranged into a compulsion in my brain and soul. Up to that point in the evening, all I could think about was how much work it was going to be just to get this raft of material sorted out before I could even begin to think about reading it all and directing it towards some kind of coherent academic process. But now Phil's words came back to me. *You'll know. You'll be hooked for ever.* With horror I realised that I was not hooked. I'd dipped a finger into the magic well and had removed it, unenchanted. The very touch of the Oswald–Hume correspondence had left my fingertips cold.

I lay in my bed until three in the morning, hands on my chest, staring at the ceiling, listening to myself breathing. I'd made a dreadful mistake, but how could I have known otherwise without coming here, without getting into the documents? I knew I had a problem. I did not make a decision to abandon my Ph.D. that night. There was still room, I thought feverishly to myself, there was still space for someone to become an academic, a good academic, without having a passion for it. In this I was wrong, but it took another couple of months – until my Oxford confrontation with Crabnook – for me to fully understand that I didn't have it in me.

I got up the next morning and went back to the desk Lady Butterfield had prepared for me, where I put my hand back in the crate, pulled out a document and then another and then another, carefully categorising and making notes. I did this all day, keeping the hearth of my brain warm, while not yet fully aware that the fire in my heart had gone out.

Just before 5pm, Lady Butterfield poked her head into the office and asked if I'd like to come and have a glass of sherry in the library.

'Yes,' I said, smiling with genuine weariness. 'That would be very nice.'

Once settled in the large, leather chairs, with the fire roaring beyond the head-high mantel, she mentioned that she was expecting her husband to return home virtually any minute. He'd phoned that afternoon from London, she explained, having decided to return from North Africa for the holidays.

'And,' she continued, 'I believe he may have his boy with him.' She took a pinched sip of her sherry, as if merely practising the movement for future applications.

'Boy?'

'Yes,' she said flatly, leaving me with not a single clue as to how I was to take that: manservant, Jeeves, driver, special friend. I never found out. We finished our sherry, talking about Margaret Thatcher and South African Prime Minister P. W. Botha, both of whom struck me as fairly execrable human beings (one even more so than the other), but whom Lady Butterfield described as 'strong people, the kind of people this world needs'. I didn't believe myself to be in a position to enter into any arguments, so I withdrew, vaguely muttering something about being raised in a liberal household. She rose to get dinner, and, as if on cue, there was a clatter from the front hallway.

Lady Butterfield stopped at the library doorway and turned her head like a hound catching a scent. Her nostrils were taut, twitching. 'That'll be Alastair.' She exited the library but did not go towards the entrance. Instead, she went off to the kitchen. I sat in a heightened state of awareness, feeling deeply out of my element. What if Lord Butterfield was to come straight into the library? Had Lady Butterfield even told him I was here? What if his 'boy' came in first? And who was his 'boy' anyway? There are mysteries to marriage; I know this now. Yet then, in my mid-twenties, I realised I was so far removed from any understanding of what might comprise these individual lives, and of what connected them, that I think it's fair to say a week in the Butterfield mansion helped me choose to make my first book a work of fiction. Many of my first clumsy attempts involved characterisations of the Butterfields, merely so that I could try to give some shape to my imaginings of what must be going on behind the doors of this relationship.

The library door creaked open, and into the room came a loud confident sniffing sound, like that of someone just finishing off a stupendous line of coke. Lord Alastair Butterfield then entered. 'Good Lord!' he said upon seeing me, as if I were an old friend he'd not expected to come across.

I stood up and extended a hand. 'Curtis Gillespie,' I said, trying to concentrate purely on exposition. 'I'm a student, and I'm here researching James Oswald.'

He took my hand and amiably enveloped it in his own, much larger, hand. 'Oh! Yes. Gillespie. Gillespie. Certainly. Marvellous.' He nodded, paused, warmly angled his head to one side. 'And who, pray tell, is James Oswald?'

After dinner at Hillweather House, during which the only topic of conversation was the £28,000 purchase price of a new dining-room table, we returned to the library. I sat quietly in the corner, waiting to see what on earth these two people could possibly have to discuss. The answer was nothing, apparently, since Lady Butterfield and I sat staring at the crackling fire for an excruciatingly lengthy period that turned out to be four minutes when I glanced at the clock. Lord Butterfield was reading *The Times*, and made a racket like rippling sheets of tinfoil every time he turned the page, fanning the pages out to their extremities, stretching them taut, before attempting never less than three times and often as many as five or six to locate the crease from beneath with his knee so that he might neatly reduce the paper back to a readable condition. He was so preposterously oblivious to the presence of other human life that such powers of snubbery could only have been achieved through intent, practice, and concentration. Lady Butterfield watched him throughout, her spine stiff against the back of her chair. She turned and looked at the far wall, saw something to her displeasure, got out of her chair, went to the wall, and fiddled with the frame of a painting, repeatedly and exasperatedly attempting to find a true line for the top edge.

'Oh, just leave it, won't you,' said Lord Butterfield, giving his paper a rather more severe rattling than had been his practice to that point.

She turned and glared at him as if he were a servant who'd challenged her, as if she did not expect to be spoken to.

'Oh, just sit the bloody hell down,' continued Lord Butterfield. 'I say, when are the children coming around, anyhow?'

She sat down, and seemed to find it impossible to look at him. 'I believe David is returning tomorrow.'

I perked up at this news. Another Butterfield added to the mix! I was scheduled to stay another few days, and began to wonder excitedly about what I might soon be witnessing. It was beyond the powers of my imagination to picture it.

'Tomorrow,' he muttered, as if greatly disappointed. 'Excellent. Good to see the young chap. How is he?'

'You could phone him, you know.'

He ignored this and pulled a small metallic case from a waistcoat pocket. When he'd prised it open I could see inside, but was only able to make out what looked to be finely ground espresso, or perhaps a bit of sphagnum an avid fisherman might keep worms in. He dipped a thumb and forefinger into the tin and produced a pinch of the material – snuff, I now understood – which he placed on his other hand, lowering it precisely into that small cup of skin joining the thumb and the forefinger. He took the tin from that hand, and then put his nose so close to the pile that he might have been touching it with one nostril. Then, with an enormous inrush of air and a repeat of the snorting sound I'd earlier heard coming from the front hall, he made the pile disappear directly up his nose, hoovering up loose grounds in the aftershock. Replacing the tin in his waistcoat, he looked back up at us, and appeared to be stunned, practically high.

'Ugh,' said Lady Butterfield, twisting her face with disgust. 'I keep thinking you're going to give that up.'

He shook his head. 'I've no major vices,' he said hoarsely but quietly. I was surprised, for some reason, that this statement went unchallenged. 'I believe,' he continued, 'that a man needs his minor vices, otherwise he invites real evil, genuine degeneration. Don't you think, Craig?'

'It's Curtis,' said Lady Butterfield sharply. 'And I would suggest we do not begin discussing what you, of all people, do and do not consider a vice.'

I opened my mouth to assure Lord Butterfield I was not insulted by the name Craig, but I was prevented from speaking by the sight of a black earthworm that began to wriggle out of his nose. It shone like a new bead of crude oil, but was really just snot.

The slimy scrawl of viscous black fluid began quite visibly working its way out of his left nostril and progressing towards his mouth as he spoke. It reached, and then began to pool treacherously, on the shelf of his upper lip. I silently thanked him for not having a moustache, but it was all too much for Lady Butterfield. She stood. 'Alastair, wipe your nose. It's positively revolting.'

Lord Butterfield quickly removed a hankie from a side pocket and covered most of his face with it. Lady Butterfield quit the room, her steps clip-clopping rapidly away down the long hall outside the library. Blowing hard and repeatedly, Lord Butterfield seemed to empty no less than a couple of tablespoons of semi-solid matter into his hankie, a hankie that may once have been white but which through decades of miscegenation had become spotted like a giraffe. I wondered if he'd ever cleaned it. Finally he removed the hankie from his face, crumpled it into a moist ball, then ran it ten or fifteen times across his septum. Satisfied, he plunged the hankie back into his pocket and looked to where his wife had just been sitting. He seemed surprised she'd left the room, but he turned to me, unleashed a brilliantly devious grin, and then actually winked. I was helpless to do anything but giddily return his grin. That night, I lay in bed thinking that the study of history, valid and necessary as it was, paled beside an ongoing investigation of living creatures such as the ones I was currently under the same roof with. I didn't quite know it then, but I was done with history.

It was in this frame of mind that I sat down at Macgregor's Café on Market Street in St Andrews to write to my father on my exquisite R&A paper. I'd yet to have my blow-up with Crabnook, but I had to have known somewhere inside me that I was going to fail sooner or later at this historical enterprise, an enterprise that had meant so much to my parents, only one of whom, my mother, had even finished High School. They were proud that I was operating at this level of schooling. Two days before I'd left Canada to go to Scotland, my father presented me with money to help with my living expenses. Smiling, he simply passed into my hand a mountainous wad of cash. 'Work hard,' he said. It was thirty one-hundred dollar bills. It was an enormous amount of money, particularly for my parents, but they seemed delighted to give it to me. And never once after my return did they suggest or hint at any feelings of disappointment or resentment that I'd wasted their money, though that didn't stop me from feeling guilty.

I'd not been working that hard into the New Year, and had seen very little of Crabnook. I was wondering about when I ought to get down to Devon again to see the manuscripts, and was waiting to hear about having them moved to St Andrews. I suppose I may have mentioned these things in the letter I wrote to my father, though I don't remember if I did or not. I can't check because we can't find the letter; my mother was unsure if he kept it, and it wasn't amongst his things we sorted through after he died. But I do remember describing to him in rich detail the town of St Andrews, its glorious stonework, the ruins of the cathedral, and the wonderful simplicity of my favourite pub, the Whey Pat Tavern. I spent pages telling him about the golf courses, and particularly the Old Course, and how it represented true golf, golf in its natural state. *It's the people's game over here*, I told him, *not just the preserve of the wealthy*, knowing that would strike a chord with his lower-middle-class upbringing and egalitarian beliefs.

I also mentioned the recent and memorable trips I'd made to the East Lothian town of Gullane, once with the golf team to play a match on the Gullane No. 1 golf course, the second time with a friend on the golf team, David Walker, to play Muirfield, the home course of The Honourable Company of Edinburgh Golfers. After just two trips, Gullane had already become one of my favourite places in the world. The same was true for the

Reverend John Kerr, one of East Lothian's great historians as well as one of its great historical figures. In his monumental 1896 study of golf in the area, *The Golf Book of East Lothian* (a book to be passionate about, so crammed to its bindings is it with tales, facts, opinions, mountains of utterly useless information, and the garrulously confident voice of its author), Kerr wrote that at the end of the nineteenth century East Lothian was 'the garden of the game . . . a feast which ought surely to satisfy the most Gargantuan golfing appetite'. After reiterating the greatest names of the golfing day who had spent considerable time along that impossibly delightful coastline – Old Tom Morris, Young Tom Morris, Old Willie Park, Old Mungo Park, Willie Park Jr, Alan Robertson, David Strath, Andrew Kirkcaldy, Bob Ferguson, J. H. Taylor, Harold Hilton, Jamie Dunn – the good Reverend, who never used a single short word when two longer ones would do, concluded that

we [in East Lothian] have thus been in the midst of golf from first to last. Here, if anywhere, has the genial influence of the great 'gulf stream' been felt. The fishing villages have become fashionable seaside resorts, and hundreds of acres, formerly useful for nothing but rearing rabbits, have become a great golf sanatorium . . . We have visitors from all the ends of the earth – princes, nobles, statesman, Lord Mayors, generals, merchants, and others who come here to play golf or to see it played, and among the golfing brotherhood there are few of any note who have not tested the qualities of our greens . . . In the propagation of the game East Lothian has been a missionary agent of great activity.

For scenery we place Gullane before any other green. It is said that from the top of the hill on a clear day you can see fourteen counties. Certainly at many points the outlook is grand, far-reaching, unsurpassable in interest and beauty. Mind and body are refreshed as the eye wanders over the Firth, sweetly silvered under the sunshine of a summer day. Beyond lie the green fields of Fife . . . eastward the busy ships carry the imagination with them to far-off lands as they disappear past Fidra and the Bass and the May [islands along the coast]; in the west the player notes away beyond Aberlady Bay the clear outline of Arthur's Seat, the massive arches of the Forth Bridge, and the lofty Lomond peaks. To the south, he has 'the garden of Scotland' in full bloom lying between the Links and the long Lammermoor Hills [*sic*], which bound the horizon on that side. Altogether it is a glorious sight.

Gullane, concluded Kerr, 'if its fine turf, its glorious scenery, and other features are taken into account, may be called the most enjoyable of all greens' (*green* then being the term used to indicate an entire golf course).

Kerr, though, must have been referring to idyllic summer days, because if it's true that the East Lothian coastline is in some places gentle and sandy (such as at Gullane), it's also true that in others it's rocky and cracked, fraught even, as if the land and the sea have been trying to overpower one another over the millennia. The water is frigid all year round, rarely blue and sometimes full of such a glowering intensity it takes on a plummy black colour. Multinationals drill for oil in the North Sea, but recreation in the water is dependent upon benign weather. In harsh storms children have been swept from piers and waves leap ashore as if they're frantically trying to escape the clutches of something evil under the water's surface. There are points of détente: the flat, marshy Local Nature Reserve at Aberlady Bay, just over Gullane Hill; the Gullane Bents (the beach); the North Berwick West Links beach.

But for the most part the land thumbs its nose at the sea, doing whatever it can to sabotage thoughts of a truce between elements. Rocky bluffs and jagged stone promontories glare seaward.

Ironically the crashing together of land and sea along this stretch of coastline instigated a geological evolution of terrain ideal for golf; from this space fit neither for agriculture nor housing has come a sand-packed, high-salinity linksland, the space Scots have termed the area between the land and the sea. It has become a seaboard (if you consider the east coast one line stretching from Dunbar through North Berwick, Muirfield and Gullane, then over the Firth of Forth to Elie, then up to Crail and St Andrews, then across the Tay Firth to Carnoustie, Montrose, Royal Aberdeen, Nairn and then on up across the Firths of Moray and Dornoch to Fortrose, Tain and Royal Dornoch) that is home to the world's most famous, most difficult and most beautiful golf courses. The sea, soil, sand and wind produced mounds and dunes and gullies and burns, fescues and buckthorn and gorse and heather, all key factors in a game that is nothing if not an exercise in the geometric avoidance of trouble. Above all, the elements combined to create a turf that only links courses can claim; a turf that is year-round firm, springy and energising to walk upon. Along this coast nature built a landscape full of beauty and pitfalls; the Scots of centuries past merely found an activity that suited the littoral topography, and called it golf. It all fit: a game meant for both a land and its people. Even John Updike was once moved to write that there was clearly 'a connection between the three salient features of Scotland: the beautiful wildness of much of its landscape, the austerity of its Presbyterian brand of Protestant Christianity, and its national passion for golf'.

'I want to come back here with you,' I wrote to my father, meaning it with hopeful sincerity. 'It would be fantastic to come here and play all these courses. You'd love them. We could play the courses around Fife. Then we could go up and play Royal Aberdeen and Montrose [where I'd played in the Scottish Universities Championship] and Cruden Bay. Then I'd want to take you down to Gullane and play the courses around there. It's stunning. We'll do it. We'll come back together.'

It would be wrong to say that I worshipped my father; that would imply a distance, an anti-relationship, that didn't exist. He was too much an active part of his children's lives for us to formally worship him, and so the thought of travelling with him was utterly appealing. For years thereafter, we talked about this trip, about travelling to Scotland to play golf together, possibly with some friends, possibly with one or two of my brothers. When I licked the back of the Queen's head and pasted my Royal Mail stamp on that equally regal R&A envelope, it seemed obvious to me that he and I would soon be making the first of what I'd hoped would be numerous trips, that we'd one day soon be teeing it up at St Andrews, or, even better, sitting in the Gullane clubhouse, looking out of the large bay windows as Gullane Hill in the near west swallowed up the last of the day's sun. I could already hear us bickering happily about the results of our match played over the austere perfection of the Gullane No. 1 course or perhaps even Muirfield. My father was just fifty-five. There was no reason to think we would never make it.

I slid my letter into the postbox at the heart of Market Street in St Andrews, smiling as I watched that red mouth of human communication swallow it up. I wondered if my father might show the letter to his friends who golfed, if he might hold the envelope and notepaper as I had, admiring its simple elegance, its historical import. I often hoped to impress him, to make him proud, to tell him I loved him without having to say the words, and I must have thought this was one of the ways I could achieve that. My mother told me, after he died, that he was proud of me long before I left for St Andrews and long after I came back. Yes, she told me, he'd enjoyed the letter, but it didn't signify anything more to him than the pleasing fact that he'd received mail from his eldest son studying abroad. And, of course, why should it have? I was reaching further than I needed to. I was trying to prove something for which he'd never requested or required proof.

2

It's best, most satisfying, if you say the words out loud. Gullane. Dirleton. Muirfield. Luffness. Archerfield. Musselburgh. Kilspindie. Longniddry. I love speaking these place-names, hearing their sounds. Even looking at the words on a map has always brought a smile to my lips. For a long time these words had been signifiers in my mind of something both real and fantastic, indicators of both past experience and future enjoyment. The memories raised were shot through with images of hole after hole of subtle, perfect links golf, though these memories were also always just a little bit hazy, involving as they did a sense of awe towards the natural splendour of this hidden stretch of coastline.

In 1987 I'd sat in Macgregor's Café on Market Street in St Andrews and written to my father, telling him that we ought to come here, to Scotland, to Gullane, but it wasn't until 1999, twelve years later, that I'd returned, not with my father, but with my friend, the writer Lorne Rubenstein. How, and why, had I left it this long? The last time I'd stood in the Gullane clubhouse had been with the University of St Andrews Golf Team in 1987. Twelve years? It seemed not just unfortunate, but irresponsible, wasteful.

Not that the intervening twelve years had been without merit. Far from it. I had worked for close to ten years in the social services, first operating housing programs for people with mental illnesses, and then for people with developmental disabilities, and along the way also received an accreditation to teach suicide prevention. It was after leaving these careers that I took up writing full-time, making a choice early on that I wanted to write both fiction and non-fiction.

Of course, it was during this time that Cathy and I got married. We had known one another years earlier at university, but had been dating other people. When I returned from studying abroad – no longer in a relationship – it seemed hard to believe that she was also unattached, and so I immediately asked her out. Using her most charming smile, she immediately said no. A sceptic the day she first drew breath, she took some persuading, but did in the end succumb to the inevitable. We married in 1992, and had Jessica in 1995.

And now, standing before me upon my first return in 1999, was the short, imperious form of Archie Baird. We were in the Back Bar (sometimes still called the 'dirty bar' by older members, referring to the fact that golf shoes are allowed inside), a cosy wood-panelled enclave that formed part of the Men's Locker Room. Lorne, Jack Marston and myself had been relaxing in one of the high-backed booths, already well into our second pint of 80 Shilling ale, and cheese and pickle toasties. Archie entered holding four or five ratty-looking old golf clubs that he dismissively tossed behind the bench seats of the booth. The clubs clattered against the wall, and Archie stood hands on hips, as if demanding to know precisely what form of deviousness we'd gotten up to in the five minutes he'd taken to change his shoes and place his golf clubs in the boot of his car. A short, compact man, Archie was a retired fourth-generation veterinarian who possessed the bearing of an army drill sergeant given to abusing underlings (though he'd actually flown with the RAF in the Second World War). The man looked as if he could still grapple a Hereford to the ground if needed, but his angina had worsened lately, and his breathing was hoarse and webby.

'Archie,' said Jack softly. 'Get yourself a drink, my friend.' Jack Marston was Archie Baird's oldest and dearest friend, and seemed a man deeply committed to never raising his voice. Archie brusquely ordered an 80 Shilling, then tried to pay for it. The barmaid pointed at Jack and grinned. Archie swung round and glared at Jack, false bile spilling from his lips. 'I told you not to do that, you old bugger.' Jack smiled, happy to have won the latest round in a contest that had been played out over decades. Archie deposited himself on the bench beside Jack and took a nettled gulp of his ale. Jack raised his glass, peered at the liquid inside it, then turned to Lorne and I. 'To new friends,' he said. 'Cheers, boys.'

We clinked glasses, sipped our beer, and agreed to play again as soon as possible. Lorne and I dissected our loss to Archie and Jack as they sat listening with great satisfaction. Clearly, we'd been sideswiped by this pair. Archie was seventy-five years old and Jack eighty-one, the two of them, as Updike once said of ageing golfers, 'warty old pickles blanching in the brine of time'. Warty pickles or not, Lorne and I had been conned. We had simply given them too many strokes, had been too sympathetic to their 156 years. Of course, being golfers, Lorne and I were nothing if not optimistic about our chances, no matter how many strokes this pair squeezed from us before starting. Golf, after all, is a game for closet optimists. You've got to believe something good will *eventually* happen, otherwise the game will drive you into the arms of the nearest prescribing psychiatrist. But Jack and Archie knew a few things we didn't. They knew the game, and they truly knew the course, having been members at Gullane for a hundred years between them. They knew before we started that they had us. I ought to have suspected as much on the 1st tee, an inconspicuous square of grass set literally on a street corner at the western entrance to town. It's a beautifully humble opening to a world golfing treasure.

'You first, my boy,' Jack had demurred.

I'd known Jack Marston for five minutes and already felt protective towards his grandfatherly nature, the cheeky smile and the dripping reddish nose that required almost constant nuzzling from a crusty handkerchief. Still stiff from the drive out from Edinburgh, I swung a little too briskly perhaps, but managed to meet the ball well enough. With some dismay, I watched it dive hard into the punishing westerly wind, squirrelling into the right fairway bunker. Jack peered so myopically into the distance I wondered why he even bothered to look. 'Where did that go? I'm afraid I can't see that far any more.'

'It went in the bunker. I can see it from here.'

'Oh, dear,' said Jack, touching his hankie to his nose, smiling mischievously. 'Isn't that a shame.' He jammed his hankie back into his pocket, and then bent over with some difficulty. For a moment I thought I might have to stick his tee in the ground for him. He did manage it, but was even less convincing about placing his ball on the tee; a ball, I might add, that looked as if it had been purchased during the same 1956 shopping trip on which he'd last purchased a hankie, a ball he had then used every day since. It was the colour of ignored porridge, and was scarred like a monster's skull. Even from where I stood, it was clearly out of round. But he swung with surprising fluidity – for any person, let alone an 81-year-old – and poked his drive about 150 yards straight down the middle of the fairway. He held his graceful post-impact position for no more than a second and a half before Archie – who was, in theory, Jack's partner – strode to the tee shouting at the top of his lungs, 'Stop admiring it, you old bugger, and get your arse out of my way!'

Jack adopted what I would learn over the next few hours was his natural expression, a kind of tolerant sweet-hearted grin. He looked at Lorne and I, as if to say, What shall I do with this man? He moved to let Archie tee off.

Archie is, in many ways, the definition of Gullane Golf Club. He's been a member for nearly fifty years, and when he married the doctor Sheila Park almost as long ago, he married into the bloodlines of one of the greatest families in Scottish, and therefore world, golfing history: the Parks of Musselburgh. Willie Park Sr won the first Open Championship played at Prestwick in 1860 (then again in 1863, 1866 and 1875). His brother, Old Mungo, also won the Open, in 1874 at Musselburgh. Willie Sr had many children, including Willie Jr and Young Mungo. Willie Park Jr won the Open in 1887 at Prestwick and again in 1889 at Musselburgh. One of the greatest golfers of his day, Willie Jr also worked with great success in club and ball construction, golf course design, and even golf writing. Young Mungo (Willie Park Jr's brother) was Sheila Park's grandfather, meaning that the very first winner of the Open Championship at Prestwick in 1860, Willie Park Sr, was Sheila's great-grandfather. There are few links to the game's history more direct than this.

Archie has served as Captain of Gullane Golf Club (where Sheila is a member of the influential Gullane Ladies' Golf Club), he's written a delightful book, *Golf on Gullane Hill*, that charts some of the history and personalities of Gullane Golf Club, and, as if all that wasn't enough, he owns and operates a golf museum right next to the Pro Shop, within chipping distance of the 1st tee. Archie also seemed to me the personification of the Scottish temperament (unlike Jack, who was born and raised in England, but has lived in Gullane since after the Second World War). He can seem abrupt, even rude at times, but underneath lurks a generous and kindly heart. First-time visitors to Scotland, even those fore-warned, are often surprised at how churlish the Scots can seem, but it's not that they are an unfriendly people. Quite the opposite. Scots are among the most gregarious and good-natured people on earth . . . once they learn you aren't English. The Scot is like a lump of coal; unlit it's a bit cold and rough around the edges, but once set alight it glows from inside, providing deep and authentic warmth.

The Scots come by their pinched temperament honestly. If you lived in Scotland, you would understand. The constant wind; the lack of sunshine; Julys like January; Januarys like January; cen-turies of either being conquered, ignored, or having their sovereignty tampered with. The Scottish scowl is not meanness but a defence, a closed gate that opens easily when the conditions allow it. Their climate and history have taught them that if they let down their guard for a minute, marauders will invade or the ele-ments will sweep them off into the ocean. They must be forever ready to fend off invasion, flood, downpour, wind, famine, English pretension, and rising green fees. Smile? Best not to until all the facts are in. It's just common sense, and there never was a Scot who did not possess common sense in (he will tell you) exactly the right degree. And so, once all the depositions are in and the wit-nesses have been heard, once it can be proven that you are no Trojan Horse, you will have a friend for life in the Scot you meet. Such is the case with Archie and the honorary Scot Jack. Even as you watch Archie bury his club into the turf so demonstrably to blame for his most recent shank, you simply cannot help but love the man. Lorne and I lost three of the first six holes, all of them difficult, all played through a constantly swirling wind. This trend had Jack and Archie in great spirits – yet how could Lorne and I be in anything but great spirits ourselves? We were in the company of kindred souls, on hallowed ground, on a landscape of pure and utter beauty. Archie lined up his tee shot on the promontory of the 7th tee, and then swung briskly, using a snappy motion in which he held his breath so forcefully his face reddened. I tried to follow his ball down the fairway.

'Curtis!' he shouted, before his ball had even landed. I looked over, the wind skirling my hair. 'Play, you daft lazy bugger.'

I beamed out a smile but could not stop marvelling at the arresting view from the promontory. Gullane Hill rises above the town of Gullane itself, and the 7th tee of Gullane No. 1 is one of the highest points along the East Lothian coast. The great golf writer Bernard Darwin (nephew of Charles) once wrote that the 7th tee at Gullane No. 1 was the most majestic view in golf. He was right. You can see the world from up there. A couple of kilometres west is Aberlady, and then Longniddry, then Musselburgh. Another ten kilometres west, when the light and air are right, you can easily make out the heart-stopping grace of the Edinburgh skyline, of Arthur's Seat, the castle, the spires along Princes Street. Late in the day, when the lowering sun is backlighting them from the west, the long Firth of Forth rail and car bridges take on the eerie look of skeletons laid out horizontally, like some laboratory props being readied for removal.

South are the gentle Lammermuir Hills, dark green and sporadically rocky, over the top of which is just a wee skip to the English border. Immediately to the east, well below the height of Gullane No. 1, is Muirfield, home of The Honourable Company of Edinburgh Golfers. Long recognised as one of the world's best, it is the course by which all others are measured for fairness and shot values. Just past Muirfield is the town of North Berwick and its greatly historic West Links. In the distance to the west, but still clearly seen, are two volcanic plugs jutting into the sky. The North Berwick Law, a small mountain south of town, and Bass Rock, an island of stone two kilometres offshore that's home to millions of seabirds, mostly cormorants, puffins and gannets. Bass Rock has been bleached putty-white from centuries of guano deposits, and in the sunshine it gleams like an overturned ceramic washtub.

By the time I got around to addressing my ball, Archie was nearly apoplectic with impatience. Jack was not paying any attention to me, but was instead watching his hyperventilating partner. I struck my drive, pulling it left down the steep hill, straight into the teeth of what to me felt like a gale. 'Gale!' Archie and Jack had laughed earlier, when Lorne and I mentioned the ear-flapping wind. 'This is nae wind. It's just a wee zephyr.'

We laughed, too, but now, walking downhill into the wind, the force of it seemed strong enough to drive us back up the hill. To make matters worse, my tee shot, which had been little more than five yards off the fairway, had gone into an area of rough that seemed to be the site of some deeply twisted agricultural experiment to develop strains of vegetation that had learned to tie their stalks in knots. The heather and whins and fescues were so thick and woven together I could feel the root systems pulling at the heels of my shoes as we waded in to search for my ball.

'This rough is brutal,' I said, starting to take on my own Scottish scowl.

'Actually,' said Archie dryly, 'it's not been very wet this year, so the rough's not up that much.'

The combination of grasses, fescues and sea buckthorn make the fairway the place to be at Gullane. I assumed we'd need an emergency application of Agent Orange to locate my ball, but, miraculously, Archie stepped on it.

'What good luck,' said Jack, forcing out a smile, but eyeing my ball as if he could not believe it had the audacity to be found. I managed to separate the ball from the woven flora and hack it out on to the fairway. Lorne and I halved the hole. The tide was turning in our favour. After another half at the 8th – Lorne and I were starting to get the measure of these two old fusties – we turned to the 9th hole. The tee shot at the 9th, a par-three, is a delightful 140-yard pitch down the hill, seemingly into the sea itself. The vista is oriented north-west, across the Firth, to Fife, to the towns of Kirkcaldy, Crail, Elie, Pittenweem, and Anstruther, all former ports of fishing commerce, though nowadays few serve the function.

Lorne pitched left of the green. I left my 9-iron just short. Archie drilled a 6-iron into the front right bunker and Jack chunked a 7-iron into the swale that fronted the small green. The momentum in the match seemed to be turning, especially after Archie, in attempting to hit too fine a shot from the bunker, left it stuck below the steep face of the sod-faced bunker. He slashed his club at the accountable patch of sand. 'Christ!' he shouted, then looked up to see Jack giggling again. It was unclear whether Jack would have preferred to win the match or witness his partner turn purple and implode. Both possibilities seemed to hold great delight. 'Oh, Archie,' said Jack gently. 'You're trying too hard, my boy.'

Archie swiped his ball out of the bunker twenty feet past the hole, then stomped out of the bunker. Lorne and I both parred, a score that won us the hole. The match was all square.

The 12th hole at Gullane No. 1 is a masterful par-five, 485 yards of trouble that is as close to a work of art as you'll find on a golf course. The tee box is set upon a finger of rock that juts out above Gullane beach. I hit a poor drive, but Lorne hit well down the fairway, long enough that it seemed he might be able to go for the green on his second shot. Both Jack and Archie were in trouble off the tee, and we didn't really need to take the chance, but Lorne sensed he was due a great shot. He had 230 yards to the hole. Lorne is both a fine writer and a fine golfer. 'It's a one-iron,' he said. 'I've got this shot.' He pulled his 1-iron from his bag. It was a gamble, but we had the momentum. A stiff westerly breeze was quartering against the direction Lorne was aiming. He swung, too hurriedly, and lost the ball badly to the right. It skittered into a bunker forty yards short of the green, up against the face so that he'd have to play out backwards.

'Acchh,' howled Archie from across the fairway. 'Lorne, you CLOWN!'

We lost the hole.

From the 13th tee row after row of concrete anti-tank blockades left over from the Second World War are visible, relics from a time when it seemed this coast would be one of the most expedient places for the Germans to launch an offensive against the Allies. Jack told us the story of how Gullane had been a no-go zone during the war, closed to all but residents and military personnel, and even as we teed off, now heading back with the fearsome westerly gale, it was easy to forget about golf. Jack had served in the war, but he didn't seem to want to talk about it on the golf course. In the bar, he said. We shall talk then. We had a match to complete, a match in which Lorne and I had now lost the momentum. Lorne had played well, hitting just the single stray 1-iron, but I'd done nothing to help the cause. We didn't win a hole after that, and we all shook hands on the 16th green. Jack and Archie had won 4 and 2.

'Very satisfying,' said Archie, as we left the green. 'It's always a pleasure to provide the colonials with a sound thrashing.'

The Comfort of His Own Skin: I'd Rather Be Me

I knew my father in many different ways, of course, and one of these was through golf, though I'm not referring just to the playing of the game. One of my earliest golf-related memories of my father is of the two of us sitting in the basement television room of our bungalow house in the dry, treeless suburbs of north-west Calgary. It was the second Sunday of April in 1975. We were watching the Masters. I had only recently fallen in love with the game, for a variety of reasons, not the least of which was that my teen years were largely unhappy (short, fat, bad skin, no friends, no sex, no drugs; in short, not much to do, good or bad). Golf was something that didn't require height, muscle, friends or girls, and so I took to it avidly.

That tournament, the '75 Masters, was one of the most exciting ever played. The quality of the golf was so gripping, the shifts of momentum back and forth between Weiskopf, Miller and Nicklaus so startling, that I decided then and there to become a golf professional (though the priesthood was also in the mix during these sexually terrifying teenage years). Everyone who watched that tournament will always remember how Nicklaus' curling forty-footer on the 16th hole broke Weiskopf's spirit, but what I remember best about that day was not the golf. While the triumphant Nicklaus was squeezing himself into the Green Jacket, I said to my father, 'Boy, don't you just wish you were Jack Nicklaus?'

He looked over at me, scratched his greying beard. 'Why on earth would I want to be Jack Nicklaus?'

'Because he's the greatest golfer ever,' I said.

'I'd like to be able to play golf like Jack Nicklaus,' my father said, stopping for a minute to make sure he had my full attention. 'But who knows what kind of person he is. Maybe he's a good man, but maybe he isn't. I'd rather be me.'

If ever there was a phrase that neatly encapsulated my father's opinion of himself it was this. It was said without fanfare, without expansion, without inflection of any sort (which in itself suggests self-ease), as if it was simply about recognising that the world is a grand lottery, and that he was quietly thankful to have drawn the right mix of numbers.

One arena, however, in which my father most definitely did not draw the right numbers was in the dental lottery. My father had very bad teeth. It was something that was with him all his life, but which he never had the resources (or, I suspect, the motivation) to do anything about. Since he ran his own business for most of his working life (Calgary Glass & Trim, in which he repaired car windshields and did all manner of upholstery), any healthcare costs for him or his family came straight out of his own pocket. We were never skimped upon as children for visits to the dentist (though my mother regularly chastised the dentist for needing to take so many X-rays), but he didn't attend to his own dental health, mostly due to the sheer cost, but also perhaps because he just didn't care about having a mouthful of straight white teeth. His teeth, he always said, were 'rotten', and a close inspection of them wouldn't have led to any other conclusion. Arranged like a haphazard, post-concert semi-circle of separate chairs, many of his teeth were yellow, some white, one a crumbling grey. It was a bit of a mess in there. The irony of all this is that I'm not sure my mother would have ever let him fix his teeth, even if we'd had the money, because she once said he 'had a beautiful smile . . . despite his bad teeth and chicken lips'. She meant it as a compliment. His was a light-hearted and inclusive grin. As kids (I was the oldest of six: five boys and a girl), we did things just to make him smile, so that we could see that grin. We would tell bad jokes, make up stories, make my mother smile (which made him smile); whatever it took. Anything to see those rotten teeth and chicken lips form that brilliant smile, a smile that always seemed to furtively emerge from the whiteness of his beard, moustache and hair, a whiteness that was the derivation of his nickname: *Ghost*. I think it must have been a friend of my brother Matt who first called him by that name, but once it had been uttered it stuck. Our friends sometimes referred to my mother as Mrs Ghost. My mother even occasionally called him Ghost. It became who he was, and even if he'd shaved off his beard, I'm sure the name would have been his for ever.

But aside from appearances, how fitting was his nickname? Was he spectral, fleeting, hard to grasp and hold? Who was my father? Do any of us ever really ask that question, of either parent, and listen to the honest answer? We cannot find the answer by standing at the mine entrance of our lives. We must go to the coalface, to our memories; a dark, cramped place. Labouring far underground in this way is of no little consequence – it's honest work – yet truth does not come away from veins of memory in ready-made blocks of wisdom, but rather in shards and lumps, some gleaming, some dull, some perfect, some misshapen. These must be gathered, reshaped, and are given utility and meaning only in combination with our own ability (and desire) to see them clearly.

My father was not a *larger than life* person. He was not *quietly heroic* or a *beacon of goodness* or a *pillar of honesty* or any of the other italicised verbal tombs in which many, myself included, had enclosed his memory after his death, though all these traits were a part of him. He had a poor education. He worked hard. He married a woman he loved, and stayed married to her, and in love with her, until he died. He had six children, all of whom grew up healthy, out of jail, and not grotesquely maladjusted. He liked popcorn with lots of butter. He smoked. He drank. He had a temper. He watched sports on TV.

But there was one quality I can see now that he possessed to a complete and genuine degree, a quality almost no one else I know possesses on the same plane, least of all myself: he was comfortable with who he was. He liked himself. It was that that drew people to him. Not his honesty, though he was honest. Not his humour, though he was funny. People drew up alongside him in the hope he might offer up a little dab of the balm that was his self-ease, as if he were an ointment they might rub over their own worried self-regard. It didn't matter that my father wasn't rich or powerful or tall. There wasn't much he could give people in measurable, quantitative commodities, and possibly that was why he was able to be himself. He never had money, influence or power. He only had himself to give. A rare thing, to be with someone, around someone, who is simply who they are. His Ghostness was complete. Authenticity is what I'm talking about. There wasn't a false note to the man. And when he told me that he didn't believe in capital punishment, but if someone ever raped and murdered Mum or Janine he'd 'like to see the bastard fry', or that he 'believed Jesus existed but that didn't necessarily mean he was God', or that he 'didn't necessarily believe in monogamy, but only lived that way because it meant something to your mother', or that it used to be so hot in Dayton, Ohio that he had to put a hankie between his butt cheeks when he played golf to stop the chafing and sweating, well, you could agree or disagree, laugh or cringe, but you knew you were getting what he thought. People came from miles around just to hear what he had to say, and if he said nothing, that was something, because it meant there was nothing to be said.

My father's authenticity was an organic part of his being. It wouldn't occur to him to lie or cheat or say something he didn't mean. This is a difference between us. Not that I'm dishonest: I tell the truth and I don't cheat. But these are sometimes acts of willpower rather than effortlessly natural stances. I have to think about it, have to remind myself, that there is a right way and a wrong way, and that the wrong way is fool's gold that only pays short-term dividends. I am tempted by short cuts. When I drive, I find the quickest route. When I play golf, I look for the shortest, not the safest, route to the hole. When I play squash or tennis or ping-pong or chess or checkers or Scrabble or a Pokémon word game with my six-year-old daughter, I always look for the opportunity to achieve the best result with the least effort, and this is the zone of temptation. I don't cheat, but I understand the impulse. I wonder if my father ever knew that impulse? And I wonder which is more common, more human; to feel what it's like to be tempted, or to never know it?

After we finished our second pint of 80 Shilling in the Back Bar, Archie went to have a quick shower. While he was gone, Jack began to tell us about his wartime experiences. It was how he'd met his wife, Doris, in Port Sudan on the Red Sea, where they'd both been stationed.

'It was a gift from above, and that's all there was to it. It was a dance at a club called the Red Sea, one of those posh clubs for expats. And for us, the servicemen, there were so many that wanted to go to this dance, we had to have a raffle for tickets, and only two men from each unit won tickets. I won one and so did my friend Ken Hall. And there were hundreds of men at this dance. Young men everywhere, but they made a point of putting two Wrens, you know, the Women's Royal Naval Service – that's what Doris did, the coding and ciphering – and they put two at every table, so that every man would have the chance to get at least a few dances in that night. There were so few women, so many men.'

Jack was staring dreamily at the ceiling. He was there. It was in his eyes. It was Africa, 1943. A sweltering night. He was twenty-five again. Lorne and I sat quietly, not needing to acknowledge our privilege. 'She wasn't at our table, but I noticed her right away, and I said to my friend Ken Hall, "Oh, I'd like to meet her." Ken set up a double date, and, well, I suppose things just went on from there. I proposed in Alexandria, and we got married in 1945, right back here in Gullane.'

Archie came bursting back into the bar, interrupting Jack's idyll. 'Let's go!' he bellowed. 'I'm ready.'

Lorne and I started in our seats, so abrupt was Archie's entrance. 'Sit yourself down,' Jack said quietly but firmly. 'You must sit yourself down for five minutes and be quiet. That's all there is to that.'

Archie groaned with exasperation and picked up the new half-pint of 80 Shilling Jack had so craftily already paid for. 'What boring old lies are you telling now?' he asked Jack as he sat down.

'His wife,' said Lorne. 'Jack was telling us how they met.'

'Ah,' said Archie, brightening. 'In the war. He drugged, then kidnapped her. No other reason for such a lovely woman to end up with this silly old bugger.'

Jack smiled. 'I remember we went for that date to a place called the Pelican Club. Just a big tent on the sand, really.'

'And did you have children?' I asked.

Jack's face dropped, and Archie took to searching the bottom of his half-pint glass as if he'd dropped a one-pence coin into it.

'Yes,' said Jack.

We sat saying nothing and it was only then I noticed the Back Bar had emptied out. Only the four of us remained. The barman had retreated to the kitchen.

'His daughter's sick,' Archie burst out, not loudly, but as if he'd just been forced to divulge a state secret. He kept his eyes on the bottom of his glass. Jack, on the other hand, looked straight at

Lorne and I. His eyes, a touch cloudy with age, were now shining. 'It's true,' he said, his voice wobbling. 'We're not sure how it looks.' It was plain across his face that his life was wrapped up in his daughter and her fate. This was a man of utter selflessness. I was struck then with the notion that Jack was what I'd wanted my father to age into. I was also reminded, through Jack, that my father was no longer in my life. Jack seemed kind, gentle-hearted, a man I wanted to know well, the kind of person you meet, are taken with, and then end up regretting your eagerness for fear that you have scared him away. Of course, it was partly because of my father that I was eager to learn more of Jack. He may have been talking of his daughter, but his words also led my mind elsewhere. Archie stood abruptly. 'Right. Let's get a move on, Marston.'

Jack looked up and pointed at his pint glass. It was still half full. 'I've got this. And I'm not moving. I want to finish this. And I'm enjoying the company if you don't mind.'

Lorne and I smiled. 'So are we,' said Lorne. We all raised our glasses again.

'As am I,' said Archie. He looked at his watch. 'But I promised Doris I'd get you home tonight at a reasonable hour, and I'm bloody well going to do it.'

'Will you just sit yourself down for five minutes, please. And stop trying to rush me through things. You've really got to relax nowadays, my boy.'

Archie let his hands search vigorously through the depths of his pockets, jingling his change, rattling his keys. The battle between doing as Jack said versus following the eternal call of his own nature was being played out across his face; he was mugging and grimacing and contorting his lips into thick and thin postures. Jack pointedly ignored his dear friend. Finally, Archie could take no more. He sat down. 'You're an old bugger!'

At that point, Jack picked up his glass and calmly drained it, not pausing once. He then placed his glass on the table and smiled contentedly. 'Nice ale, that,' he said, grinning at us and then turning to Archie.

'Marston!' exclaimed Archie, who burst from his seat. 'You!'

Jack giggled and leaned over to Lorne and I. 'Gentlemen,' he said. 'This has been a great pleasure. We will do this again.' We shook hands.

Archie snatched from behind Jack's head the clubs he'd so casually tossed there. For the first time, I noticed that these clubs seemed to be not just ratty but actually quite old. All were wooden-headed and wooden-shafted. As curator of the golf museum he'd founded next to the Pro Shop, Archie had amassed a considerable collection of historic golf paraphernalia.

'Those look old,' said Lorne to Archie. 'Are they yours?'

'Some of my favourites,' he nodded. 'Club meeting tonight for the Ladies, and I told them I'd do a little history lesson on clubs for them.'

Jack spied the clubs, one in particular. It was a stunning piece of wood; pear-shaped when whole, but which had been cut in half to make the club, and of a blond colour, like the fruit of an overripe banana. Jack picked up this club and examined it.

'Eighteenth century?'

Archie nodded.

I gasped. 'Eighteenth century?!'

'Some of these are from the nineteenth.'

'But, but . . . how much are those worth?'

Archie grabbed the lot of four, holding them together by the shaft, scrambling them about so casually he might have been holding four hockey sticks. He eyed them, and then spoke a number that caused Lorne and I to gasp.

'Are you serious?' I said.

Archie held out the blond pear-shaped club, unimpressed with himself as only a Scot can be. 'Paid three pounds for this one in a shop in Edinburgh years ago.'

'But you were just throwing them around back there.' I pointed to the space behind the bench seats. Lorne started laughing. As an older friend of Archie's, he seemed not at all surprised by Archie's cavalier way with the clubs.

'They're golf clubs,' Archie said, as if by way of explanation. 'They knew how to make a club back then. Running them about a bit isn't going to do them any harm. They've lasted two centuries, a little bit of a knock isn't going to hurt them.' He paused, seemed to become bored with the topic, and then noticed that Jack was slipping towards the bench seat again. 'No!' he shouted. 'Let's go. You're a dodgy old bugger!'

Jack looked at us and smiled, shrugged. He leaned over to shake hands again.

'Jack,' I said. 'It was a treat. We'll meet again.'

'Yes.'

'We'll be thinking of you,' said Lorne. 'I hope it goes well with your daughter.'

'Thank you,' he said in a whisper. 'That's very kind.' His eyes went shiny, and a drip appeared at his nose (and it did go well in the end for Jack's daughter). He pulled his handkerchief from his pocket and applied it to both nose and eyes, then dragged it haggardly across his mouth. He looked old at that moment, looked his eighty-one years, but then he smiled and was young again, gloriously young and so alive that, for a moment, I think I wished I was him, that I'd lived his life, and that I'd acquired his directness and grace and simple amiability.

Archie barely said goodbye before bustling from the room. Jack followed, but stopped at the door and turned. 'My dear friend Archie,' he whispered. 'He just doesn't like goodbyes. He had a wonderful time today.'

I stepped out from behind the booth, and went to Jack. 'I just wanted to say something,' I muttered, pausing, now embarrassed. Jack looked at me expectantly, willing to listen. 'You remind me of my dad,' I said, not bothering to take the time to tell him anything about my father, that he was no longer alive, or even that I meant it very much as a compliment; my highest praise, in fact. 'That's all. I just wanted to say that.'

Jack put a hand to my upper arm, squeezed, smiled again. 'I'll keep that,' he said. 'I will.'

Meeting Jack that day decided me. Of course, Jack and Archie, Archie and Jack, formed a nearly symbiotic pair, as I was to find out. It was, and still is, difficult to think of one without the other naturally arising in my mind's eye, in the way, perhaps, that you can't click a pen without the nib appearing. I would come to understand and benefit from the kindness and generosity of Archie. But through no design or purpose higher than the random nature of the universe, Jack in a single meeting initiated in me a complex set of recollections, regrets and promises. The past, present and future – all fingers of the same hand – touched me at once, and it seemed at that moment as if I wasn't quite making the most of the combination.

Jack not only reminded me of my father in many direct ways, but he also leapt out at me as a kind of representation of everything my father lost by dying so young. Both men had worked like slaves since their teens, and Jack's sensibility was decidedly working-class, as had been my father's. Both men owned their own businesses; Jack the Marston's Fruit & Vegetable Shop on Gullane High Street, and my father Calgary Glass & Trim. Both men had large and loving families, full of kids and grandkids. And each had, of course, a passion for golf, as well as a genuine talent for playing it.

I'd known Jack for one day. He was eighty-one years old, healthy, happy, robust, cracking jokes, playing golf, downing drinks and behaving in a manner so decent, so free of pretension, so in love with the world around him, that to meet him and not warm to him was an impossibility. In this, he was most like my father; he didn't put on airs, and he was easy to like. In Jack, I saw – quite suddenly, in a vision I'd not had before – what my father might have been had he lived into his eighties, instead of dying at sixty. I was happy, truly, to have met Jack, but he touched an ember of sadness inside me, and brought it into flame.

I had never written about my father before, had never been ready, but now, effortlessly, I was. This understanding materialised without any foreknowledge that its arrival was imminent or even inevitable. But now I wanted to write about my father, and to write about this place, Scotland, the place he'd so wanted to visit, that I wanted him to visit with me. The journey we'd never taken. Why did I feel this way now? I don't know for certain, and can only guess that he needed to be fully gone for me to bring him back, to find the space inside myself for him. It had taken this long. And in a way he'd never have guessed (and knowing him now, in a way he'd be embarrassed about), Jack prised that space free, opened my hold, as it were. And never would I have guessed what the ensuing trawl through my own and other's hearts was going to net.

Lorne and I were left to finish our pints in the declining natural light seeping through the high glazed windows along the back walls of the bar. When we left the clubhouse and stepped out on to West Links Road, Gullane Hill and the golf courses were dark, but as the sun failed in the west there was still a delicate halo of light bathing the back side of the hill and spilling weakly over the top. It would be completely dark in ten minutes. The faint nonsensical music of sandpipers, plovers, oystercatchers, curlews and dunlins drifted over from Aberlady Bay, but a throng of robins and chaffinches were chattering before bed in the stubble fields out by the ruins of Saltcoats Castle, not far from the A198 back to Edinburgh, the great stony city only eighteen kilometres distant. And yet I was so bewitched by the setting, so separated did I feel from everything that wasn't Gullane, the city might as well have been three worlds away.

We walked to the car park out back, speaking little. I knew I would bring my family here; it felt obvious, a given. A small car had left the Gullane car park a few minutes earlier, and it was now on the road west to Aberlady, or Musselburgh, or perhaps even Edinburgh. I could only make out the dull glow of the tail lights. I tried to follow them, to see if I could get a sense of the curvature of the road just from tracking the departing red eyes, but it was only a few seconds before the darkness swallowed them and the car was no longer visible. It was night.

Part Two

On Gullane Links a man envies none, and has only pity to spare for the rest of the world.

John Geddie, 1895

1

The two of them came hurtling down the steep twenty-five-foot slope of the dune, strides comically elongated by the pitch, sand rooster-tailing in golden spumes behind them. The light winds coming off the sunlit Firth of Forth collected the rogue grains and salted them with it. Jessica made it down safely, but Cathy lurched forward at the bottom, gaining her footing with all the elegance of a foal fresh from the womb. Both were laughing hysterically. Grace was in the backpack on my shoulders, sound asleep, limp as a sack of grain on the back of a labourer.

It was less than a year after meeting Jack and Archie, and now I was back, living in Gullane, with my wife, Cathy, and our daughters, Jessica, who was five, and Grace, who wasn't yet one. On one of our first days in East Lothian, a Sunday, we decided to walk the coast from Gullane to North Berwick. It hadn't looked that far on the map. We'd just bought a car from a dealer in North Berwick, and the plan was to walk there and drive back. Along the way we crossed mountainous rows of sand dunes spiked at their heads with marram grass; at one set of these dunes, on the huge West Sands beach just outside North Berwick, Cathy and Jessica had raced to the top, and then dared one another to race back down to the bottom.

'Again!' shouted Jessica. 'Come on, Mum. Let's do it again.'

Cathy shook sand from her shoes, her hair, her coat pockets. 'Next time,' she laughed.

'Awww,' said Jessica, as we again turned our feet eastward. North Berwick was now at least within view. Yes, we were on our way to pick up our car, but Jessica had a higher purpose, a mission of her own. She'd left behind in Canada her best friend Astrid. Earlier that summer Astrid's grandmother and grandfather had visited from Sweden. And when we were telling Jessica that we'd be moving to Scotland, we told her it was near Sweden. What an opportunity, she now thought! She'd made up an elaborate note to Astrid's Mormor and Morfor, and stuffed it in a bottle. I corked it for her.

'Is it tight?' she asked.

'It's tight.'

'Because water can't get in, Daddy.'

'I know. It's tight.'

'Are you sure?'

'Yes.'

'Let's see.'

Finally I'd managed to convince her that it was watertight. And so we'd set off. We'd left Gullane at noon. It was now four o'clock. Archie had told me of a shortcut early in the route, and we'd faithfully taken his advice. It had seemed shorter than strictly following the beachline, as we cut through the dense stands of hawthorn and buckthorn hard against the 3rd, 4th and 5th holes that make up the northern boundary of Muirfield. The path veered into the bush at the middle of the 5th hole, and we'd emerged from the trees and dunes on to the beach near Dirleton and Yellowcraigs park, soldiering on from there.

Jessica had done marvellously well, but now, four hours down the road, we were all starting to flag. The dune scramble had taken the last of our energies. Finally, after what seemed another hour, we reached a spot along North Berwick's West Links Golf Course where it looked as if we could cut across the course to High Street, where we were supposed to pick up our car. East Lothian residents make jokes that the whole of the coastline from Edinburgh to Dunbar, a stretch of perhaps forty kilometres, is nothing but one long string of golf holes. It's not far from the truth, with Old Musselburgh, Royal Musselburgh, Monktonhall, Longniddry, Kilspindie, Craigielaw, Luffness, Gullane Nos 1, 2 and 3, Muirfield, North Berwick West Links, North Berwick East Links, Dunbar Winterfield and Dunbar Golf Club. And this list does not include courses that no longer exist, such as links at Archerfield or the infamous course at Seton Sands, just outside Musselburgh, where in 1567 Mary Queen of Scots was found playing 'at the kolf' just days after the murder of Lord Darnley, a bit of post-trauma recreation for which she was heavily castigated in the pulpit by none other than the Haddington-born Reformer John Knox. ('One of the eventful turns of an eventful life,' Reverend Kerr, with uncharacteristic brevity, had written in his *Golf Book* of Mary's run-in with Knox. Archie, when taking people through his golf museum, was always fond of saying that Knox's primary criticism of Mary was that she played golf just six days after Darnley's murder, and that she ought to have had the decency to wait at least seven.)

Knox (who, to be kind, was a man free of modesty and self-doubt) was also at the centre of one of the greatest debates in golf's early days, that of Sunday play. Though he was critical of Mary for her golfing habits, he himself was known to be keen on the game, even on the Sabbath. The good Reverend Kerr captured the debate in his own inimical style, while simultaneously managing to re-interpret military history and slide a knife into English ribs.

> Our greatest Reformer, John Knox, who was an East
> Lothian man and a golfer, did not believe in a Sunday
> observance that was wholly made up of religious exercises.
> Tradition has it that he was seen more than once golfing on
> Leith Links on Sunday afternoon. Certainly his idea, and
> the idea of our early Reformers, indeed we may say the true
> Scottish idea of Sunday, was that the early part should be
> given to worship in the House of God, and that after
> divine service all were free to indulge in bodily recreation.
> The old Session and Town Council Records of which we
> hear so much, dealt chiefly with offenders who neglected
> worship altogether, and golfed during the 'tyme of preach-
> ing or the tyme of sermounes', as the hour of worship was
> called. If, as no doubt was the case, an attempt was made to
> prohibit golf and other games on the Sabbath, this was due
> to the adoption of the Puritan idea of the day which was at
> first introduced from England, and finally imposed on
> Scotland by Cromwell and his Independents – thanks to
> the stupid blunder of General Leslie at Dunbar.

But on this particular Sabbath day, in the year 2000, as we wandered across the marvellously firm West Links turf, there was little golfer traffic, which we couldn't have been happier about. The last thing we needed as a family at that point was to have one of our troop felled by a golf ball. Despite crossing this most historic and beautiful of golf courses, our by-now bedraggled caravan was badly in need of a different kind of oasis. Yet when we got to our shortcut gate, up by the 6th tee, we found, naturally, that our oasis was a mirage. 'MEMBERS AND RESIDENTS POSSESS ACCESS TO THIS GATE' read the sign. The sturdy iron bars resolutely resisted my less-than-noble jail-cell bid for freedom. 'Come on!' I said, gripping and tugging. 'Shit!'

Cathy let her shoulders slump. 'Oh, I just don't know if I have the energy to walk back down the beach again . . . and then all the way into town and around.'

'When can we go to the place to throw my bottle to Mormor and Morfor?' said Jessica, loudly, a whine on the way. A fourball came off the 5th green towards us. 'And I have to go to the bath-room.'

Grace stirred behind my ear. I was about to pull her off my back, just to help me think, when there was a rattle at the gate. We turned to see a man about my age with a moustache smiling mercifully at us. 'I've got a key,' he said happily. 'I was out doing my lawn there, and saw you. I thought you might want to get out.'

'Oh, thank you,' said Cathy. We picked ourselves up and stepped through the gate. He closed it behind us, and we looked to his 'house', an imposing white mansion, one of a string of palaces that line the south side of the course.

'You've been out for a walk,' he said, still grinning.

'Sort of,' laughed Cathy, brushing some strands of her long black hair from her face. 'We came from Gullane.'

'Gullane!' he half-shouted. 'Crikey! I've lived here all my life and I've never walked from or to Gullane. Heavens.'

We explained that we were on our way to the local car dealer-ship where our car was waiting to be picked up, and that our plan had been to walk to North Berwick and then drive back to Gullane. I had thought the dealership would be right across the road from the golf course, but he told us it was at least another twenty minutes' walk. 'But twenty minutes is nothing if you've walked from Gullane.'

We thanked him for letting us through the gate, and set out again towards the town centre, but we didn't get more than a couple of hundred metres when a Renault people-carrier pulled up beside us. It was the same man.

'Hop in,' he said. 'I'm just going in to town anyway, so I can give you a lift to the car dealership.'

'Are you sure?' I said. 'We could walk, really.'

'No, no . . .' he said, pausing, searching for words, clearly trying to fabricate any sort of excuse to make us feel less like the ramshackle colonial refugees we so clearly were. 'I, um, I . . . had to pop out to get some milk anyhow.'

We all tacitly agreed to let this excuse stand in for his generosity and piled into his car. The seats were masterpieces of comfort, shaped to our bodies, nicely reclined. The air conditioning was humming quietly. I could have sat in that car for a month. The drive to the dealership was short, but uphill, and it would have taken us longer than twenty minutes. We passed a grocery shop on the way into town, but I said nothing, and as he dropped us off we thanked him so profusely, almost giddily, that he had to be delighted to see the back of us.

Spilling through the front door of the car dealership, Grace began yelping with hunger. Jessica had found a stick on the beach that she'd refused to give up, and she now began swinging it like a golf club in very close proximity to the new showroom vehicles. Cathy and I sat heavily in the big plush chairs against the wall, lacking the energy to control our children. I looked at my legs and noticed some bleeding scratches from when we'd passed through the nettle and buckthorn stands just north of Muirfield. At this point, a sales person approached with an expression of alarm, his eyes nervously flicking left and right to ensure there were no genuine customers within an infectious distance. 'Can I help you at all today?' he said.

'We're here for our car,' I said. 'A Renault we purchased. The salesman's name is Matt Cannon.'

'Right, right,' he said, running off to find the man responsible for bringing these people into the dealership. Grace had by now emptied the bottle we'd brought for her, and was loudly complaining for more. Jessica was poking her stick into the wheel well of a sports car.

Matt strode quickly out of the back room, casting an uneasy eye at the chaos in front of him. 'Hi there,' he said, in his Florida accent. He'd married a Scottish woman, and was now living in Gullane, virtually across the street from us. 'Bad news. The car isn't ready yet. Well, the car is ready, but the Post Office was closed, so I couldn't get the tax disc. We'll have to wait until tomorrow.'

'That means the bus back,' said Cathy listlessly.

'And we have to get to Woolworth's, too,' I said.

Matt stood over us, nervously holding his hands together.

'Where is the Woolworth's, anyway?' said Cathy.

'Quite a ways, actually,' said Matt. 'Especially on foot.' At this, he directed a quick glance to Jessica, who had turned her stick into an épée and was duelling with a car antenna. 'But, look, I'll drive you. I, uhh, I have to go that way. Let me just get my car, and I'll drive you up there. And the bus stops right in front.'

We decided to split up after Matt dropped us off at Woolworth's. Cathy would do the shopping with Grace, and I would take Jessica to the pier, the mission being to release into the sea the bottle containing her message to Astrid via Astrid's grandparents in Sweden. We agreed to reunite at the Scottish Seabird Centre on the pier. The North Berwick pier has different jetties and platforms that jut straight into the Firth of Forth, which, at that corner of East Lothian, is essentially the North Sea. The pier is a small village unto itself with many different levels and various structures atop those levels. The marvellous Seabird Centre anchors the east side of the pier. 'Sweden is just across the water,' I said to Jess, pointing east. 'Astrid's Mormor and Morfor will get it for sure.'

'That way?' she said, pointing in the same direction I had.

I nodded. There were two boys, maybe fourteen years old, fishing from the jetty, but they ignored us. After I gave her the all-clear, Jess leaned back and heaved the bottle as far as she could into the sea . . . about five feet. Thirty or forty feet would have been a lot more useful, since it didn't look to me as if the current was going to get the bottle in its grip just a few feet out. We watched it bob up and down. At least it was staying afloat.

'Look! Look, it's already going to Sweden. How are Mormor and Morfor going to get it? What if someone else picks it up? How are they going to get it to Astrid?'

The two boys fishing turned to stare at us.

'Message in a bottle,' I explained.

'Aye, right,' said the brattier-looking of the two. Something told me the moment we departed they'd pick up stones and start aiming for it, but I said nothing, shuttling Jess away instead, assuring her all the while that her message was going to reach Sweden, and that perhaps Astrid would then throw one back into the ocean that would wash up on the Gullane Bents. We got back up to the top level of the pier and walked along its concrete prow, heading for the Seabird Centre, where Cathy and Grace by now might have returned to check out the gannets on Bass Rock. Near the end of the concrete walkway I glanced back down to the jetty where Jess had just thrown her message off to Astrid.

The bottle was no longer in the water, or at least it was no longer at sea. I couldn't find it. Then I saw one of the little imps who'd been fishing go prancing off the side of the jetty and down to the rocks where the waves lapped against the stone. The bottle, I could now see, was bobbing in the chop near the rocks. The boy reached down to grab the bottle, which was a move not completely without risk, since many of the stones were slick with sea moss and kelp. But he managed it, plucking the bottle from the water and then scooting back up on to the jetty, showing it to his fishing pal, brandishing it like a bit of treasure. They both burst out laughing and my heart sank. Jess wasn't tall enough to see over the railing, and so I said nothing, but I knew those boys were going to break it open, read the note (in which Jess had told Astrid how much she missed her, how she was her favourite friend, all about the different foods she was eating), and that they would have a grand old laugh over it. I didn't blame them. It occurred to me that I might have done the same at their age. It was just their age, that was all; it was too easy to find a little girl's dreams silly and worth denigrating.

But then a thing happened, a thing that made me ashamed for thinking ill of those boys. They touched heads briefly, or so it looked. Then the larger of the two, the less bratty-looking one, took the bottle from his friend, who gave it up willingly. The boy went straight to the lip of the jetty, holding the bottle with some care. He got a good solid footing, and with a huge arm-behind-the-head hurl, heaved the bottle as far as he could out into the sea. It sailed through the air, and landed at least fifty or sixty feet from the jetty, well past the small waves that were working their way back into shore. The bottle bobbed and weaved, hesitated, then pointed its spout away from us, aiming not for the shore but the sea, for Sweden. The two boys laughed once more, but this time I heard it for what it was, not a meanness, but with a certain kind of maturity, as if this message-in-a-bottle thing was a fable they'd simply outgrown, like Santa Claus or the Easter Bunny, but which they fondly recollected. They picked up their rods and went back to fishing. I felt like running down to the end of the pier and adopting them.

'Jess!' I said, hoisting her up above the guard rail, so she could see the ocean. 'Look, the bottle.' I pointed and it took her a minute to find it, but she did.

'My bottle!' she cried. 'My bottle! It's going to Sweden, already. Look. See, Daddy, I told you. I told you it would go to Sweden.'

My arms were around her waist, and her curly longish hair was loose and fluttering in my face, the salty September breeze turning it against my cheek like light stalks of fescue grass. We watched together as the bottle bobbed, drifted, tacked slowly but relentlessly seaward, the odd glints of refractory sunlight becoming gradually less frequent. It was now all about the current, about fate. I held on tight to Jess, and she rested her hands on my forearms. 'You were right,' I said. 'I think it's going to make it.'

After dinner we went for a stroll, a digestive, and to see the light begin to fail on the waters of the Firth. On the way to the beach from our flat on the High Street we passed through the one neighbourhood in Gullane that contained, in a nutshell, the money. The Hill is the part of town that climbs the shoulder of Gullane Hill, so that its homes look out over the golf courses, the beach, the Flats (the rest of the town) – basically, over everyone else. The smallest section of a small town (Gullane has a population that hovers around 2,000), the Hill is a grouping of perhaps fifty mansions and large homes whose inhabitants surely have a combined net worth higher than many small African dictatorships. As we crossed Erskine Loan on the way to the beach we passed two elderly ladies out for a constitutional of their own. They said 'Good evening' in what sounded to me like the plummy tones of Oxford or Cambridge. Jessica was naturally drawn to the elderly Labrador they were dragging around the streets, a fuzzy, heavy-tongued thing they called Ariadne, 'after the Strauss opera, of course'.

'Are you visiting from America?' one of them said, wrapping her pink cashmere sweater around her neck against the slight evening sea-chill.

'We're from Canada,' Cathy replied. 'But we're living here. For a year.'

They seemed to need a moment to square such an unexpected piece of information. The more Thatcheresque of the two ladies smiled as she spoke, putting a tentative hand to the pearls around her throat. 'Oh! You're living here? In Gullane?' She said the word Gullane as 'Gillan'.

'Yes,' I said. 'In Gullane,' pronouncing it 'Gullan'. This was to be the first among literally hundreds of exchanges we would have around the pronunciation of the town's name. 'How do you say it?' new friends would continue to ask us throughout the year. But it is very simple, really. If you live up the Hill, if you are rich, you pronounce it Gillan. If you live in the Flats, if you aren't rich, you pronounce it Gullan. Of course, aspiration and reverse snobbery also come into play. If one is poor or middle-class but aspires to a higher rank, one utilises Gillan. But if you live up the Hill and want to be known as a good sport and a person of the people, you splash out Gullan as broadly as possible. As I said: simple. One friend I made during the course of our time in Gullane told me that he would never utter the name of the town in conversation until he'd heard the other's usage, at which point he would adopt that pronunciation. It was safest, he said.

Ian Finlay, in his 1960 travel diary entitled simply *The Lothians*, revealed perhaps more about himself than his knowledge of the area when he wrote:

> The generally accepted pronunciation of the name today is Gillan, although one meets occasionally people who, either out of an apparent profundity of special knowledge or because they prefer to be thought a little different, call the place Gullan. The old name was Golyn, and . . . in 1612 Parliament merged it in the parish of Dirleton on the grounds that it was 'any decaying toun, and Dirleton is ane thriven place', while its last vicar evidently consoled himself for a shrinking congregation by joining the increasing community of smokers, a 'filthie habit' for which James VI, perhaps with a glimpse of the rare foresight which he sometimes revealed, deposed him from office. The modern Gullane as one passes through it on the main road is not particularly interesting [and its] fame today is founded principally on the cult of golf. It lies very near the strategic centre of what is probably the greatest concentration of first-class golf courses in the world, a vast chain of links which, broken only here and there, stretches from North Berwick to Leith.

Even Andrew Hajducki, who wrote *The Gullane and North Berwick Branch Lines*, a study of the history of the railway in the region, considered it necessary to comment on the town's name. 'The pronunciation of Gullane,' he wrote, 'is variable and (to some) a matter of controversy and although those who arrived in third-class carriages would have referred to the village in much the same way as it is spelt, i.e. "Gullan", the more affected first-class passenger would no doubt have booked to "Gillan"; the author offers no guidance here!'

Finlay and Hajducki were not the only writers who felt compelled to comment on this hitch in the local pronunciation. The prolific writer Nigel Tranter also thought the Gillan/Gullan debate emblematic of greater divisions in Scottish society (meaning, I think it's fair to say, the English, public-school influence in Scotland, or, as was said to me more than once throughout our year in Gullane, the class system). Though Tranter lived at Quarry House just outside Aberlady for most of his life, he spent his last years in Gullane, living up in the elegant housing estate that rings Goose Green. This was where he died early in 2000 at the age of ninety-two. For half a century, Tranter was one of Scotland's most distinctive writers, parading for his readers a stream of novels and biographies that chronicled his nation from its birth right up to his death. The man was simply prolific beyond normal human accomplishment; so much so, in fact, that it's hard to imagine a classic actually emanating from his pen, cruel as that sounds. The ink could barely have been dry on his previous epic before he rifled off another historical adventure about William Wallace or Robert the Bruce or the Loch Ness Monster. He wrote the first of his eighty novels in 1935, and published a wide variety of non-fiction besides. In his range from history to adventure to mystery, coupled with his staggering productivity, he was a kind of East Lothian James Michener. Yet Tranter was a serious writer, a fluid stylist and, best of all, just a little bit misanthropic. He loved the odd, the strange, and he loved most of all taking the piss out of the stuffy folk around him. After noting that he considered Aberlady a much more traditional East Lothian village than Gullane, he adds that, though it is larger than Aberlady, it also feels newer, which is not the case,

> . . . for Gullane or Goolan or Golyn was an ancient village and parish also. But it lost its parish status as far back as the early seventeenth century when King Jamie Saxt deposed

its vicar for the filthy and detestable sin of smoking tobacco, and removed its church to Dirleton, the next village two miles further to the east. It has won its church back since then, but never its parochial standing. Nevertheless, the ruins of the ancient Kirk of St Andrew, Gullane, dedicated in the twelfth century – and therefore in fact much older than the Aberlady Kirk, indeed one of the oldest churches in Scotland – still stand, with Norman chancel arch, in the kirkyard [a kirkyard not forty metres from the 1st tee of Gullane No. 1, and which directly borders Archie's museum] . . . But by and large Gullane is a modern place, its new houses vastly outnumbering the old – and expensive ones outnumbering the other kind – its traditions of much more recent origin and very largely connected with the game of golf. Completely ringed with golf courses instead of ancient demesnes – Muirfield, Gullane Numbers One, Two and Three, and Luffness – this is scarcely to be wondered at. With its excellent bathing beach contributing, it has become a most popular place in consequence for prosperous folk to live, within a convenient distance of the capital city for businessfolk, and for others to retire to, especially from the upper ranks of the services, and so on. I have heard it described by an old Aberlady resident as 'nae mair'n a bluidy stuck-up doarmitory suburb' – but that perhaps is unkind and prejudiced. Money admittedly does talk with a much louder voice in Gullane than its neighbouring village, and inevitably the accent is more Anglified than Doric. In this connection it is recorded that there are three distinct occupation layers in Gullane, and each gives the village a different name. Those on the Hill – that is, those whose houses occupy the higher and more desirable sites – plus those who would like to be taken as living there, refer to it as Gillan; those further down, along the main street and near the shops, call it Gullan; while the small and diminishing residue of the original indigenous population, tucked away in odd corners, still pronounce it by the ancient name of Goolan.

'Right, on we go, Ariadne.' The dog seemed more interested in what the gutter had to offer and resolutely refused to take the step up to the pavement. 'She's somewhat blind, I'm afraid,' offered the Thatcher clone, as she pulled rather sternly on the leash, choking and lifting poor Ariadne at once. When she made the pavement, Ariadne ambled off with her keepers, one of whom looked back and said properly, 'Enjoy your time in Gillan.'

'Bye, Ariadne,' said Jessica, waving at the Lab's receding rear end.

The bottom line of the sun's arc was just touching the spires of Edinburgh's skyline on the western horizon. It was a clear but cool evening, and we didn't linger long at the beach. We'd seen enough of the coastline that day. The next day, I picked up the car. The registration was W766 EGG. A completely white car with a yellow number-plate. An egg, I told Jessica. Our car is an egg.

X

'C'mon, sweetie, let's go. We're late. Get a move on.' Jessica didn't seem too concerned with what I'd said, and didn't seem too bothered, either, when Cathy went into her room ten minutes later to hurry her along. It was her first day of school. The walk from our flat to Gullane Primary School was no more than five minutes, east along the High Street, through the narrow walkway between the houses down a short hill (towards the location of Gullane railway station prior to its abandonment before the Second World War), then back out into the fields leading to the school on the south-eastern and lowest part of the town. When we arrived we went with Jessica through the front door of the school, and checked in at the office. We were late, and there was a class already in progress in the gymnasium beside the office. The school administrator met us, ticked off a name in a book, and then led us through the gym to the classroom for Primary 1 and 2.

Jessica followed along, eyes wide open, mouth closed; it wasn't fear, just exposure to the strange. The classroom was bright and spacious, and full of drawings and artwork, and the walls were covered with letter and number recognition schemes. The class had started a couple of weeks before, but the teachers said we were not to worry. Primary 1 was all about basics and finding your feet. Mrs Inglis, a tall, attractive woman with a dominating sense of cheer, came over to meet us.

'Ahhh!' she said, loudly, so that the whole class could hear. 'This is our new student from Canada, Jessica Gillespie. Everybody say hello to Jessica.'

'Hello, Jess-i-ca,' they chorused.

Mrs Inglis spoke to us in a lower voice. 'This is grand. She'll do just fine today. I'm sure of it. You're welcome to stay and watch for a bit if you like, but you can go whenever you like, too.'

We nodded and moved to the side, while Mrs Inglis took Jessica by the hand to the group of kids seated on the floor. They'd just been in the middle of reading a book. Before she let Jess sit on the floor, she said to the class, 'Now Jessica has a special friend today, and for the whole time that she's getting used to being in school here, and that's Isla.' A red-haired girl in the middle of the pack grinned and waved to Jessica, who tentatively raised a hand, unsure about waving back. 'And so if she has any questions she can ask Isla, but if she can't find Isla, or if Isla isn't here, then she can ask anyone else for help. Isn't that right, class? . . . Isn't that right, class?'

'Yes, Mrs Inglis,' they said.

'Right,' said a satisfied Mrs Inglis. She looked at Jess. 'You can sit down now if you like, Jessica, and perhaps we'll continue reading our story.' Jess went over and sat down right beside Isla, who reached over and took Jessica's hand, holding it lightly but firmly. Jessica smiled at her, then both of them turned their faces back up to Mrs Inglis, who looked to us and winked. Jess had already forgotten we were there.

We turned and eased our way out of the classroom. Cathy reached for a tissue in her pocket. I used it after her. We went to a door that seemed to lead outside, but it was locked. We tried to leave the way we'd come in, but when we got to that door, it too was locked. It was our daughter's first day of school and we couldn't get out. A teacher spotted us trapped like fish in a bowl behind the door window. She came over and opened it for us, giving us a rather sceptical eye. 'Can I help you?' she said.

Cathy spoke, and her voice was hoarse. 'Oh, we're just here dropping off our daughter . . . in Primary 1.'

The teacher took a closer look at us, and her expression softened. 'Ohh,' she cooed. 'First day?'

We nodded.

'Ah, right,' she said, leading us out through the gym. 'That's always hard.'

Trying to smile away our embarrassment, we thanked her as we left. Walking down the street, back up to Lammerview Terrace where a sitter was with Grace, Cathy shook her head and stuffed the tissue back in her pocket. 'It's just so humiliating,' she laughed. 'The only person in our family that can keep it together is five years old.'

The Comfort of His Own Skin: I Don't Need to Look

My father did not finish High School, making it only as far as Grade 11 before dropping out to go to work for the National Cash Register company as a repairman, after which he went on to start Calgary Glass & Trim. I never fully understood why he didn't finish school. It wasn't something he talked about, though my suspicion was that he just didn't think it would do him any good. He probably knew he'd never go to university, and he must have thought that to get out into the world, learn a trade, and start working was the best way forward. He wasn't wrong in this, because he was a wizard with his hands. There wasn't anything he couldn't fix, wasn't any technical, electrical or material problem he couldn't resolve. Certainly one of the more recurring images of my childhood is sitting around the kitchen table helping him fix the stove or the toaster or a clock, passing him a tool, holding down a wire (though my guess is that his children were more hindrance than help in terms of efficiency). I've inherited that love of working with my hands, though not his talent for it.

But it wasn't just his ability with materials that was impressive. He was a smart man. And he knew it, too. This was the funniest thing about him, that for a man with so little education, he had very few doubts about his ability to think through a problem, or to properly analyse a complex set of facts and arrive at a synthesis of those facts. And yet he rarely spoke in this way. It was only when challenged or provoked that he displayed his intellectual abilities. I just don't think he cared enough about arguments of an intellectual nature to fully participate.

Though it's more an anecdote about memory than it is intellect, the incident I remember best regarding his faith in his mind was an argument he and I had one day when I was perhaps sixteen.

There had been a terrible aeroplane crash somewhere in the Middle East, and the papers had duly reported how all 121 passengers had died. A couple of days later, this crash came up at the dinner table, and I reiterated how awful it was that 121 people had died.

'A hundred and twenty-nine,' my father said.

'No, a hundred and twenty-one.'

'A hundred and twenty-nine people died,' he said.

I was as sure of the number as I had ever been sure of anything. I could even see the newspaper headline in my mind's eye. 'Dad, it was a hundred and twenty-one. I read it in the paper. It was a hundred and twenty-one. I'm positive. One hundred per cent positive.'

'Do you believe everything you read?'

'Don't try to be funny. It was a hundred and twenty-one.'

He shook his head. 'It was a hundred and twenty-nine.'

I was getting exasperated. Why didn't he just acknowledge that I was sure of what I was saying? Especially since I *knew* I was right. 'I know I'm right. Why don't you go back and look at the paper. You'll see.'

He gave me a level stare. 'I don't need to look.'

With that he returned to his meal. Someone else at the table raised a different topic and that was that. Still, it bothered me for days. Albert Camus once wrote that the sign of a vulgar mind is the need to be right. One night after everyone else had gone to bed, I took my vulgar mind and turned my fingers black with ink scanning through the old newspapers we collected under the kitchen desk before tossing them out every couple of weeks. Eventually, I found the article. The headline confirmed what I'd said, 121 PASSENGERS KILLED IN DESERT CRASH. I think I actually cackled with glee. I tore the article out and took it into my room, expressly so that I could show it to him; but not just to him. It would have to wait for dinner, a family dinner, in front of every-one else. This was a coup.

The next night, we all sat down as usual for dinner. The normal cacaphony of eight, plus a whining dog (our cocker spaniel–poodle cross, Tommy), plus, I imagine, a guest or two, since dinners at our house were invariably more dorm frenzies than quiet family sit-downs. There was a lull in the conversation about halfway through the meal, and I leapt into the void.

'Dad, remember that airplane crash?'

He put down his knife and fork.

'Well, I'm still pretty sure it was a hundred and twenty-one.'

He smiled, and must have sensed what was coming. 'Is that right?'

'And I knew you wouldn't believe me, so I actually went back and found the newspaper article.' With a flourish I pulled the article from my back pocket and produced it for all to see. I showed the table the headline. 'See. "*A hundred and twenty-one passengers killed in desert crash*".'

There was a hubbub around the table. My brothers and sister were all grinning. This didn't happen often, or ever. Had the Ghost been caught out? Was the infallible fallible? Even my mother seemed to be holding her breath. My father took the article from me with a world-weary sigh, as if he was being forced to do some-thing he didn't want to do. He lowered his eyes to the bottom of the article, found what he was looking for and began to read, '. . . and with the eight crew members, the total number of dead in the crash is confirmed at a hundred and twenty-nine.' He folded up the article, handed it back to me, picked up his knife and fork, and calmly cut into the chicken on his plate. I held the folded arti-cle in between my thumb and forefinger as the table erupted with laughter and heckling from my siblings. This was even better than Ghost being caught out. I'd flown too close to the sun, and had crashed down straight into the middle of the kitchen table. My brothers and sister mercilessly pulled me apart.

It took years to see, but what I take from that now is that he didn't need to look. During the first phase of the argument, he didn't need to look. And I do not doubt that he never did look, never would have looked, and never would have thought of it again, had I not kept picking. He knew he was right. Whether anyone else knew he was right, he couldn't have cared less. That wasn't the point.

$$\lambda$$

The water was scorching my hands, as usual, as I cleaned up the lunch dishes. The infelicities of the taps made it impossible to find a middle ground between cold and scalding, so cleaning dishes was always a bit like poking a hand into a fire to snatch out a sizzling hot dog. I was just shutting off the taps when I heard a shriek from the living room. It was Cathy.

'Curtis, get in here! Quick. Get in here!'

I left the water running and with dripping hands bolted into the front room.

'What?!'

'Look,' said Cathy, pointing at the floor. 'Jess, put that toy over there by the table. Watch.'

Jess did as she was told, and then Grace eyed it, and took off, crawling, actually crawling over to the toy she so clearly had her mind focused on. We laughed, shouted. 'Way to go, Grace!' Jess went over and gave her a hug. 'Yay, Grace.' This was new and we'd been waiting for some time for her to start crawling, since Jess had started at about seven months. Grace was now ten months old. Unsurprisingly (now that we see her personality emerging), Grace had paid no attention to any timetables other than her own. She looked up at us, her face a cross between surprise (that she'd some-how managed to find herself at the toy she'd wanted) and annoyance (over the fact that we were acting so surprised). For the next twenty minutes, we put her through what can only be called torture, placing objects of intense desire – such as teething rings, fuzzy bunnies and music boxes – well out of her reach just to see her crawl over to them.

Despite the great success of her day, Grace wouldn't fall asleep that night. She seemed upset about something, almost frightened, as if she'd seen a sinister shadow against the wall of her bedroom and couldn't stop looking at it. She was exhausted, and even seemed as if she wanted to fall asleep, but could not. Cathy held her for at least two hours, tried to put her to bed a couple of times. Each time the result was the same: fear of something, shrieking, spastically arching her back as soon as she was laid in her crib. Perhaps she was still adjusting to the shape and smell and energy of a new bedroom. Or maybe it was only the frustration all small children experience at the always-in-flux divide between mental and physical prowess.

Cathy needed relieving, as it was about midnight by this point, so I took Grace and sat in the front room with her across my lap, with her large flannel blanket across both of us. Having done all the hard work – the childcare equivalent of loosening the jar lid for someone else to twist it off – Cathy went to bed and left me to oversee Grace as she slowly calmed down. I turned off all the lights, but left the television on, and the queer garish colour of it played against the far wall. The sound was off and we could hear the October wind whistling off the North Sea. We were warm under our blanket, just the two of us, allied against the night. Grace went quiet, but stayed awake. We were settled into the big green chair by the window, and it was warm and comfortable, and I wouldn't have been anywhere else on earth at that moment than folded up in a chair with my ten-month-old daughter.

I woke up. I didn't know how much later it was. The TV was still on. Grace was flat across my lap, though still mostly under her blanket. The heat from our shared position made a kind of aura around us, and made me think of cuddling in my mother's lap, something that still must appeal to all of us in one way or another at some point in our lives. Grace was sound asleep, and through the flickering greens and yellows of the TV – playing some absurd cop movie from the '70s – I could examine my daughter's face now that she was asleep. She had her mother's nose, small but broad, delicate eyelashes, cheeks so comically pudgy that I knew we would tease her about it when we looked back at baby pictures. I was smiling, but a spear of loss soon struck home, found its central mark. The moment was almost too great for me. Even as I had it, here with her, the two of us alone, a father and his daughter, this moment was already gone. The future was going to be too much to bear, and as I looked into the years to come I wondered just what kind of father I was going to be.

I had always been horrified by men who cling, who suffocate their children with the pillow of their love. I felt sufficiently aware of the awfulness of it that I thought I could recognise it and avoid it. Cathy would be there to help if I strayed. It hadn't been that hard to date with Jessica, but as I sat there, with the wind groaning outside, the queer colours flickering inside, my daughter sighing in sleep before me, I began to understand why some parents act this way. Cathy and I knew, or had hoped anyway, that Jessica would not be our last child. Each moment, each marker, in her life passed as it did, and we celebrated and enjoyed them. First word, first solo walk, first potty. But the urge to hang on to them had never been that severe, never been that psychologically difficult to let go, because we planned to experience it again with another child. But Grace is our last child. And so, with no more children to come, each marker Grace passes through will be the last we will see of that in our own children. Hence the urge to preserve it, to coddle it, to over-celebrate it, and to infantilise both your child and your relationship with that child. But love is not meant to be caught in amber; it's not a solid, but a fluid – light and clear like spring water. To try to hang on to your child's past has to be to somehow lock both of you into that past. I vowed then and there to release my children, to try to love them with a free and blithe spirit, as I already knew Cathy would, more naturally than I ever could.

This, it occurred to me then, was my parents' gift to me – meaning that they applied their love in the form of a light mist, not a stream through a fire hose. I never doubted that they loved me. Only once do I ever recall my father saying that he loved me, and that was the day before he died. And yet I never doubted it.

I hit the remote and turned the television off. The room was lit up by the darkness of the night, its shadows drawn of moon and cloud and wind. Grace stirred as I picked us both up, but she did not wake. I kissed her forehead lightly as I laid her in her crib; she rolled over on her side, put a nibble of blanket in the space between her upper lip and nostrils, and stayed asleep. I left her room and noticed from the hallway that Jessica's bedside light was still on. She'd taken to wanting it on as she fell asleep, since she claimed it helped her 'sleep better'. She'd gone through many such strategies of her own devising: over the last few years she'd needed to go to bed with socks on, then with a woolly hat on, then with her winter coat on, then with nothing on, then with a music box playing, then with two music boxes playing, then with the window open, then closed, then with no bedsheets, with stuffed animals under the pillow, the quilt, the bedframe, beside her, on top of her, under her. There were as many permutations as there were sleeps.

She was snoring softly. Her own flannel blanket – covered with animal shapes we'd never actually been able to decode; they were either sheep or dogs, we thought – was wrapped like a belt around her waist, but covered no other part of her body. I covered her up, kissed her goodnight and shut the light off. She mumbled and put her face into the pillow.

In our bedroom, Cathy's bedside light was still on, and she was reading, which seemed odd, given the hour. I whispered something about Grace having finally gone down, but there was no answer. I went over to that side of the bed, and saw that she'd fallen asleep while reading. Her book was open and she was still grasping it one-handed, her other hand under her cheek. It took a firm pull to loosen the book from her grasp. I got in bed, and read for ten minutes from my own book, *The Orchard on Fire* by Shena Mackay, and as I shut off the lamp I wondered, not for the first time, why her delicate, brilliant prose had not yet made her a worldwide household name.

The light of the moon above the Lammermuir Hills to the south poured into the pale darkness of our bedroom, throwing a cast of shapes and shadows against the far wall. Rectangular, clearly delineated, yet of unknown outline or origin, the shapes and light were strangely comforting despite the fact that they were mysterious. There was both clarity and no clarity, at once an understanding (that the moon's backlighting was creating the shadows) and a lack of understanding (of which objects were interrupting the moonlight). I lay on my back and watched the shapes change over the course of half an hour as the moon floated across the dark night stage, its path the determinant as to what got splayed across our bedroom wall, unable to predict how these shapes would silkily mutate. I was able to guess where, and in what size, the shapes would be etched against the wall; I just didn't know quite what they would look like or precisely what was creating them. Sleep came late, in a state I had come to recognise as familiar, my default condition; impatient for the future to arrive, yet fearful of missing the beauty and significance of the present, even as I consciously watched it sink into the past.

2

I popped into the Goose Green bakery on the High Street. Katriona, cheery and cherry-cheeked, huffed and puffed out a quick hello, as she served the stream of people that came every morning to the town's only bakery. With my bread under my arm, I went next door to the newsagent to pick up some papers and some milk. Shafqat Rasool was behind the till, engrossed in his own newspaper, which was always the same exotic-looking Pakistani journal featuring that looping, gorgeous Urdu alphabet.

'How are you today, Mr Rasool?'

'Struggling, Mr Curtis, struggling.'

'Oh,' I said, trying to commiserate. 'Why's that?'

He lifted his nose up, as if an interesting scent had just come across his counter (which perhaps it had; our flat had not been equipped with a shower). 'Life,' he explained slowly, 'is a struggle. And I am alive. Therefore I struggle.'

I put the milk and papers on the counter in front of him. It appeared as if he'd also been doing some stocktaking; there was a sheet of paper on the counter, with ticks beside a long list of words, all of which were written in Urdu. 'Ah, well,' I said, nodding. 'We're all in the same boat.'

'I don't think so, Mr Curtis, I don't think so.'

'No?'

'We all have our own boat, I think. Some of us have big boats, yachts like, and some of us,' he waved his hand around the shop, 'have dinghies.' He smiled his forlorn, irresistible smile.

'Some of us prefer dinghies,' I said, adopting as weary an expression as I could so as to express my solidarity with his plight. He laughed as Eeyore might, if Eeyore ever laughed, and then he dolefully suggested I do everything within my powers to have a good day. Once back home, with my coffee beside me at my desk, I phoned Jack. We'd talked on the phone a couple of times but had not actually seen one another yet. The phone rang four or five times, and I almost hung up, since there was no machine to take a message. But then there was a jangle on the other end. Doris answered.

'Oh, yes, Curtis, hello,' she said in her soft East Lothian coastal singsong. Because of the Edinburgh influence, the accent along Gullane way is much softer than in serious working-class East Lothian villages such as Tranent and Prestonpans, many of which had their heyday during the area's peak of coal production a century earlier. Doris, at seventy-eight, was and still is the oldest person living in Gullane who was actually born there. 'I'll put Jack on straight away.'

There was a brief pause, before a chuckling sound rose from the background. This was Jack's way, I would learn. You could always tell him coming by his chuckle, the way some people's smell or footsteps announce their imminent arrival. With Jack it was a little boy's chuckle, and it couldn't help but bring a smile to your own lips.

'Hello, boy,' he said, picking up the receiver. 'Ow you getting on then?'

'Good, thanks.'

'Ah, well, that's wonderful. The girls settling in okay?'

'Great, yes, thanks.'

'So you want to play golf?'

'I was talking with Archie yesterday and he booked us a time for one this afternoon. What do you think?'

The chuckle. 'Not me, boy. Not a wind player. Don't like bad weather.'

'Really,' I said, playing up my surprise. 'You can't play golf in Scotland without wind, can you? I thought the Scots said, "If there's nae wind it's nae golf!"?'

'Well, I'm English, so there you go!' he laughed. 'Anyway, this is not wind we're talking here. Wind is fine, it's good. But I'm telling you that the forecast is for gales. You'd better bring your wellies and waterproofs.'

'They forecast that?'

'Gales,' he emphasised with the satisfaction of the already-decided. 'Pelting rain and massive winds.'

To be sure, the weather was looking unpromising. The winds were stiff, flag-flapping from the east, and a dull tin-coloured herd of clouds was hustling in from the North Sea as if a shepherd were beating them on with a long cleek. I paused a moment to consider what a person living in Scotland would mean by gales. Could it be the same as a North American gale, or was it some-thing altogether worse?

'Righto,' I said. 'Maybe later in the week.'

'Count on it, lad . . . Now then . . . are you getting lots of work done?'

'Of course, Jack! How could you suggest otherwise.'

He kept chuckling. 'Because you don't seem to be doing much work to me.'

I laughed back at him. 'Well, you know, man wasn't made for work alone.'

'True, true. But that's not my point, if you see what I mean. I mean, are you doing *any* work?'

'Jack!'

'Am I right, though, boy?'

'Well, let's just say that you and Cathy are certain to get along.'

'Ah, right, a clever woman, no doubt.'

'Well, I'd better get back to work then.'

'Right. I don't want to keep you, son.'

I rang Archie up, and told him what Jack had said about the weather.

'Marston? Did he tell you what he did to me this morning?'

This morning? It was only nine o'clock as it was. 'No, he didn't.'

'I rang him this morning, and he picked up and he said, "Archie, my boy, do you realise that I'm standing here talking to you naked as a bluejay?" Can you imagine? Ach, the thought of it! That bloody Englishman standing there without a stitch of clothing on. It boggles the mind, it really does. I've tried to get the image out of my mind all morning. Anyway, okay, it's not so good right now, the weather. But listen Cartiss, ring me again at eleven just to make sure it's playable out there.'

'Okay,' I said, looking out of my window to the rain that was now beginning to fall. The vista from the back of Lammerview Terrace caught the gorgeous sweep of the Lammermuir Hills to the south as they ran in a stately line west to east. The weather was wonderful in the west, but the smoke from a chimney down in the village below was heading west, so I stood up again and looked out to the east to see what was coming. Black thunderclouds over

Dunbar were now massing in rows like infantry battalions waiting
for their General's arm to drop. 'Are you sure it'll be fine?'

'No.' With that he rang off.

But the weather did improve, dramatically. When I called Archie
at eleven, the wind had lessened slightly, and the black gang of thunderclouds had passed to the south-east and were now loitering over
the Pentland hills south of Edinburgh. One o'clock it was. When I
got to the 1st tee of Gullane No. 3, Archie had not yet arrived, but
Jack was standing there, swinging his driver, loosening up.

'Jack!' I said. 'What are you doing here? I thought you weren't
going to play.'

He grinned. 'I was sitting around the house dickering about
going out or not going out, and Doris said I just ought not to go
if I didn't want to, and to stop moaning about it. But then I
thought, Oh hell, what kind of complainer does that. And
look . . . it's turned out wonderfully.'

I did a 360. *Wonderfully* was not entirely accurate. Yes, it was
sunny, but the wind, as usual, was howling angrily, whistling
and warping. Up until my time in Scotland, I'd never actually
heard the wind whistle out in open spaces, with no small porticoes
or pathways to reverberate off. But it was whistling here, was
moving so quickly that a skirling trill was going on in the tunnels
of my ears.

'Has it really been a year already?' Jack said. 'Since we had that
game? Since we met that day?'

I nodded, smiled. 'I know. Hard to believe.'

'Well, it's great to see you, son. I'm delighted you're back.' Jack
stopped and looked at me, quite seriously, surveying my face as if
he'd noticed I was missing a couple of teeth or had a bloody nose.
'I have to say, though, you look a bit weary, boy.'

I laughed. 'Grace didn't sleep so well last night.'

Jack laughed along with me, and Archie appeared from around

the other side of the Starter's Hut. He raised one hand and came towards us as fast as he could. He'd had angina when Lorne and I had first played with him the year before. It had got worse, and just that past spring he'd had triple bypass surgery. Yet here he was, not five months later, out for a game of golf, undeterred. I was about to tee off with two men, whose combined age was quadruple my own, one of whom was eighty-two, the other who was seventy-six and had just undergone major heart surgery, and I already knew I'd feel as if I was holding them back, such was their energy and the sheer speed with which they played.

Archie marched directly to the tee and dropped his quiver bag, pulling out his driver and placing a tee peg in the ground almost in the same single fluid motion. He didn't seem in the least surprised to see Jack present. 'Right,' he said, waving his driver at both of us. 'A game. Handicaps. Young Mr Gillespie is a three, I believe, I'm a sixteen and the crusty Englishman to my left is a seventeen. Call the difference fourteen, three-quarters of which we'll call eleven. Gillespie gives Baird and Marston eleven. We'll play 10p skins. Right.' He turned to face the hole, and, without even the remotest hint of a practice swing, took a short stab at the ball, sending it dead straight 150 yards down the fairway. He pulled his peg from the ground, pocketed it, and went to stand splay-legged at the back of the tee. 'Come on!' he half-shouted. 'We haven't got all day here, have we? Stop confabulating and play.'

Jack let his head fall into a slow, short back and forth. 'Try to imagine,' he said to me, but with enough volume that Archie could easily hear it. 'Try to imagine what would happen if you put all that aggression in a frame bigger than what Baird has now. It's truly frightening, it is.'

Archie jiggled his tees and coins in his pocket, pretending not to have heard us. 'Come on, Cartiss, on you go.'

I teed off, as did Jack. We made our way along the 1st hole of

Gullane No. 3, a tricky par-four of 320 yards. Gullane No. 3 is the shortest and the newest of the three Gullane Golf Club courses, measuring just 5,600 yards at a par of 68. It was opened in 1910. The shame is that the vast majority of visitors through Gullane never even set foot on Gullane No. 3, thinking that it's either too short, or that the number assigned to it is an indicator of quality relative to the other two courses. Nothing could be less true. Yes, Gullane No. 1 is the championship course, the course where they play the final Open qualifying during those years the Open is staged at Muirfield. And yes, Gullane No. 2 is a brilliant golf course in its own right, nearly as hard as No. 1, and which was often used in the past as an Open qualifying course. No. 2 also has the advantage of having been designed by Willie Park Jr, the brother of Sheila Baird's grandfather. But Gullane No. 3 is the kind of golf course you fall in love with. It's short, but it's hellishly difficult if you're hitting it crooked. And the greens are small, tight, undulating, and heavily guarded by bunkers. It runs up and across Gullane Hill and Gala Law (a kind of subsidiary corner of Gullane Hill) and then down into the flats hard against Luffness New Golf Course and the Aberlady Bay Local Nature Reserve. 'You'll never make a fool of No. 3,' Jack had said to me on the phone a couple days before. Archie had agreed. 'Architecturally, it's the best course we've got here. If you told me that I only had one course to play for the rest of my life, and that it had to be No. 3, I'd be delighted about that. I'd die happy.'

We marched off down the khaki-coloured fairway, past the old rail tracks, across the ancient Saltcoats Road, and down near the ruins of Saltcoats Castle. The first three holes of Gullane No. 3 are all at the bottom of the hill, and are played virtually straight out from the middle of the town, south-west towards the potato fields, then, at the 4th hole, the course turns west, up the hill, towards the Nature Reserve and Aberlady Bay. Jack may have been a sixteen handicap and Archie a seventeen, but they were already fleecing me by the 4th hole. We all parred the 1st, but they had strokes, and therefore net birdies. We all parred the 145-yard par-three 2nd hole. On the 300-yard par-four 3rd, both had strokes. I birdied it, but Archie parred it, with a stroke, giving him a birdie, and Jack birdied it, with a stroke, giving him an eagle. I was one under par after three holes, but was down thirty pence. Jack went on to shoot 78 that day, four shots under his age. It wasn't the last time I would witness it.

Of course, the golf wasn't the chief pleasure of the day for me; it was the company, though at more than one point, I wasn't sure that Jack or Archie were deriving the same pleasure from the company that I was. When I'd first played with them, a year earlier, it was clear to me that they were best friends. I was wrong. They were closer than best friends. As we marched up and down the fairways, they bickered, they fought, they argued. On the 3rd hole, Jack claimed an automatic skin for a birdie.

'I'm afraid not,' said Archie. 'We didn't clarify that on the first tee.'

Jack turned on him. 'Baird, we always play automatic skins. That was your rule. You always insist on that.'

Archie remained resolute. No automatic skins. On the 4th hole, Jack conceded a putt to me that was about three feet. Archie challenged the concession, which irked Jack.

'Oh, but Archie, he'd make that. It's a tiddler.'

Archie looked at me, and may have even winked. 'Marston, that was not a putt to concede. It was four feet at least. And I've yet to see young Gillespie make a tiddler. Once he makes one, I'll happily concede the next one.'

'Ah, but Archie, you said yourself once that a putt discussed is a putt conceded. Those were your very words. I can hear them even as I speak them.'

Archie seemed to have no reply to this and so took a different tack, pushing ahead to the next tee, the 5th, from which there is a stunning view of the whole of the Firth. 'Cartiss,' he said. 'Do you see those?' He pointed across the water to Fife, his finger indicating the West and East Lomond Hills. I nodded. 'The Paps of Fife,' he said, cackling. Jack had pulled up beside us, and was laughing as he considered the hills. They did look incredibly breast-like.

'Ah yes, the Paps,' said Jack. 'Not much cleavage, really.'

Archie turned on Jack. 'Marston! Shocking! A man of your age, talking like that. You ought to be ashamed of yourself.'

Jack grinned. 'The Good Lord may have taken away the ability, Archie, but he hasn't taken away the desire.'

Archie nodded soberly, as if to concede the truth of Jack's statement, and their exchange put me in mind of the early twentieth-century British Prime Minister A. J. Balfour's article on growing old as a golfer. (It was also Balfour who, during a speech to a golfing society, uttered the famous quote – one Archie frequently invoked – that, 'A tolerable day, a tolerable green, a tolerable opponent, supply, or ought to supply, all that any reasonably constituted human being should require in the way of entertainment. With a fine sea-view, and a clear course in front of him, the golfer should find no difficulty in dismissing all worries from his mind, and regarding golf, even, it may be, very indifferent golf, as the true and adequate end of man's existence.') In his 1894 article in *Badminton Golf*, Balfour wrote that ageing severely affects one's performance in most sporting pursuits,

> . . . and growing old is not commonly supposed to be so agreeable an operation in itself as to make it advisable to indulge in it more often in a single lifetime than is absolutely necessary. The golfer, on the other hand, is never

old until he is decrepit. So long as Providence allows him the use of two legs active enough to carry him round the green, and of two arms supple enough to take a 'half-swing', there is no reason why his enjoyment of the game need be seriously diminished. Decay no doubt there is; long driving has gone for ever; and something less of firmness and accuracy may be noted even in the short game. But the decay has come by such slow gradations, it has delayed so long and spared so much, that it is robbed of half its bitterness.

A fine sentiment, and undoubtedly true in most cases, but before me I had two men still hitting far enough to be dangerous, and with short games deadly enough to suffocate any hope I had of winning a majority of skins. Archie had played the first four holes well, but Jack had played them even better, and had won all the skins to that point. He teed off and stroked yet another perfect shot down the middle of the short par-four 5th. Again, he held his stance for a fraction longer than was necessary and Archie was on him in a shot. 'Get off the bloody tee, for Chrissakes! Quit standing there like a statue.'

We played down the 5th fairway and it was along that stretch of turf that I remembered just why I had always loved Gullane so much. The weather that afternoon had become very pleasant; the wind was ever-lessening and there was only broken cloud remaining, so that the sun actually stuck its nose out every now and then. The intermittent sunshine meant that the waters of the Firth were changing colour and depth throughout the afternoon, one minute a light blue, then kelpish-green the next, even going almost a light magenta along the northern shore near the Elie cliffs. Tankers, tugs and liners languished in the soft tide. Jack caught me staring sea-ward. 'I never get tired of that,' he said softly, following my gaze. 'Never. I've been up this hill thousands of times in my life and it's never been the same twice.'

Golfers had been having similar reveries from this hilltop for centuries. 'There is at Gullane,' wrote John Harrison in the *Scotsman* in 1885, 'all that the heart of man can desire; we mean, of course, the heart of a sensible man. He is a "duffer" indeed who cannot play golf on Gullane turf; and he is a wall-eyed wretch who, as he plays, does not enjoy the beauty of Gullane Hill.' Harrison can't match the nostalgic fury of D. J. Croal, writing his Gullane reminiscences in 1895:

> The place is rapidly being spoiled, the air of primitive quiet is going from it; the lack of architectural taste on the part of somebody or other has already vulgarised a piece of the finest, if least pretentious rural scenery in the South of Scotland. How different the place from what it was even fifteen years ago! On a fine September day in '80 or there-abouts, it was possible to play round after round with a sense of absolute possession, for the only living things to be seen were the geese and an aged black cow that used to ruminate near the smithy. One day now gives the green as much work as it then got in a week . . . let us go back another fifteen years and find Gullane very much as nature made it for golf. The game at that time lisped, so to speak, with its infant accents. August was as quiet in the village as March is now; September knew no break in the peaceful torpor of the year . . . [golfers] had to be content with a bare allowance of thirteen holes; and with putting-greens that were at the mercy of the rabbits . . . The backbone of the course was the same then as now . . . This was Gullane thirty years ago, when the racing stables were still pretty full, when trainers occupied the houses now held by city

men, when Luffness was known only to the plover and the wild duck, and when North Berwick was little else than a dirty fishing place. Golf was then only beginning to take firm root in the county. The promised land had not yet been entered upon. Yet the game, as it seems to me, was played with rather more hilarity then than it is now . . . Gullane, in this unalloyed state, was delightfully reposeful.

Yes, what a shame that Gullane had become so overrun, so despoiled, the village so hideously serious a place in which to play the game. Nevertheless, we did manage to continue on through our round, our games unalloyed, our demeanours reposeful, more or less. Nearing the end of the round, Archie had racked up a few skins, though Jack had taken the majority. I'd earned precisely none, despite the fact that I was only a couple of shots over par for the round. We came to the 16th tee, and Jack stopped me and pointed to a spot over in the left rough. 'Let me tell you something,' he said. 'About Baird.' Archie perked up and listened in. He was smiling broadly, so he must have known which story was coming.

'Years ago,' continued Jack, 'these holes were a bit different. This wasn't a par-four, it was two par-threes, and you used to have to tee up over there for the green we're using now, do you see what I'm saying?'

I nodded.

'So, one day, oh, this had to be twenty years ago, I was playing a match with this character here,' he jerked a thumb at Archie, who was now grinning ear to ear, 'and we came to this hole. It was a tight match, I think I was one-up. Well, I put my tee shot to about a foot. A kick-in birdie. And do you know what he does?'

I shook my head, and Archie began to laugh.

'He inspects the position of where I'd teed my ball and decides that it was six inches ahead of the markers. He made me replay the shot.'

'Well, of course, I did!' bellowed Archie. 'Those are the rules, Marston. I didn't make them up. You played ahead of the markers. Not my fault.'

'Would you have made me replay it if I'd hit a terrible shot? No, I don't think so. You'd have said not a word. But only because it was a great shot . . . really, one of my best . . . only because of that you made me re-tee it.'

Archie shrugged. 'I can only reiterate . . . such are the rules.'

'I will never forget that,' muttered Jack, as we trudged down the fairway. It was clear to me that this was not the first time this incident had been discussed in the last twenty years. On it went. They continued to bicker and take every opportunity to insult one another. ('Our wives call us the Two Grumpy Old Men,' they said in unison on one hole.) And yet it was so obviously a kind of symbiotic relationship, the kind of relationship strong enough to withstand any abuse. Their bickering was just a small gargoyle on the upper façade of a grand and dignified structure; the fangs were bared for ornamental purposes only. The evidence of this was quiet, but plain to be seen. Each man took every chance he could get to graciously pull the other's trolley ahead, always without saying a word, always taking it as far as possible. They picked up tees for one another. Archie would take a divot, Jack would pick it up and hand it back to him. Jack would sink a putt, Archie would pick the ball out of the hole and hand it to him. They repaired one another's ball marks. When I was on the other side of the fairway from the two of them, I would look across to see them striding side by side at every opportunity, talking amiably, laughing. They were competitive, but inseparable, like brothers. Until we finished, that is, at which point an argument broke out in the club lounge over who was to pay for drinks. 'You better not be buying that!' Jack half-shouted to Archie, who was standing at the bar. 'You'll be in big trouble if you pay for that, and that's a fact.'

Later, when Archie got up to leave, Jack held out a hand.

'No hard feelings, old boy.'

Archie grinned. 'You daft old bugger! Of course not!'

Jack turned to me with a world-weary expression. 'See what I'm saying? There's not even any point in making a nice gesture.' He returned his attention to Archie, who was standing cheerfully jingling the coins in his pocket, eagerly anticipating whatever Jack had to say next. 'I'm your only friend, Baird. You know that, don't you? I'm the only one who can put up with you day in and day out.'

Archie smiled and searched for the right words. A few members (some with nicknames as colourful as the Ferret and the Poisoned Dwarf) were lounging about, chuckling as they listened, no doubt familiar with the patter. 'Marston,' pronounced Archie, 'I believe I bear your friendship with considerable grace and equanimity, and I consider it the highest honour to be among your throng of admirers.'

Jack chuckled and raised his glass to his dear friend, pausing a beat. '. . . Likewise,' he said.

Gullane is a one-street town. I don't mean that literally, of course. There are many tight little side-street neighbourhoods, warrens, really, down in the flats along Muirfield Crescent and Muirfield Station, where former council houses have now almost all been sold for private ownership. And there are the wider, upsweeping boulevards of the Hill, where the mansions of the gentry are positioned so calmly above the fray. In a town of just 2,000 people there are at least five tiny but distinct communities in and of themselves, ranging from the out-and-out wealthy of the Hill, to the comfortably upper-middle-class located north of the High Street but not fully up the Hill, to the solidly working-class in the flats surrounding Gullane Primary School. And though the boundaries are demarcated clearly enough, the names do help distinguish things. The house names, that is. Historical precedent has decreed that in Great Britain people with a certain income and standing tend to feel compelled to own country homes with names, as if a simple address is not enough. These names almost always lean towards the simplistic, the nature-oriented or the idyllic. Pineview. Larkwing. Duneside. Rosebud. Iona. That sort of thing. Such is the case in Gullane, where there are scores of named houses (most of them, of course, up the Hill). In Gullane, there are many house names that invoke in one way or another the key factor of living smack in the middle of such beauty, namely, the view. Seaview, Forthview, Firthside, and so on. I'd not paid a whole lot of attention to these names during our first month in Gullane, but it was through the simplest of house names that the distinctions between neighbourhoods, and their respective physical and socio-economic attributes, were made clear to me. One day, the three of us walked Jessica to school together. We passed a ramshackle old house next to the asphalt path leading from the High Street down to the flats, the council houses and the school. Much to my delight, it was obvious a subversive soul owned the house in question. Nailed to the fronting of this small and rather squat house – which looked out on to nothing more than asphalt and a brick wall – was an ornately decorated, highly visible sign. In the kind of jaunty nautical lettering that might have denoted the name of one's sailboat, the sign said, *Nae' View*.

In any event, despite the variety of streets and neighbourhoods in such a small place, Gullane is functionally a one-street town in that the only road with any real and regular vitality to it is the

High Street (which also happens to double as the A198, which cuts through town on the way from Edinburgh to North Berwick). And on either side of this street, in amongst the various side streets, are the two town commons, though only one of these, Goose Green, is the 'official' common. It's just up from the Goose Green bakery, and is a wonderful expanse of manicured grass, featuring a small children's playground that became our regular hangout with the kids.

The other 'unofficial' common is the Children's Golf Course, owned by the Gullane Golf Club. The six-hole 'course' isn't really much more than a field about the size of two football pitches, and it sits squarely below the old High Street smithy (now a flower shop), and is bordered by the Mallard Hotel (where I'd stayed as a visiting student golfer with the University of St Andrews) and the 18th hole of Gullane No. 3. In terms of visibility, it is certainly more of a town common than Goose Green, because you can see it from the High Street, whereas Goose Green is not visible to those simply driving through town.

One bright afternoon, Jessica and I went to play golf at the Children's Course. On occasion I'd taken her with me to hit golf balls at the range in Canada, but this was to be her first ever actual game of golf. She was excited, as was I. Leaving the flat, she'd slung her stubby pencil bag over her slender little shoulder and announced to Cathy, 'Bye, Mum. Dad and I are going to go play some golfing.' I felt a brief flush of pride striding down the High Street with Jessica at my side, she with her short half-set of clubs, me with just my wedge and putter. I imagined driving down the street and seeing a man walking to the course with his daughter, and the vision brought a smile to my face. *But don't forget,* I silently reminded myself, *this is about having fun. She's just starting out. Be patient.*

On the way to the unattended 1st tee, we passed the sign that said, in no uncertain terms, that adults were not allowed on this golf course unless accompanied by a child. Bravo, I thought. At the 1st tee, Jessica took a tee from the pouch of her bag. 'I'll just stick one of these in, Daddy,' she said, getting down on her knees. She tried to push it in the hard ground with the tip of her index finger, repeatedly failing.

'There's an easier way, Jess. Want me to show you?'

'No,' she said quickly. 'No. I like this way.' Eventually she did manage to get the peg stuck in the ground, and she placed her ball on it. 'See,' she said, turning her face to mine. 'That works.'

I nodded, and motioned towards the flag, which was about forty yards away. 'Aim at that one, okay. Do you remember how to hold the club?'

She ignored me and took her miniature 3-wood in her hands, with the left hand separated from the right by at least a foot, as if she were holding a hockey stick. She stood over the ball with her legs spread so far apart she might have been expecting earth tremors.

'Sweetie, it's easier if you keep your hands together and stand a little more upright.'

'It is not.'

Patience.

She took a swipe at the ball, missing by at least a couple of feet, and the momentum she'd generated carried her around in a corkscrewing fashion so that she finished facing the opposite direc-tion. 'Wheeee!' she said. 'Oooh, that was fun!'

I looked at her ball, which was still perched undisturbed on her tee. 'You missed the ball, though.'

She turned and stared at the ball. 'Oh, yeah.' She giggled, and stood to the ball in exactly the same way as she had before.

'Jess, sweetie, it really is easier if you . . .'

'I like this way.'

'But . . .'

'I'll get it this time.' She stood and swung in the same way, and though it would be inaccurate to say she hit the ball, she did at least make some sort of contact, off the toe of the club. The ball shot away at a right angle to the hole. 'Look, Daddy! I got it!'

'We're going to that other hole over there . . . but, yeah, that's great. Good one.' She stood on the tee, admiring her effort. 'Okay, you have to stand back now, Jess, so that I can have a shot.' She moved back, I played and on we went. Thankfully, the course was empty. After a hole or two of continually missing the ball, I suggested that she try holding the club in a different way, any different way, from the hockey grip she'd been favouring to that point. 'Any way you like, Jess. It doesn't matter. But maybe some other way would work better.'

She thought about that for a minute as we stood on the 3rd tee. 'Okay,' she said. 'I've got an idea.' She got on her knees again to poke her tee into the ground, and then when she stood up she took the club in her hands more or less as I'd suggested fifteen minutes earlier. 'Watch, Daddy, I'm really going to hit the golfing ball this time.' Still standing like she was playing leapfrog, she swung violently but made a precise contact, hitting the ball squarely off the middle of the club. Unluckily, she'd lost her footing, and therefore lost what little ability she had to influence the direction of the shot. The ball went screaming at shin height off the course, past the boundary railing, across East Links road, between two parked Land Rovers, and off the ancient stone fence in front of the Mallard Hotel, causing it to ricochet up and over the Land Rovers, back on to the road and over on to the apron of grass fronting the course. The whole thing had taken a couple of seconds.

Jess turned to me, her eyes wide, not sure if she was going to be reprimanded or congratulated.

'Wow,' I said, quickly glancing up and down the length of the open field. We were still alone.

She grinned and pushed some of her curly hair away from her face. 'I hit that one good, didn't I, Daddy?'

'No kidding.'

The next couple of holes passed without event, and as we came to the 5th tee I decided it was as good a time as any to try to start introducing her to some of the game's etiquette. After all, I rather piously reasoned, it's never too early to teach a kid how to behave properly. 'You know, Jess,' I said to her as she marched to the tee ahead of me. 'Normally, in golf, the person who won the previous hole gets to tee off first on the next hole.'

She stopped and looked at me. '. . . Okay.' Continuing on, she made a move to put her tee in the ground.

'Jess, do you know what I mean?'

'Yeah.'

'Well, what are you doing, then? Why are you putting your tee in the ground? Shouldn't you offer to let me tee off first?'

'Why?'

'Because I won the last hole.'

'No, I did.'

'You did not!'

'Yes, I did. I beat you.'

'Oh, come on, you had at least ten shots on that hole. I only had three.'

'You did?'

'Yes. And let me tell you, three is a lot less than ten.'

It was only when she stopped and looked at her fingers, and began counting with them to compare three against ten, that the shame kicked in. I was arguing with a five-year-old about who got to tee off first.

'You're right, Daddy. Three is less than ten. Six less.'

'Seven less.'

'What?'

'Never mind. It's okay. You go ahead.'

'No, you go. It's okay.' She backed away, and wouldn't return to the tee until I'd finished.

The 5th hole is about sixty yards long, and runs along a narrow gravel path, Saltcoats Road, that separates the Children's Course from the rough along the 18th fairway of Gullane No. 3. I took my wedge, addressed the ball, made a compact half-swing, and watched as the ball landed five yards short of the cup, took two hops, and plopped straight into the hole.

'Jess!' I shouted. 'Jess!' I shot my arms in the air. At that exact moment, a car happened to be passing along Saltcoats Road with its windows down. 'Did you see that?' I shouted. They gave me an excited thumbs-up. 'Jess, a hole-in-one! Can you believe it?!'

She'd begun walking to the tee, holding her peg in preparation. She stopped beside me. 'Good one, Daddy. Do I get to hit now?'

When we stepped through the door back at the flat, Jess shouted out, 'Mum, we're back.' Cathy and Grace came through to the front entry.

'How was it?' Cathy said.

'Oh, it was great!' said Jessica, pulling her bag off her shoulder. 'And you're not going to guess what happened!'

'What?' said Cathy, looking to me for hints. I decided not to give any, curious to see just how Jess would describe my hole-in-one, a thing most golfers never even see, let alone experience; and here was Jess, having seen an ace during the first round of golf of her life.

'I hit one off a wall and over a car. You should have seen it!'

X

The Face: The White Shadow

The best word I can come up with to describe the picture in my mind's eye is impassivity, though perhaps that's not quite the right word, since what I mean to suggest is more the attempt at impassivity. There are many things I recognisably share with my father, and probably many more that I don't recognise, but one I do know very well is the over-reaction to cheap emotion and maudlin entertainment, followed by a pathetic and usually comic attempt to hide the over-reaction through the aforementioned attempt at impassivity. Either that, or an all-out attack on the manipulative and/or aesthetic qualities of the offending material. To wit: *The White Shadow*, a mediocre television show from the late '70s and early '80s that revolved around a white basketball coach hired to run the team at an inner-city Los Angeles school populated by nothing but black students. Growing up, my siblings and I were all devoted television-watchers (not much has changed) and this was one of the shows we watched without fail, for reasons I'm unable to recall. Also for reasons I'm unable to recall, my father used to watch it with us every week.

During one episode, the coach had to help one of the young players through a particularly bad time at home. Maybe there were drugs involved, or spousal abuse. I don't remember much, except that the coach risked his job by helping the player resolve the family crisis. At the conclusion of the episode, the young black player, who didn't talk much, was standing in the gym with the old white coach, who talked a lot. As the closing credits ran across the screen, the young player silently stepped forward and gave the coach a simple hug. End of programme.

There was a rustle as we all got up to get a drink or a snack before the next programme. Then my brother Conor noticed something. 'Ha!' he cried. We all looked over. 'Look! Look at Ghost. He's crying. Ghost is crying.'

Sure enough, our father was sitting in his chair, his eyes wet with tears. We were absolutely over the moon with glee. 'He's bawling! Ghost is bawling. Awww, was it that sad? Boo hoo!' We were relentless in our teasing, but through the whole thirty seconds of abuse we gave him, he just sat there, didn't wipe his eyes, didn't get up, didn't growl at us. He just tried to remain impassive, as if to suggest that this was purely physiological, and was not something he was in control of.

Of course, I'm now the same, though I do try to cover it somewhat. There was a commercial on TV a few years back in which a young boy wasn't allowed out of the house to play with another young boy, something to do with racism. The final shot of the commercial was of the excluded boy standing on the stoop clutching his teddy bear. I saw this commercial perhaps a hundred times, and was a mess by the end of it each time. Cheap straight-to-video melodramas get me reaching for the tissues ('Manipulative trash,' I say hoarsely to a smiling Cathy), and close-ups of exultant athletes crossing finish lines or winning cups bring on runny noses and wet cheeks. It's physiological.

Still, I don't think I've quite managed the impassivity my father achieved during those moments when we caught him out, though I wonder now if it was less about reserve than it was a coded message. Was he just trying to say something to us without having to say it, since the words themselves would have been mocked or ignored? *You'll understand. You'll grow up, marry, have children, lose friends and family. Then you'll understand.*

3

It was impossible to imagine a worse afternoon to begin driving lessons, but Cathy was insistent despite the rain and wind, and despite the fact that we had errands to run and tickets to buy prior to attending the Gullane Community League Autumn Ceilidh that night. She didn't want to keep putting it off. Besides, she reasoned, Jess was in school for the next couple of hours and if we took Grace along in the car, she'd probably fall asleep.

Cathy drove back in Canada, but that was with an automatic transmission and on the other side of the road. Worse for her was that reliance on me to get from place to place was proving too much of a strain. 'But isn't that the way things ought to be?' I'd said.

'Meaning?'

'Well, you know, woman needs man. Woman cannot adequately negotiate the world without the assistance of a man.'

Her mouth went tight.

'. . . or, or maybe we can just go out and do some practising,' I said, reaching for the keys.

It certainly made sense for Cathy to drop any reliance on me to get around. Her days seemed forever full, and in the short time we'd been there, she'd already made many fast friends in the village. A gang of mothers with their non-school-age children would regularly congregate for coffee at one house or another (and when it was her turn to host, I tended to make my way into Edinburgh to work). But that certainly wasn't the extent of it. She went for runs along the beach. She took a course on the Art and Architecture of East Lothian in Haddington, and boned up on Scottish history. She took Jessica to swimming lessons. She visited Edinburgh regularly, and even sometimes managed to get out for a game of golf. And for many of these activities, being able to negotiate Scottish roads and left-hand shifting was an asset.

'I want an open space,' she'd said, once we'd got the Egg moving with me behind the wheel. 'Somewhere where there's lots of room, but not other cars. Or people. I don't want anyone watching this.'

The nearest space we could find to fit that description was the car park at the Yellowcraigs beach access, behind Dirleton. It was a large open field, not paved, but so well-used through the summers that it was as flat as a tarmac lot. The lashing rain had slickened it up somewhat, but it still looked safe enough for a beginner's lesson.

'All right?'

Cathy nodded, did a quick visual inspection at all compass points. At the far south end, there was one car, a Volkswagen van, not running, possibly unoccupied. 'Okay.'

We swapped seats, strapped ourselves in. Cathy adjusted the mirrors, moved the seat forward, changed the speed of the wipers, fiddled with the radio.

'You're going across the parking lot, not the country.'

She turned to me, eyes half-lidded. 'I need to feel comfortable. It's important.'

'Right.' I waited a moment until she'd fully comforted herself. 'Whenever you're ready.' I looked in the back seat. Grace, trapped in her car seat, was quizzically turning her head back and forth between us, as if too much in her understanding had shifted and she was having trouble squaring up the new world order.

'Okay.'

I explained as best I could how to nudge the gas while slowly releasing the clutch, waiting for that little pull of engagement that told you to go with the gas and let out the clutch. Cathy nodded, and then popped the clutch so violently Grace started to cry. 'It's okay, sweetie,' I said turning around. 'Mommy's just learning how to drive.'

'I know how to drive.'

I turned back to Grace. 'Mommy's just learning how to drive . . . this car.'

'That wasn't so bad, though, was it?'

'You popped the clutch and stalled the engine.'

'Well, it was my first time.'

'That's true. It took me quite a while to learn.'

'It is not going to take me *quite a while*.'

I tried to demonstrate again with my hands the sensation of the relationship between gas and clutch, putting my palm on her thigh so as to use pressure to help her understand when to give it gas and when to smooth out the clutch. On her second attempt she popped the clutch again, but in a less violent manner, allowing the Egg to actually stay running and get moving. We trundled across the grassy car park.

'Hey!' shouted Cathy. 'All right.'

The engine was now whining in first gear, and we were

approaching, more or less straight on, the Volkswagen van. 'You'll need to turn or stop,' I said. 'Cathy? Turn or stop. Cathy?!'

She turned and hit the brakes simultaneously, but forgot about the clutch and the Egg shuddered to a halt. 'Do you think anyone's in that van?' she said, peering out the front window, which was becoming increasingly foggy given how much time we were spending in the car with the engine off.

'Not now that they've all leapt screaming from the rear window.'

'That's funny.'

She started up again, popping the clutch time after time, but with noticeably less violence, less grinding. On her fifth attempt, she drove straight at the people cowering in their van, but did a nice little buttonhook and shifted into second while doing so.

'Look at that!' I said.

She looked over at me, grinning, and we kept on practising for the next half-hour or so. We went out again the next day, and the next, and by the third day we received the final sign that she was ready to take to the road. Cathy had been taking the Egg through its paces for about ten minutes when I looked into the back seat. Grace was sound asleep.

X

The haggis was thrust in front of us on paper plates, accompanied by steaming mounds of neeps and tatties (neeps being mashed turnip with a little milk and allspice added, and tatties being creamed potatoes flavoured with nutmeg). It could hardly have been called a surprise since the poster we'd seen on the Post Office window advertising the Autumn Ceilidh had promised a 'traditional Scots dinner'.

'Gross,' said Jessica, looking at us with a mixture of horror and disgust. 'What is this?'

The cheerful woman who'd put the plate in front of Jessica laughed and said, 'Food of the gods, little one. Try it out, now.'

I looked at the paper plate before me. The plate itself was already turning soggy at the centre, due less to the haggis than the watery yellow pile of neeps dominating the middle of the plate. 'How bad can it be?' I said.

Cathy eyed me sceptically, a look that clearly identified the Royal Taster. I picked up my fork, and went straight to the heart of the matter. Holding a pint of 80 Shilling in my left hand, in case of emergency, I put a modest amount of the haggis on my fork. The smell was surprisingly unrevolting, and in the midst of it I thought I detected oregano and rosemary, even a little cumin. Raising the fork to my lips, I tried not to think about what went into the making of a haggis, but couldn't help remembering what a Scottish friend of mine had once said back in Canada. 'They finish processing all the real meat from the animal,' he said. 'Then they pick up all the stuff off the floor, toss in some oats, spice it, grind it, and stuff it into a sheep's intestine. It's bloody great.'

It was in my mouth, and though it wasn't bloody great, it wasn't bloody awful either. Amazing what you can do with spices. Chewing boldly to give Jessica the confidence to try new things, I finished it off, and immediately went for another forkful. 'Give it . a shot, Jess,' I said.

I might as well have been eating live beetles. 'Gross.'

Cathy took a forkful of tatties, and offered it to Grace, who was seated in her stroller. She rotated her whole upper torso away from it. A voice came over the loudspeaker. 'Ladies and gents. Ladies and gents. Just to let you know, we'll be starting the music in about ten minutes. If you can finish up your meals, then we can get the tables cleared away, and get started with the dancing.' There was a bustle throughout the Town Hall, which was located right below the High Street, across from Bissett's Pub; both of which were certainly less than 100 metres from our front door, highlighting both the beauty and curse of living in a small town with three pubs – you can get hammered and walk home. Perhaps this had something to do with both the camaraderie of the locals and the frightening levels of alcohol intake.

We choked down a few mouthfuls of haggis, neeps and tatties, and disassembled the rest to the outer edges of our plates, so as to give the impression that the food had at least been decently sampled, if not technically ingested. A team of volunteers scurried about the hall, which was the size of a small school gymnasium. They worked in pairs, one person holding open a green garbage bag, the other piling dirty plates and plastic utensils into the maw. In a matter of minutes, there was no remaining evidence that haggis, neeps and tatties had been on the premises; this was not a bad thing. Everybody helped re-arrange tables and chairs, during which the band tuned up, making a lot of squeaking, screeching and wheezing noises with their fiddles and accordions.

Ian came over. He was a friend of Archie's, an older gent, and I'd nearly killed him the day before when Archie introduced him to me. I'd firmly grasped his hand and shook it warmly, causing him to actually double over with pain. 'Arthritis,' said Archie. 'Devastating.' When Ian reassumed his full height there was a tear in his left eye. I apologised, and he good-naturedly waved it away. 'Some days he can't even hold his cards when we play bridge,' Archie had carried on. 'Not that the daft bugger would know what to do with them anyway.' Ian smiled weakly, still in a lot of pain. 'These are my friends,' he'd said.

'And how are you tonight?' Ian said, smiling at us as we awaited the start of the music.

He was a tall, angular man, and though I'm six feet tall I had to lift my hand considerably to lay it softly on his shoulder in lieu of shaking his hand. 'We're well, thanks.'

He reached out and touched my hand on his shoulder. 'That's the way,' he laughed. 'All ready to do a few wee jigs and whirls?'

'I suppose I'll be forced into a few, though maybe Jess will do a few in my place,' I said. 'This is great, though.' I looked around the crowded room. The event had been organised as a fundraiser for the Gullane Community League, and there had to be a couple of hundred people, anyway. And it wasn't just old fusties, either. There were kids, babies, teenagers, mums, dads, grandparents. The whole lot. It was a party, and everyone there from age one to ninety seemed delighted to be part of it.

'First one in thirty years,' said Ian.

'What?!'

'Aye. When I was younger we used to have these things all the time. Not recently, though. But, yes, you're correct. This is grand, isn't it? I'm so glad you've come to town when we've decided to have another of these.'

'I can't believe you don't have something like this a couple of times a year.'

He nodded. 'We ought to. But . . . why we haven't? I don't know.' He winked and left us, heading to the bar. At that point the leader of the band took the microphone. 'Right!' he said. 'Here we go. I think we'll start out with some easy Highland reels.' The band struck up and I sat down, ready to enjoy the music from my seat. Cathy scowled at me, and took Jess up to the dance floor. A heaving mass of people whirled and twirled through the tight space, spinning one another around, pointing their toes in a variety of directions. It looked pretty chaotic from where I was sitting, but a person with a microphone was calling out steps, unintelligible to my ear, and so I assumed there was meant to be a pattern. Cathy and Jess were standing in the middle of things, randomly hopping and skipping around, and didn't look out of place. Grace, still in her stroller, had fallen asleep the moment the music started.

When Jess and Cathy returned to the table after the first dance they had Jess's friend Isla with them, the red-haired girl who'd been designated as Jess's special friend her first day at school. They were holding hands, and when they sat down on the other side of the table, they started whispering to each other and giggling. Isla's mother Phyllis came over and sat with us, but just as we were starting to talk about the school, and the way Jess and Isla had already become fast friends, the band leader shouted out, 'Okay, and now we've got an old-time favourite, the Canadian Barn Dance.'

Phyllis leaned towards us, and broke into a devious grin. 'Ohh, that's brilliant! A Canadian Barn Dance! You must be experts at this!'

I happened to look up and across the room, where I saw Ian looking over our way. He was laughing and nodding, and gave me a thumbs-up.

'Canadian Barn Dance?' said Cathy. 'I've never heard of it.'

'I've never even been in a barn,' I said.

The floor filled up and groups of four began parading around the room. Every single person in the room, save the Canadians, knew the steps. It seemed to involve traipsing around for a few paces, kicking out your feet every now and then, at which point the tempo would change, instigating the swinging around of women by men, until another tempo change, bringing about the slower traipsing and kicking. Clearly, years of practice were required to master it.

'What do you think?' said Phyllis.

'I have never seen a Canadian perform this dance,' I said, struggling to keep pace. 'And why would we do it in a barn? We do have dance halls, you know.'

The evening passed with one intricate jig, reel, or fling after another, each of which seemed second nature to every person in the hall, young and old. The goodwill in the room was so complete that by the last number, a kind of line dance that called for a good deal of running around and then under rows of bridged arms, I was actually able to imagine some day enjoying at least this kind of dancing. The evening ended with what they called a 'soft penny'. This called for people to line up about forty feet from a bottle of single-malt Scotch and whisk coins along the floor towards the bottle. The person whose coin ended up nearest the bottle took it home. It was a brilliant fundraising ploy. After all, what Scot is able to resist the thought of a bottle of single malt for the price of a 50p coin?

Walking home, the combination of the cool night air, the humidity, and the sweat we'd worked up dancing gave us a little chill. Cathy asked Jess if she'd had a good time, and whether she'd like to do it again.

'Yes!' said Jess. She paused a moment, and I thought maybe she was just trying to identify in her own mind what exactly had been her favourite part of the evening. She stopped walking and looked up to us. 'But would we have to eat that stuff again?'

The Goose Green Bakery was warm, filled with the scents of fresh grainy bread, sweet rolls, cinnamon, and coffee; a tempting haven on a crisp autumn day. It was worth stepping inside for a whiff even if you weren't needing anything. The place had the look of an old one-room schoolhouse, with large bright windows and rough-hewn floorboards. There was a small hearth that through the autumn and winter burned fragrant and warming clots of bristly peat. It was so cosy-looking, this little fire, that you almost wanted to crawl into it. Katriona brought me a coffee and a scone, dropping them down on my table.

''Ow are you, then?'

'Recovering,' I said.

'From what?'

'The ceilidh, Friday night. A couple extra pints. Too much haggis.'

'Oh, you're a brave soul to eat that,' she said twisting up her face, before pointing to the notebook and pen I'd laid on the table. 'Working today, are ya?'

I nodded. 'Might as well try to get something done every now and then.'

'Shocking,' she said, shaking her head. 'Cathy doesn't mind? You skiving off all the time?'

'I guess not.'

We both laughed.

'Oy,' she said. 'I'm raising money for charity, for the local kid's charity. Would you like to contribute?'

'Sure. What is it you're doing to raise the money?'

'It's on Friday,' she said, grinning. 'Down at the pub in Dirleton. I'm going in early in the night, and the longer I can go through the evening without talking, the more money I raise.'

One of the other staff, Yvonne, spoke up from behind the counter. 'I'm betting on ten minutes!'

Katriona whipped around. 'Shut it, you! I can do this. I'm going to go all night. You watch.'

'I'm in for this,' I said. 'How about one pound for every thirty minutes?'

'Aye, that's great. Cheers.'

She left the table and I poured out my coffee from the cafetière in front of me. It was true that I was going to do a bit of work that morning, but I didn't dare tell Katriona that I was also planning on playing golf later that afternoon, with Jack and Archie in 'The Doctors', a weekly gathering they'd invited me to. The premise was that whoever wanted a game on the designated day only had to show up at the 1st tee at 1:30pm, prepared to golf, drink, and gamble away the exorbitant sum of £1, thrown into the kitty for the best net score. Those that turned up would put their golf balls into a big hat, at which point someone would pull them out and randomly arrange the balls in groups of three, denoting who played with who. It was a nice way for someone to get a game if they felt like playing, and it was also a good chance for newcomers to meet people, since one's partners were decided at random.

'It'll be good,' said Jack on the phone the night before. 'It's a good way to meet new people, to get you to meet people from around the village and around the club. It's good fun.'

And so we met at the 1st tee. I ended up playing with Jack and Willie Robertson, who'd been the Head Greenskeeper at Gullane for twenty-one years until his retirement in 1997. Jack hit first, sending his tee shot straight and well down the fairway of the 313-yard par-four. I hit next; solid, down the middle. Then Willie stepped up. A wee man with a ready, half-manic grin, he proceeded to produce the most distinctive and unusual golf swing I have ever seen. I want to say the ugliest, but Willie was far too nice a man to ever apply that word to any of his activities. Gripping the club with hands in the wrong position (right above left, instead of left above right) he was physically incapable of achieving a real shoulder turn. Swinging in this manner, it's possible to damage your internal organs. The Scots even have a name for this peculiar way of holding the club – *cack-handed*.

Luckily, Willie did not injure himself, though soft tissue damage never seemed far away. He took the club back as far as his restricted grip would allow, in a steep upward path, raised himself on to his tiptoes, and then swung down on the ball so abruptly it seemed reasonable to conclude that he had no interest in making contact with the ball. It was difficult to look at, and seemed grievously inefficient. Still, there did seem to be precedents in the

Gullane area for cack-handedness, even as far back as 150 years ago. Reverend Kerr, in his appendix to *The Golf Book of East Lothian*, transcribed the reminiscences of many local and visiting players, including that of a Mr Edward Blyth. 'Of local Gullane players,' wrote Blyth in about 1860, 'there was one, a blacksmith, whose name I cannot recall, who played with the left hand below the right; no doubt having acquired this from the use of the sledgehammer; he was an excellent golfer, very difficult to beat.'

Willie managed to poke his tee ball a hundred yards down the fairway, splitting the short grass with actuarial precision. This was no fluke. Throughout the round, Willie did not once hit a ball into the penal Gullane rough. Perhaps, as the man responsible for nurturing the evil herbage for over twenty years, he knew the punishment was so severe that any measures taken to stay out of it were warranted; even if it meant swinging cack-handed. He never hit the ball further than about 120 yards, but he was eerily straight. His putting was equally unaesthetic. A lifting action, he seemed more interested in tamping down some gnarly spikes of grass behind his ball than with actually directing the ball holeward. But again, it worked. Not once did he three-putt. Willie's game, if it could be called that, had an almost metronomic efficiency. It was not pretty, but it was all he had and he made it work.

'Why do you swing like that?' I asked Willie about halfway through our round. 'It's very odd.'

'Aye,' he muttered amiably. 'But I cannae swing any other way. I've tried holding the club all those other ways.'

Other ways? How many other ways could there be? Willie interrupted me as I was working out the permutations.

'And ah'm not the only one, either.'

'You're kidding?'

'No,' he said phlegmatically. 'Some good players, too. Four or five blokes round here do it. One's a nine handicap.'

'That's not possible.'

'Ah'm telling ye,' he reassured me.

After my fourth ball lost, by the 8th hole, it was becoming ever more clear that a cack-handed Willie might have been on to something that a more traditionally-minded Curtis was missing.

'Getting a bit expensive for you, Curtis?' he said dryly, after he rammed in a forty-foot putt for a two on the cliffhanging par-three 9th hole. Low clouds hustled by us on their way out to sea. 'Running low on balls, boy?' Jack added, joining in the fun. 'I've got extra in my bag here.' He grinned at Willie, and Willie broke from a dead stony glare into his manic-glee face, though it was unaccompanied by laughter.

'I may have to take you up on that,' I said. After we teed off on the 10th, I walked up the precise middle of the fairway with Willie as we went to his ball. 'Do you ever lose a golf ball?' I asked, half-joking, almost afraid of the answer. We got to his ball. It was laying on the short grass, not quite sparkling since that would have required sunshine to achieve such an effect. But it was certainly looking perky, sitting so nicely, so clearly visible. I was a hundred yards on, in the rough, naturally, though in a potentially findable location.

'This ball here,' he said, pointing to the one on the fairway that awaited his latest stab. 'I've been playing with this one for the last twelve rounds.'

'Twelve rounds?!' After a quick mental calculation I realised that it had been quite some time since I'd played twelve consecutive *holes* with the same ball.

'Aye,' he poked his 3-wood at the ball, sending it another hundred yards directly at the pin. 'That's nae half bad. I'll do fifteen rounds or so, likely, with it. I like to change them up every now and then.'

Slack-jawed, I trudged up along the left rough of Thucket

Knowe (the 10th hole named after its right-side mounding, designed to resemble Arthur's Seat in not-so-distant Edinburgh, which is almost always visible to the west: 'thucket' apparently being an old Scots word for *like* or *resembling*, and 'knowe' being *hill*). I found my ball, miraculously, and, not so miraculously, hit my next shot further into the left rough, up near the green. We lost it.

'Let's just move on,' I said, after we'd looked for the ball just a minute or so. 'We aren't going to find it in this.' We duly moved out of the shin-high, thatched, matted fescues, my trouser legs wet, my shoes gleaming with damp. 'You're the one responsible for this rough, aren't you?' I teased Willie.

Manic grin, but no words.

'Why do you think he never hits it there?' laughed Jack.

It made sense. It was just the smartest way to play: to hit it straight. Jack knew it. Willie knew it. His ruthlessly utilitarian game was designed with an eye for survival, and was not at all concerned with what anyone else thought. It was the epitome of function over form. It was, in short, Scottish. *No pictures on a scorecard*, a Scot might say. *It's not how, it's how many*, another would say. And though golfers the world over say these things, it seems only the Scot truly takes them to heart and applies them to his or her game. It certainly wasn't a Scot that brought the fluid and graceful modern swing to the game. But as I watched Willie send yet another ball scampering down the middle of the fairway after I'd sent another arcing gracefully to some new hiding place in the deepest fescue, I stopped to wonder exactly what the Scots *had* brought to the modern game the world now plays. Yes, Scotland is the spiritual home of golf, its true birthplace, but is that their only claim on the game?

After all, there are currently only a handful of good professionals from Scotland (Colin Montgomerie, Catriona Mathews,

Mhairi Mackay, Paul Lawrie, Andrew Coltart), and too seldom are the game's top administrators Scots (many Royal and Ancient members and executives are English). The Scottish Golf Union, which ought to be one of the world's leading golf organisations, has been criticised for its disorganisation, particularly in the area of handicapping systems. The Scottish Tourism Authority has had a disastrous last few years, and has been notoriously hamfisted at bringing visitors to Scotland in the numbers that its golfing facilities and other attractions would seem to warrant.

And yet there are areas of supremacy in Scottish golf. Perhaps one can legitimately say – this is no small thing, and may even be the most important thing – that the ultimate authority of Scottish golf resides in one place: in the nature, challenge and mystique of its golf courses. Scottish golf courses are astounding for their quality and variety and number, not to mention the intangibles of history and aura. You've got the world-class (Muirfield, the Old Course, Gullane No. 1, Troon, Prestwick, North Berwick West Links, Turnberry, Royal Dornoch, Royal Aberdeen, Nairn, Western Gailes, Gleneagles [Kings and Queens], Kingsbarns, Loch Lomond, Carnoustie), the merely great (Luffness, Elie, Cruden Bay, Murcar, Barassie, St Andrews New), and the irreplaceable historical treasures (Machrihanish, Fortrose and Rosemarkie, Montrose, Braid Hills, Crail, Tain, Panmure, Brora). And these are just the elite courses; there are many others that are quite brilliant by any standard other than Scotland's (Longniddry, Dunbar, Burntisland, Downfield, Bruntsfield, Royal Burgess, Golspie, Glasgow Gailes, Boat of Garten, Stirling). There are hundreds of others. No course architect alive can claim to truly understand his or her profession unless he or she has visited and studied the Scottish courses from which so much can be learned (the most educational of which include Muirfield, Dornoch, the Old Course, North Berwick, Troon, Turnberry and Prestwick).

The second area in which Scotland is without doubt a beacon of light in a sometimes otherwise gloomy golfing world is the pace of play. A round of golf rarely takes longer than about three and a half hours across Gullane Hill. Scots are always alive to their position on the golf course in relation to their starting time. The Scottish golfer is somehow intuitively aware of even the most minute degradation in the speed of their play, as if some sort of Global Positioning System had been surgically implanted in the cerebellum of each tiny Scottish newborn. Even out with Jack and Archie, on a calm day, with the course empty and holes open in front of and behind us, I can recall numerous discussions such as this:

'We're not quite on the move today,' Jack will say.

'You're too busy admiring your shots,' Archie will reply.

'We'd be moving along faster if you didn't keep telling these long-winded stories, Baird.'

'I wouldn't have to tell stories if you weren't dawdling around so much making us wait.'

'I'll move faster, then, if it means I don't have to listen to any more of those stories.'

At which point, I might have said to both Jack and Archie that there was, in fact, no one behind or ahead of us, that it was a gorgeous day, that none of us were needing to be too serious, and that anyway what's the harm in spending a little extra time in such glorious surroundings with such good company. Both men would stop dead in their tracks, rotate their gazes on to me, and consider me with utter mystification, as if I were thick beyond belief.

The point being not that we could be playing faster, but that, to a Scot, golf is *meant* to be played fast. To do otherwise is to participate inadequately in a centuries-old tradition. There can be no worse insult for a Scot than to be labelled slow. Quick play is not just an element of the Scottish game, it very nearly *is* the point of the game.

Access is, I think, the final point in which Scotland can claim to be leading the world, though even here there are problems. The good, the bad and the ugly of access to Scotland's golf treasures can be neatly summarised by discussing that course just around the corner from Lammerview Terrace, a tidy little track known as Muirfield (or as some local wags call it, Gullane No. 4). The difficulty can be reduced to a neat conundrum: anyone can play Scottish golf courses, but not everybody is allowed to play Scottish golf courses. In short, visitors, if they are organised enough to book well in advance and can afford astronomical green fees, can easily play courses such as Muirfield, Troon, and Western Gailes. It's easier to play Muirfield, one of the world's great golf courses, than some of the flat parkland courses in Edmonton, which are not among the world's great golf courses. This is one of the marvellous things about Scottish golf.

But Scottish golf also has a deep and ugly vein of misogyny running through it. Of the three golf clubs in Gullane, two (Muirfield and Luffness New) are almost as resolute, as fervent, in their no-female-members policy as Gullane Golf Club is not. The Secretary at one of these clubs once said to my face that the 'lack of female members makes for a very happy club indeed'. This discrimination is inexcusable, no matter how such clubs try to justify it through the sorely misguided invocation of history and tradition. Members believe a total lack of change preserves something unique, that it keeps history intact; in truth, it only belittles them and their history, but they choose not to see it that way.

I had ample time to ponder these and other issues as Willie, Jack and I continued to look for balls I'd rifled into the heavy stuff. Still, though I'd lost five balls in the first ten holes, my game came together enough over the inward half that I was able to salvage some respectability in the clubhouse as we gathered for a drink afterwards. I sat beside Jack. 'How many of these fellows are actually doctors?' I half-whispered.

He looked around the room, as if identifying the odd one or two that might have been dentists or veterinarians, and so might not therefore qualify. 'Well,' he mused. 'I should think . . . none, really. Well, maybe one or two. I'm not quite certain, to be honest.' Jack looked at the table in front of us. 'Another, then?'

I looked down. I had taken two sips of my pint. Jack had clearly spilled his on the rug, because there was only foam left at the bottom of his pint. I'd not seen him take even a sip, and apparently Willie had also spilled his drink somewhere. Jack was up to the bar in a shot, and back immediately with three more pints, and three whiskies to boot. Somehow I managed to keep up with him, and then it was time to head home. He offered me a ride, and on the way told me the story of the Dirleton Castle Golf Club, the oldest golf club in Gullane, and the oldest artisan club in the world which still meets regularly (though there were others that formed earlier and then died out, such as the East Lothian Golf Club and the Tantallon Golf Club). Jack had been a member of Dirleton Castle almost since moving to the village in the late 1940s.

It wasn't more than a kilometre from the club to our flat, so when we got there he pulled his little blue car up against the curb and shut off the engine. The daylight was going soft, the street was empty, and the winds had died down, lending a quiet, almost conspiratorial element to our conversation, as if we were two spies meeting to exchange snippets of microfilm.

'It's a great club,' Jack said of Dirleton Castle, 'a great part of the tradition of this village, and of Gullane Golf Club. It just hasn't always been recognised as such.'

I asked him what he meant.

'It was this way,' he said, twisting himself in his seat just slightly, so that he was facing me more directly. 'The village, back in the middle of the nineteenth century, was made up of two classes, the poor and the rich. And it was a much greater divide then than now, of course. Well, back then the poor people started to play some golf, too, once the gutty ball replaced the feathery around 1850.'

(An aside: this is a long-standing distinction made by many, Archie included, in that the durable gutty ball, moulded from the rubber-like gutta-percha, completely changed the game from one only the rich could play – since the fragile feathery ball, made of leather and feathers, cost more to make than a golf club – to a game all could play, because the gutty was a cheaper mass-production rubber ball. The golf greens were on common land, and once they had the implements with which to play, the poor had as much access to the golf green as any: hence Scotland's tradition as the land where golf is the game of the people.)

'The village was full of artisans,' continued Jack, 'right? You know, joiners, shopkeepers, farm-workers, basically anyone that worked with their hands. And they decided to form a club, and they called it Dirleton Castle Golf Club, which limited the membership to anyone who lived in Dirleton parish. That was 1854, long before Gullane Golf Club was formed in 1882. Are you with me?'

I nodded, smiled. Jack continued, telling me that for decades Dirleton Castle played golf across Gullane Hill because it was common land. Animals grazed on it, trainers trained their horses on it, and people played golf across it. But in 1882, a group of people decided to form another club and play out of Gullane. That was the Gullane Golf Club. They all played on the same course, these different clubs, though for a long time, nearly a century, you didn't have to be a member of Gullane Golf Club to belong to Dirleton Castle.

It was really only at the turn of the twentieth century that Gullane Golf Club eventually took a kind of predominance over the Dirleton Castle Golf Club in terms of the course ownership, but Dirleton Castle did continue to maintain its right to play for a pittance of an annual subscription, mostly through historical precedent. For the last century or so they existed side by side as separate clubs using the same courses. Dirleton Castle members were under no compulsion to become Gullane Golf Club members, though many, such as Jack, joined Gullane anyway. 'And then,' Jack continued, 'about twenty years ago, Gullane Golf Club decided that all Dirleton members had to become Gullane Golf Club members in order to use the courses. It was, well, it was a little controversial. But Dirleton Castle is a big part of this community, of Gullane, and it should survive. And Gullane Golf Club sees, I think, that the artisan clubs are a big part of the history of golf in the area. I think it's good to co-operate.'

Unfortunately, not everyone felt quite as conciliatory as Jack. It was in 1983 that the Gullane Golf Club formally subsumed Dirleton Castle, in the process limiting the Dirleton Castle membership to 100, and restricting their access to Gullane No. 1. Still, this agreement did go some ways towards preserving Dirleton Castle, since now the Castle would be part of a more stable, financially secure operation.

But the relationship between the two clubs, both before and after 1983, has not always been a completely comfortable one, and though Jack, for one, easily and regularly crosses the fence, as it were, the fence does still exist. Many Dirleton Castle members fraternise only with fellow Castle members, and choose to use the local pubs like the Golf Inn, or even the Visitor's Centre, rather than the Gullane Golf Club clubhouse. Dirleton Castle members do not even post their club notices and competition results in the Gullane clubhouse, but use instead an enclosed notice board screwed to the outside wall of the old High Street smithy. Given the fact that I was brought up in a very working-class home, I immediately sympathised with Dirleton Castle (though the logic of the Gullane Golf Club loyalists also seemed clear). But this failure of disparate segments of the membership to fully emulsify seemed to me a matter of class, reflecting the earliest years of the joint usage of the golfing greens between the two clubs. The irony is that the Gullane Golf Club was originally formed with the membership of many Dirleton Castle members, the thinking being that locals could then bring along non-local friends for a game of golf (since all Dirleton Castle members had to live in Dirleton parish).

On this delicate matter, Reverend Kerr, a Dirleton Castle member and also one of the founders of the Gullane Golf Club, has much to say, phrasing the early 1880s debate in terms of a battle between those (primarily Dirleton Castle locals) who wanted to keep the game and the green free and public and those (the Gullane Golf Club mixture of locals and city folk) who wanted to create a private fee-charging club and co-opt the green as their own.

The historian and Gullanite, Dr Audrey Paterson, in her privately published and highly informative *History of the Dirleton Castle Golf Club, 1854–1981*, puts it quite plainly. 'It is obvious from various sources that this was a period of intense frustration between the two local clubs. As many players had dual membership, loyalty and impartiality must have strained with the mounting tension. The whole issue centred on the ground used for golf which sounds simple yet was very complicated with unclear rights and questionable ownership.'

Perhaps it was no surprise that a frictionless joining of the two clubs didn't result in 1983. Local history is taken seriously in these parts, is seen as an ever-climbing wall of solid stone and mortar, of lives and incidents, rather than as a rebuildable, malleable sand castle. Memories are long. 'They're all about clans up here,' a visiting Englishman said to me on one visit. 'Always remember that about the Scot: it's about the clan.'

I've never belonged to a private golf club in my life, and neither did my father. In my father's case it was certainly a wholly financial decision, though even if he'd had the money, I'm still not sure he'd have been one to join a swanky club. I feel the same way. The public course ethos appeals to me: women, children, men, all playing on equal terms. No silly dress codes. No arcane rules about certain types of food in certain areas. No need to wear a tie just to sit down and have a drink. Such rules are not about golf, they are about clubs, private clubs, separation, status. Dirleton Castle Golf Club has always been, and one hopes always will be, about golf and nothing but. For a century these men met simply to play the game. I know which club my father would have joined (and possibly the only club he would have been allowed to join). My heart went out to Dirleton Castle, and I suspect if I had lived in Gullane for the rest of my life, it would have become my home club, too. It would be a delight to belong to Gullane Golf Club, but an honour to belong to Dirleton Castle.

Jack and I finished talking about Dirleton Castle Golf Club. The air had gone completely still outside the car. With our windows down I could hear kittiwake gulls and arctic terns squawking crankily behind the row of houses to our left. It felt calm and though it was not cold outside, there was no heat to speak of in the air. It was a moment to make you shiver. Winter was coming.

'Thanks for the game, Jack.' I held out my hand. 'It was a good day.'

He took my hand, grinned that sweet grin. 'My pleasure, son. My pleasure.'

I got out of the car, hoisted my clubs over my shoulder, and waved to Jack as he drove off. But he was concentrating and didn't see me wave, just kept his eyes focused ahead, kept looking forward. I wished he'd seen me wave. I wanted him to notice that I was paying attention to his departure.

4

I rose early one mid-November day, a day when the light was failing and the winds were weak, when all that was left in the air was the hash-like scent of burning straw and a suspended mist. The smell of the burning straw transported me back to grade school on the prairies, and to the frigid deep winter walks back and forth between home and St Dominic's Elementary, when my friends and I would periodically pass one construction site or another in our new treeless Calgary suburb of Dalhousie. If the gruff, joking men were planning to do work beneath the surface, they had to thaw the ground first, which meant heating and defrosting it from above. The men in their yellow construction helmets would lay a blanket of straw over the top of the area that needed defrosting, and would then set it aflame, letting it slow-burn, sometimes for days, adding straw as needed. We stood around the sites swaying like participants at a mystical ceremony. Thin whorls of smoke levitated upwards, lazily gathering into pods which burst open at head height, allowing us to inhale, while being enveloped in, the dreamy grey-black perfume of the burning straw. There was something deeply intoxicating about a fire burning over frozen ground, the smoke mixing with the ice. If it had been my choice, I'd have breathed in that smoky air all day instead of the real thing.

I'd risen early specifically to go for a walk over to Aberlady Bay and the Local Nature Reserve. The night before, I had finished, with tremendous admiration, Nigel Tranter's *Footbridge to Enchantment*, his series of essays about the Nature Reserve that directly borders the golf courses at Gullane and Luffness, and which is part of an overall Site of Special Scientific Interest that covers all of Aberlady Bay and most of Gullane Hill. I stuffed my feet into my wellies in the front hall and shouted out, 'Back in a couple hours or so.'

Cathy came through from the sitting room holding Grace. 'Are you off on your walk?' she asked. Grace was happily pulling at her mother's hair, and seemed deeply aggrieved to find it attached to a scalp. 'Graaak!' she said, as if explaining her frustration.

'Off to the Nature Reserve. Time to see what the other side of Gullane Hill holds.'

I popped in to Mr Rasool's to pick up some chewing gum. 'Hello, Shafqat,' I said, as I did every morning.

He held up a hand, palm outwards, in a vaguely heiratic gesture; a shamanistic crossing-guard. 'Hallo, Mister Curtis,' he said in his melancholy baritone. As many times as I'd been in Mr Rasool's – almost as often as the number of days we'd been living in Gullane – something struck me for the first time that morning. Only that day did I hear an echo, and it bounced back to my conscious mind right away. The way he pronounced my name, in his marble-mouthed way, always supremely deadpan, sounded precisely like, 'Hello, Mistah Kurtz.' It wasn't the most welcome literary reference first thing in the morning. I kept on hoping throughout the year that he would never follow 'Mister Curtis' with 'he dead'.

I set out straight up the hill, directly through the middle of the golf courses, a route that would take me over the rocky hump of the hill then back down to the dunes, the rocks and the Firth. From there it was just a jaunt along the coast of no more than a mile to the Nature Reserve. I gained the height of the hill, up around the 3rd tee of Gullane No. 1, and kept walking due west, towards the shore, towards Edinburgh, the skyline of which in the day's meagre light was just a charcoal sketch. There were a few golfers out on the course, and I avoided coming near them. Crossing the hill, I spied the Paps of Fife in the distant gloom, and noted they still had no cleavage. The paths through the course were clear and it was easy to make my way, especially since there are no trees on Gullane Hill, except for the odd lonely globular stand of spiky sea buckthorn (the branches of which were reputedly used to weave Christ's crown of thorns). As I walked, grouse burst from the long grass and were outlined against the pale pewter sky. To the south, settled in front of the Lammermuir Hills, the dun-brown and black-green fields were starting to take on definition.

We'd been in Gullane for nearly three months and I'd yet to make it to Aberlady Bay or the Nature Reserve, though I'd seen it many times from the farther reaches of Gullane Nos 1, 2 and 3. It promised so much, this huge scythe-shaped flora and fauna sanctuary that directly borders the lower parts of Gullane Nos 2 and 3, and Luffness New. I'd had so many different views of the terrain from the golf courses. From the 13th tee of Gullane No. 1, you could see the massive ranks of concrete block anti-tank traps left over from the Second World War scattered in amongst the tall dunes. From the promontory of the 7th tee of Gullane No. 3, it seemed as if Aberlady Bay was so close you could almost dip your spiked shoes into it. And from the 12th green and 13th tee of Gullane No. 2 you felt as if you were more inside the Nature Reserve than the golf course, so close was the boundary line. The Reserve, with its dunes and lochs and ponds and shrubs, beckoned as some mysterious place might, a bazaar in a foreign city, a forest outside a strange town. To my surprise and shock, many of the locals had told me that they had never been down to the dunes and marsh flats beside the bay. Too far to walk, many said. I had these voices in my head as I crossed the hill, wondering to myself how you could be this close to so much beauty and never know it.

But as soon as I left the golf course, stepping down across the 8th fairway of Gullane No. 2, it seemed as if a different voice entered my head. It was a voice many in town would have known, a voice that will always resonate throughout Gullane and Aberlady, and particularly across the marshy, austere beauty of the Nature Reserve. The voice was that of Nigel Tranter.

Many of Tranter's novels used East Lothian, and Aberlady Bay in particular, as settings, but it is this work of non-fiction, *Footbridge to Enchantment*, that is the best guide to his thoughts on his home. It's a warm, thoughtful series of essays, in essence a lover's guide through the marshy curves of Aberlady Bay and the Nature Reserve. Tranter published these essays over the years under his 'Country Notebook' series in *The Scots Magazine*. Like any lover, he was protective about his flame, kept his hands cupped around it, was not always aware of his blind spots. But that's what makes him, and this book, such a great pleasure to read. *Footbridge to Enchantment* will always have a special place in my bookshelf. One of the fascinations of reading Tranter's nature writing is that his voice is so proper in its grammar and yet so demotic in tone. It's a delicious combination, as if Evelyn Waugh had written lovingly of coal miners. He's a writer who might say in one paragraph that 'few dogs of my acquaintance are really of the stuff of heroes', and that 'owls are queer brutes', followed shortly in the same section by the admission that 'I quite enjoy watching a really good-going mobbing, a bully having caught a pack of tartars, a tough being cut down to size. Such sights promptly read me practical lessons on what we should all do about our domineering politicians, overbearing bureaucrats, petty dictators, trade union bosses, and aggressive delinquents generally. Most would be the sweeter for a good mobbing at regular intervals.'

From his house near the Peffer Burn footbridge, Tranter walked through the Nature Reserve nearly every day, holding his pen and paper, stopping frequently to jot down notes and scenes. He once said that he wrote all his books on the run, composing as he walked, a habit he'd developed while in the army during the Second World War. He was ninety-two when he passed away, just before we arrived in Gullane. How I'd have loved to have met him, or even to have seen that tall, rambling figure traverse the landscape, stopping to make a note, to gaze at the geese, to check the rhythm of a sentence by speaking it out loud to himself, thinking he was alone in amongst those massive dunes, that place that even he said didn't look like much at first sight. 'Just a notably empty and unusually flat and roadless corner of the coastline,' he wrote, and so 'strangely remote to be within sixteen miles of the Capital of Scotland'.

It was this area that Tranter loved most about East Lothian, so much so that he chose to live practically right on it. Quarry House was just steps from the footbridge, his footbridge to daily enchantment in the Local Nature Reserve, an area, says Tranter, that actually has no 'true and accepted name'. Most maps just splash the words Gullane Links over the top of the whole area, which is not at all accurate, since the Gullane and Luffness Links cover only Gullane Hill and Gala Law. Some maps refer to the marshy part of the Nature Reserve as the Yellow Mires. Some locals call the whole area Jovey's Neuk (which is but a small nose of land at the Gullane Bay beach-head). Tranter adds:

> Not that it is to be wondered at that it has no solid or established title, for the place just was not there when the names were being given out. Indeed the old maps show a quite different outline to the coast here, imaginative as early cartographers tended to be in such matters. The fact is that most of this curious area has come out of the sea in comparatively recent times – and, who knows, may equally well go back to it, just as quickly and entirely.

He goes on to explain the geography of Aberlady Bay, 'a vast triangular indentation of the Firth of Forth estuary, drying out at low water, with a mouth more than two miles wide' with a huge sand bar just above the height of the floor of the bay. The sand bar is, therefore, 'the first part of the whole to emerge as the tide ebbs'.

I strode out on the emptied floor of the bay, the sand from which is essentially responsible for golf on Gullane Hill. The sand from the bay, dry at low tide, has over millennia been blown by the strong winds up and across the volcanic plugs of Gullane Hill and Gala Law (the larger plugs along the coast being Bass Rock and the North Berwick Law). The result of all this sand and wind, says Tranter, is 'a curious ridge and valley formation, running east and west, ever changing, ever extending, with some summits reaching approximately seventy-five feet in height'.

In a short period of time, these dunes and ridges can catch and nurture the seeds of the sharp-tipped marram grasses, and the 'tussocky bents', so that a flora can begin. Yet the whole area is made up of such hardy and transient materials, and is so prone to nature's whimsy, that it changes constantly. This change is tantalising and ephemeral, because if you miss a beautiful dune one season, it may be gone the next. The Scottish wind is nature's trickster. You walk in awe through these dunes as you come across tiny hollows, places where the wind eddies and bubbles, where the sand has been sculpted into bonsai hoodoos, and you know it's all impermanent, fragile and to be admired, because the next big wind may take it down. 'After all,' says Tranter, 'one of the major enchantments of the area is that it seems to be always in a state of natural transformation, a place of perpetual transition. The coastline alters yearly, eating in here and drawing back there; whole new ranges of sand-hills develop; wind blows new deep gullies and canyons, and fills up old ones with soft sand; the spiky marram grass lays down just enough top soil for sea-turf to follow it, and then a succession of other flora.'

As a Site of Special Scientific Interest, the area is protected from further development. The scientists call the sandy mounds 'mobile dunes', with 'unstable' vegetation; in other words, a place open to change, depending on the seasonal variations in the weather. If there is a particularly bad winter or a severely windy spring, the dunes closest to the sea might take on a noticeably different character from the previous year. The secondary rows of dunes, the 'fixed' dunes, are more stable and have a richer growth of grassland with a bit of shrub and bush here and there sinking some talons in to hold down the earth. Further inland, past the dunes, the sand has blown up on to and over the hill creating the perfect links turf conditions golfers all over the world have travelled to East Lothian to experience.

All this you can see from the perches of Gullane Golf Course, particularly from Nos 2 and 3, but also from various westerly spots of No. 1. The first time I saw the Nature Reserve's magnificent dunescape I was transfixed, and became even more so when I learned of its mutating character. As Tranter so accurately notes, 'To the uninitiated it is often almost unbelievable that a substantial range of hillocks, perhaps a quarter of a mile long and a score of feet in height, rippling green in the breeze, was just not there three years ago.'

The word 'uninitiated' is the key, because once you have been initiated, once you have been for a few walks through that dry, sandy, wheat-coloured dunescape, you will understand how quickly things can change. The footing is never all that secure along the loose sandy base, and in places it seems as if the marram grass is all that keeps it from blowing away.

It was also amongst this dramatic landscape, incidentally, that Robert Louis Stevenson had his hero David Balfour await rescue in the novel *Catriona*. Stevenson was intimately familiar with the East Lothian coastline, and even had poor Balfour jailed in one sequence within the hideous confines of the old Bass Rock prison, when it was still inhabited those many centuries ago. But as Balfour awaits his escape boat behind the Gullane dunes, he comments that, 'as we crawled into that multiplicity of heights and hollows, there was such a shining of the sun and sea, such a stir of the wind in the bent grass, and such a bustle of down-popping rabbits and up-flying gulls that the desert seemed to me a place alive'.

Balfour was right. There is a huge variety of flora and fauna here. Foxes, rabbits, red deer, whooper swans, green woodpeckers, pheasants, dozens of other birds, sea buckthorn, sycamore thickets, the great horned poppy, sweet briar, spearmint, teasel, thistles, gorse, wild gooseberry. It's all there. And the various plants, adds Tranter, seem to have a common denominator; the 'prickliness of practically everything, the spiky jagged quality of almost all that grows and flourishes in this sandy paradise. For each blade of marram grass is armed with a tip sharp as a needle, and the entire area is thick with every kind of thistle in the book. The buckthorns and the sweet briar, the hawthorns and the teasels, the wild gooseberries and the yellow gorse – all one approaches with caution and touches at one's peril.'

Of course, being a true Scot, Tranter would necessarily have failed to include the spiky jagged quality of another species indigenous to the area, namely the Scot. They grow hardily under trying conditions, and flourish surprisingly well. If ever there was a people to approach initially with caution and to touch at one's peril, it is the Scot. However, as with the flora of the Nature Reserve, once a certain familiarity is achieved – once you know where you can and cannot stick your finger – it's easy to see the beauty, no matter how austere they may at first appear.

It was with Tranter in particular and the Scot in general on my mind that I refocused myself and found I was standing in the middle of Aberlady Bay, near the old Italian midget submarines and rusty jeeps the RAF had placed in the middle of the bay's sand bar during the war to use for target practice. I'd been standing there for some time, I guessed; when I'd first stopped, the heels of my wellies were firmly poised on the moistly packed sandflats of the bay bottom. Now there was water around my ankles. I took a measured glance at the lip of the bay, upon which the Firth of Forth had been gently lapping when I'd arrived at the subs. Water was now spilling over its edge as if over a ruptured dyke. The tide. Trust a prairie boy to forget about that. It had to be at least half a mile back to shore, and my mind was – it's the only word – flooded with images of the tide charging in and carrying me out to sea, lost for ever, ripped from the world before my time, torn from my family's bosom. Ever the romantic, I wasted a good minute writing my obituary before turning on my mud-heavy heels and sprinting for shore through the two-inch deep water. I could feel my heart trying to claw its way out of my throat as I ran what I'm sure was the most unaesthetic half-mile dash in sprinting history, gambolling through the incoming surf towards the nearest spit of land. It was only when I was about two-thirds of the way there that I remembered Nigel Tranter had even once written about the possibility of getting caught by the tide:

> I find that visitors to the area – and this no doubt refers to the locals too – can be much concerned about the possibility of being cut off by the tide out on the great sand flats. This is understandable, even sensible – but in fact no one, birdwatcher, wildfowler or ordinary walker out on the bar need fear for his life if he will but grasp and remember a simple piece of local geography. This is that the tide does not in fact come in straight over the bar, but creeps around behind it from the west, via the mouth of the Peffer Burn. This may sound even more alarming, especially in the darkness – but it means that the bar itself, and especially the extreme eastern end of it where it becomes the sand spit, is the last to be covered of all the bay. In other words, one can always walk out, even when the tide is swirling around one's knees in mid-bay, merely by heading north-east – that is, towards Gullane Point. And if it is so dark that one does not know in which direction is Gullane Point or north-east, then use Inchkeith lighthouse as a beacon, putting it as it were at ten o'clock on a watch and head for two o'clock. One will find the water shallowing all the way – and the tide comes in over the levels at less than walking pace.

Of course, I didn't quite remember it in this detail as I was gracelessly sprinting to shore. Once firmly back on land, I turned and surveyed the killer tide that had nearly sucked me out to the frigid North Sea. It was gently rippling in the same way it had been a few minutes earlier. The water, lapping against the rusted husks of the subs, appeared to be no higher than before. I stood there for another thirty minutes, watching the tide, calculating its depth and ferocity, both for future jaunts out and so that I could report to Cathy just how close she'd come to being widowed. There was no appreciable change in the depth of the water. From shore, the tide seemed as benign and harmless as a dribble over the lip of a child's inflatable swimming pool. I returned home, and if golfers heard me as I crossed back over the hill, they might have wondered what I was chuckling about.

The Face: Sly Bugger

My father was a card sharp. Not a professional, mind you, just a very shrewd and nerveless poker player. From the age of about fourteen on, my brothers and I and our friends played cards regularly. All sorts of games: cribbage, hearts, gin, blackjack, poker, anything involving a deck of cards and the opportunity to gamble. The stakes were always small, because none of us had much money. But whenever the poker game was held at our house (which was often, since we had a large kitchen table and three or four readily available players), our friends always asked the same question before coming over.

'Is Ghost in?'

Our answer was always the same. 'He says no. But he will be.'

The sequence of events thereafter was guaranteed, almost ritualistic. We'd all be seated around the table. Myself, my brother Bruce, brother Conor, sometimes my brother Keith, sometimes my brother Matt, often Ed Miner or Dennis Rempe or Rich Haigh or Gord Weigele or Danny MacDonald, or any of half a dozen others, all friends of ours. We'd all be seated, sipping a beer, arranging chips, shooting the breeze. Someone, maybe Rich, would say, 'Where's Ghost? Is he in or what?'

I'd shout out to the basement or the garage or the family room, 'Ghost! We're starting. Are you in or out?'

There would be no response; then, wraith-like, he would silently materialise at the kitchen doorway. All our friends would smile and greet him. He'd nod back.

'In or out?'

He'd shake his head wryly, as if we were too stupid not to have learned yet that inviting him to the table only meant we'd lose our money.

'Come on, you chicken,' one of us would say as he hesitated. 'Afraid you'll get burnt?'

He'd release a theatrically heavy sigh, as if he were being forced into something he didn't really enjoy. 'All right, I'll just go borrow twenty dollars off your mother.'

'Borrow!' we'd taunt. 'Do you think you'll keep it?'

He always won, of course, but it was the way he won that so infuriated us. A number of the games we played (such as Guts or High Man In) called for the player betting the pot having to beat every man at the table. The sucker who'd bet the pot would scan the table waiting for someone to challenge his right to take his winnings. Player after player would fold and throw their cards in, and since each and every one of us was forever anxious to inflict a burn on the other, we would normally announce ourselves loudly and triumphantly. But not Ghost. In the hubbub at the end of a hand, he would say nothing, would wait until one of us actually *believed* we'd won, until we had physically touched the money at the centre of the table.

'Hey.'

The person – Bruce, say – would stop, his fingers still on the cash.

'What are you doing?'

'I'm . . . I'm taking my pot.'

'Have you seen all the cards?'

'Yeah . . . well . . . except for . . .'

Then Ghost would lay down his hand, a winner, and would sit still. He wouldn't reach in. He wouldn't gloat. He'd simply wait until Bruce, or whoever, had removed his hands from the cash pile. Then he would take his winnings. We'd all howl and laugh and taunt the sucker he'd burnt. But we never learned, never. We always assumed we'd won if he didn't say anything right away. We never learned to see his cards first – always his cards above anyone else's – before touching the cash we thought was ours. That was what he loved, not the winning so much as watching us touch the cash, letting us think for a second that we'd won. He savoured it, even though it was as if he'd immunised himself against facial expression when he asked, 'What are you doing . . . Have you seen all the cards?' The sly bugger.

5

'Daaahhhh.'
   'Yes,' I said. 'I see it, too.'

A wobbly finger came up and pointed, ET-like, out the window. 'Daaahhhh!'

We must have stood together at our back window for fifteen minutes. The sun came up and as daylight started to win out over the night, the Lammermuir range smouldered progressively along its upper edge like a fuse burning towards the ordnance pile of the Edinburgh skyline. We could see full daylight in the east where the hills ran out at Dunbar, and yet it was dark in the west over Edinburgh. I held Grace at the window. She'd been up early, of course, and was now just staring at the sun unmelting itself over the hills. Every now and then she did her ET-point out the window; in awe, I said to myself, since she was obviously stunned, even as a one-year-old, by the beauty of this vision. But then I remembered that ten minutes earlier she'd pointed the same finger of awe, uttered the same sigh of wonder, at the soggy piece of drooled-upon toast she'd thrown on the kitchen floor.

Though it burned gorgeously and limpidly early in the day, now, in the first week of December, it was apparent that the sun had simply given up trying for the winter, as if it meant to fulfil its minimum obligation, but had reverted into some sort of power-saving mode until spring, a kind of semi-hibernation. During these short, misty days the sun would glimmer weakly as it crossed the sky in a low unconvincing parabola. Even at its daily high-point, it would tremble unsteadily in the air, like a gin-soaked old fustie who can't quite get out of his deep chair, and instead gives up and settles back in for an evening of tea and the BBC. The mornings almost without fail remained calm and soft, but the wind and haze would gather towards noon, struggle to assert themselves, and then die by mid-afternoon, when they surrendered along with the light. The sun would go pale, the sky wan and flushed of colour. All that would remain was the hushed whisper of the breeze, the smell of burning straw, and the soft mist of your own breath as you stepped into the cool night air, cosy and safe bundled up against the damp chill. This is perhaps the one time of year, November through January, when there are virtually no visitors to Gullane, indeed, when it half seems as if there are no residents of Gullane at all, when the night streets have a doom-laden Ripperesque feel to them. It is the most spiritual, beautiful and evocative of Gullane seasons.

It was on such a night that we first went for dinner to the house of Stan and Julie Owram. Stan is the Manager of the Gullane Golf Club, a Yorkshireman by birth and a robust, friendly presence, as is Julie. They live in Mayday, the house owned by Gullane Golf Club, which directly abuts the clubhouse. It's a lovely, grey-stoned Edwardian building, with a small stone wall running along the front, and tiny gate that wouldn't keep a mewling kitten at bay.

'It won't budge,' said Cathy, taking her hand off the gate latch.

I stepped into the breach. 'Here,' I said. 'Just let me give it a try.' I grabbed the black metal latch of the thigh-high gate, and pulled it inwards, outwards, upwards and backwards. There appeared to be no give in any direction.

Two ladies in elegant evening dress passed us. 'Lovely evening,' they said haltingly, eyeing us as we stood at the gate. They carried on. It just so happened that a Seniors' dinner was taking place that night at the club next door. A parade of aged, well-dressed people wandered past us as we conspicuously grappled with the gate.

'We'll just have to hop over.'

'Curtis, I'm wearing a long dress.'

'Well, it won't open. I don't think it's meant to. It must be ornamental.'

'It's not ornamental. Why would a gate be ornamental?'

'How do I know? But it obviously isn't meant to be opened. Let's just hop it.'

'Evening,' said another couple ambling by on their way into the club dinner.

We grinned and nodded. The lady of the couple turned her eye back over her shoulder as they passed, at precisely the moment I had started climbing over the gate. I waved limply. She kept on walking, whispering something to her husband as they continued.

'Come on,' I hissed to Cathy. 'Let's just go.'

'Oh all right,' said Cathy, hiking up her coat and dress underneath. She straddled the short gate, and at that precise moment the front door of Mayday opened, casting a rectangular beam of light cleanly down the walk to where Cathy was standing legs akimbo, skirt hiked.

'Be right there,' I said.

'Do they not have gates in Canada?' said Stan in his droll Yorkshire accent.

'Usually they're not ornamental.'

'Daft bugger,' laughed Stan.

We came in and got comfortable, got a drink in our hands. Stan and Julie had come to Gullane from Teesside, where Julie had worked in finance with an insurance company. Stan had worked for years with a building society before moving over to work as Secretary at the Northumberland Golf Club, one of Newcastle's best clubs. Then, three years ago, he'd been lured to Gullane to take on the vacant General Manager's job.

'It's a fabulous spot,' he said. 'I mean, just look at the place. The beach, the golf courses, close to Edinburgh, great local people.'

Julie signalled us in for dinner, and we went into the dining room that doubled by day as Julie's watercolour studio. With a dismissive, it-was-nothing wave of the hand she put before us duck stew, couscous, homemade courgette relish.

'So,' Stan said, fixing an eye on me. 'Have you been asked yet how to pronounce the name of the village?'

We both laughed. 'Just a few times,' Cathy said.

'Oh, I know,' said Julie. 'It really is the funniest thing. Who would have thought it, in a village of two thousand?'

'Does it really matter?' I said.

'Oh yes,' said Stan, slowly emancipating a smile. 'Don't you think it doesn't.'

'Have you met any of the local historians?' asked Julie.

We shook our heads. 'I suppose I'm one, though, too. I did some graduate work in history,' I said.

'Oh, they're everywhere! There's something about this place. There's Michael Cox, Audrey Paterson, Maurice Timson, Beryl Robinson. Not to mention Archie. All these people live here. It's amazing. And there's even a Gullane History Society. You can't swing a cat in this town without hitting a historian!'

'Golf, history, nature, friends,' I said. 'What more could you want in a place.'

Stan swallowed a mouthful of the duck stew, then slowly released another grin. 'Be careful out there,' he said, looking at Cathy and I in turn. 'You might end up wanting to stay.'

The Golfer: Who Else Can You Blame?

My father was a quiet man, in that he didn't often make pronouncements or dispense advice. Occasionally, his epigrammatic side would come out, and he would say something meant specifically for our benefit, but usually any information of an educational or philosophical nature had to be gleaned askance, caught passing out the side door of an unrelated discussion or observation. In 1980, Ghost and I were following a then-prominent Canadian pro in a tournament in Edmonton. He sliced his drive into the trees on one hole, jailing himself in an elegant grove of fir trees. His ball had come to rest behind a gnarled trunk, and he had no shot. The air went neon with his language.

'Fuck!' he exclaimed. 'One bad shot all fucking day, one shot in the bushes, and this is what I get. This is bullshit!'

My father and I watched this display with something approaching disbelief. I wondered what he thought of all this. I had never seen Ghost become even mildly upset on the course, let alone angry. Walking off to watch a different player, I said, 'Boy, that guy was pissed off, eh?'

'He's the one that hit it there,' my father said, shaking his head with disgust. 'Who else can you blame?'

I nodded as we moved on, and though I never forgot his words, it wasn't until many years later that I started trying to apply it to more than my golf game. It sounds so simple, but it is, of course, the pure randomness of our fates in golf that makes it the most existential of sports, particularly in links golf, where the bounces and bumps and breaks often defy the laws of physics. Many of us are unable to accept the misfortunes that come our way, blaming our grip, our spikes, a gust of wind, the cough of our partner. The parallel to life is obvious. But if my father ever had excuses he kept them to himself. In bad times, or when under pressure, I never once heard him make excuses for the state of his game or his life. *Who else can you blame?*

Jessica ran to the door when she heard the bell ring, and then came dashing back into my office. 'Dad, for you.' She left the room and sped back to her bedroom, whereupon she shut the door to her planet behind her. Her friend Jennifer was visiting, and they had forbidden entry to aliens. I went to the front hall.

'Curtis,' said the man. 'Michael Cox.' He held out his hand.

'Nice to meet you,' I said. 'Thanks for coming.'

We went into the living room. A retired college placement counsellor, Cox sat perched on the edge of the sofa, as if there was an odds-on chance that a brawl might break out at any moment. My only fear for him was soon realised, as Grace crawled into the room, drooled generously on his trouser leg, and then retreated. A small, wispy-haired man, and one of the founding members of the Dirleton and Gullane History Society, Cox bore a striking resemblance to the wise and placid Yoda of *Star Wars* fame.

'The thing about any history book to do with a local parish church,' he replied in answer to my question about what he'd been up to lately, 'is that you can take your normal print-run and cut it in half. Really. It's awful. People just aren't as interested in local church histories as they ought to be.' He put a blue-veined hand to his square glasses, adjusting them so that they sat in exactly the same manner as before. 'You might do five hundred copies for a regular monograph, but if it's a church history, well, you'd better just do two hundred and fifty copies. I'm quite serious about that. It's shocking.'

As for the town of Gullane itself, Cox told me, golf was clearly its kiss of life. It had been a town that, at various points in history, had lost its eminence in farming, church affairs, state affairs, horse racing, everything. Today it's a bedroom community for wealthy Edinburghers, but that hasn't always been the case. Three things saved Gullane from utter obscurity: golf, the train, and the car.

'Of course,' added Cox, 'there has been human habitation here for five thousand years, so it's not as if the town would actually die.' He described some of the more significant archeological finds in the area. Stone and Bronze Age relics had been found regularly throughout the surrounding fields and even up on Gullane Hill, though most of the finds, including quite a few burial sites and cairns, had been made nearer the shoreline.

Such treasures had not always been treated with the respect they deserve. Even before meeting Cox, a local greenskeeper had told me the story – at a course not to be named, on his insistence – about some digging he'd been doing years before. He was at work, trying to reshape a pot bunker, when he happened upon a stone. Picking away with his spade, he soon uncovered something more than a stone. In fact, it was a slab of rock that was obviously an ancient toppled tombstone, or perhaps even an old table top. He called his boss over. The oldtimer, a grizzled veteran of decades of golf-course management in the area, quickly scanned the horizon for signs of potentially interested parties, then laid into the young worker.

'For Christ's sake,' he said hurriedly. 'Cover up that God-awful thing right this minute and fill that bunker in.'

'. . . but—'

'Ya daft shite,' said the veteran. 'Just tell the members the bunker face was collapsing too often. Whatever. We'll tell them something. But if we show this thing to anybody, we're going to have bloody archaeologists crawling all over this course.'

The young man did as he was instructed, achieving two sad results with one spade: halting the progressive understanding of our past, and changing the character of a difficult and artistic golf hole for ever (one being so much more painful than the other). I chose not to share this story with Michael Cox.

'At any rate,' Cox continued. 'It wasn't really until the sixth century that an actual settlement can be documented to have existed in Gullane. There were churches built around the time of the Battle of Hastings, 1066, of course, and the ruins of the Church of St Andrew that still sit in the entrance to town are all that's left of what was a twelfth-century granite structure.'

Isn't it sometimes overwhelming? I wondered out loud. To be interested in local history in a place that is so full of it? Wasn't it sometimes daunting to work on projects, especially as an enthusiast, rather than a professional?

He cleared his throat nervously. 'Yes,' he said. 'Well, no.'

From medieval times, he continued, Gullane had been a religious centre of sorts. The kirk of St Andrew was established very early on, but in the early 1600s huge sandstorms blew through the region. Easterly winds howled off Aberlady Bay and over the Hill, carrying most of the bay's sand along with it at low tide. The silt storms covered the town, and left massive deposits slithering and building and duning along its eastern base, where the 1st tee of Gullane No. 1 is today. Something had to be done. In 1612 an Act of Parliament decreed that due to 'conintuewallis blowne sand' the

Parish headquarters were to be moved from Gullane to Dirleton. The Parish of Dirleton was then formed, and it has been there ever since. Gullane was deemed by the government of James VI to be 'ane decaying place'. Sand was a hazard even then.

Dirleton didn't necessarily benefit from the transfer of the Parish HQ. Its castle was razed in 1650 by none other than Cromwell as he made his bloody way through the countryside en route to declaring the Protectorate. It was just one year before that, in 1649, that a trial had been held in the castle and three local 'witches' had, as Cox put it with tremendous understatement, 'paid the ultimate penalty'. Somehow the hairs on the back of my neck stood to a sharper point than they might have with a more graphic rendering of their fate.

Cox looked at his watch. 'Well, I'd best be going.' He stood up and vigorously adjusted his glasses.

'Thanks, Michael,' I said. 'I enjoyed it.' There was so much more to discuss, and we agreed to meet again.

'Yes, well,' he said haltingly. 'Good. Yes, you'll have to come out to the meetings of the History Society. We tend to have good turnouts.'

'I'd like that,' I said, imagining a gathering of half a dozen retirees sitting in someone's house, sipping herbal tea, eating trimmed cucumber sandwiches, discussing the merits of erecting a monument to the world's largest potato, dug in 1886.

'Do you take drinks and cookies and stuff to someone's house?' I asked. 'I'd be happy to bring something.'

Cox stopped, peered at me like the turtle disgusted with the rabbit. 'We have the meetings in the Town Hall,' he said. 'We might get a couple of hundred people. It depends on the weather.'

'Two . . . Oh. Right.'

What is it? I wondered, as Cox left. Why would history, especially local history, be that attractive to people? Why in Gullane, a town of 2,000 people, were there hundreds of historical enthusiasts, half a dozen practising amateurs, and a couple of genuine historians? Certainly the area had its share of past conflict, as the Reverend Kerr, with typical understatement, noted in his *Golf Book* (a book that had quickly become my Bible, the Reverend my spiritual guide through the region), saying that East Lothian, with 'its ivy-clad castles and hollow shells of ruined towers recall the memories of many heroes whose names are connected with the most stirring incidents of Scottish history. It would be difficult to name any outstanding event between the Roman Conquest and the Battle of Prestonpans which has not left its mark upon the eastward Lothian.'

Perhaps the resident fascination with local history had something to do with golf, with the obsessive qualities inherent therein? Such a fanatical approach to the marriage of history and golf was expressed by a Mr Lang, writing in the fourth issue of *Badminton Golf* at the end of the nineteenth century, when he said that, 'To write the history of golf as it should be done demands a thorough study of all Scottish Acts of Parliament, Kirk Session Records, Memoirs, and, in fact, of Scottish literature, legislature, and history, from the beginning of time . . . A young man must do it, and he will be so ancient before he finishes the toil that he will scarce see the flag on the short hole at St Andrews from the tee.'

I wondered if history was in fact as esoteric as I had once thought? Did these people, Michael Cox and the rest of the local History Society, really care that much about their village's past? Or was it a kind of bequest to the future of Gullane? Maybe they just didn't have anything better to do. It wasn't until long after meeting Michael Cox that day, indeed, not until long after I'd stopped consciously thinking about it, that it hit me. Local history was only partially about the past, only partially about the future; what it really attended to was the present, or more correctly, those occupying the present. If no one preserved the past for the future, if no one took the time to infuse the past with significance, the implication was that the present would also very quickly cease to matter (or worse, that it was utterly insignificant even as events were being played out). Wasn't that really what local history boiled down to? A way to tell our daily selves that we mattered, that we were at or near the centre of things. What was the alternative?

I went to the next meeting of the History Society and paid my membership fee. It was a dreary, heavy night, but the Town Hall was full. There had to be at least a couple of hundred people in attendance, and I was happy to lend a hand when they needed to set up some extra chairs at the back.

An e-mail arrived, confirming that our friends Rich and Charlotte were going to be stopping in Gullane to visit us the following week, on their way home to Toronto from five years of living in Melbourne. Rich was a law professor and Charlotte a ballet company administrator, and they were spending a few months making their way back. Rich had been one of the groomsmen at my wedding, had delivered the Toast to the Groom, and he and Charlotte had stayed at my apartment the weekend of my wedding. Rich had long been one of my closest friends, and when I met up with Jack at the 1st tee of Gullane No. 3 for a game we'd arranged with Archie as well, I told him Rich was coming to town, and that I'd love for them to meet if possible.

'Right,' he nodded. 'Next week. Does the lad golf?'

I thought about Rich's golf game, about whether it would stand up to Gullane No. 1. 'Yes,' I said, making a mental note to tease Rich about my hesitation.

'Good, well, we'll have to see. It's getting close to Christmas time and Doris has a lot of things that need doing. Now then, are you going home for Christmas?'

I nodded.

'That's a long way to go for a few presents, son.'

'If I even get any.'

'Haven't you been a good boy?! I'll have to ask Cathy about that.'

Archie and another man came barrelling around the starter's hut, Archie nearly exploding at the seams with energy. 'Gillespie!' he howled from at least twenty feet away. 'This is our dear friend, Douglas Macrae.'

A portly, friendly-faced gent, who looked younger than Archie, and certainly younger than Jack, stepped forward and shook my hand. Archie addressed Douglas and said with academic precision, 'Young Mr Gillespie is an idle Canadian living in Gullane so that he can play golf all year round.'

Jack joined in the laughter, but chastened Archie. 'And I suspect trying to get a little writing done.'

'I'll see it when I believe it,' said Archie, striding stiff-kneed to the tee. 'Right. Let's cease and desist with the jabbering and flabbering and get on with the game. It's December. If we stand here all day and let Marston bore us with his stories, it'll soon be Christmas.'

'Baird, I was here ready to tee off, waiting for you. I was the first one here.'

'Irrelevant,' Archie pronounced. He poked a tee into the ground and placed a battle-scarred ball on it. 'The point is to be ready to play when the moment arrives.' He swung and nearly topped the ball, sending it scuttling sixty or seventy yards into the left rough. 'Acchh! Too much violence! This is what you do to me, Marston. You make me lose focus. Come on then. Let's go.'

'I had nothing to do with that, Baird,' said Jack, stepping to the tee. 'Don't blame that on me.'

Douglas, a soft-spoken, kindly soul, turned to me and shook his head. 'It's all a bit sad, sometimes, isn't it?'

It was to be Archie and I against Jack and Douglas, in a match for the sum of one pound per player. We all managed to make it off the tee and down the fairway, and perhaps twenty minutes later we were already marching up the hill on the 4th hole. I wondered, not for the first time nor the last, exactly what kind of drugs these men must be on. Was it golf? The beer, perhaps? Or the combination of activity, alcohol, and companionship? Whatever it was, I thought, breathing hard from the slope, I wanted some of it. Jack was ten paces ahead of me, lugging his trolley decisively towards his ball. Archie and Douglas were off to the right, where both had sliced their drives. The decades: one man in his eighties, two in their seventies, and me.

'Nice drive, Marston,' Archie shouted out from the other side of the fairway. 'Must have hit a stone.'

Jack stopped, shook his head, grinned. Only the heavy breathing induced by the slope stopped him from returning the insult. We got to the top of the hill, and it was here that the world exploded into another dimension, that it opened out and up and away, as if a carapace had just that second been prised off the sky. The Paps of Fife were easily visible across the Firth to the north, the Forth Bridges and Edinburgh stood out in relief against the western horizon, the Isle of May was clear in the eastern mouth of the Firth leading out to the North Sea. Though it was the first week of December, it was a calm and dry day, perhaps twelve degrees celsius. I was sweating from the climb up the hill and took my jumper off. It was early afternoon, and so the sun was already passing Edinburgh in the south-west, but across the sky from north to south a lone low band of cloud hung in the air like a scrim of pale grey-green diaphonous silk, motionless, so that sunshine streamed not directly at us, but from above and below the cloud. It was a benevolent glow. Across the Firth the shipyards of Kirkcaldy gleamed, and before us the dappling waters of Aberlady Bay glittered and shimmered, seemed alive with tiny, thrashing silversided smelts. It was almost too bright to look at.

'I don't think I've ever seen that,' said Jack. 'The sun like that on the water.'

We finished the hole and Archie came huffing over to the 5th tee. 'It changes every day,' he said. 'It's never the same. Never. I've come up this hill five thousand times, and it's never been the same twice.'

'It's the light,' said Jack, staring towards Edinburgh. His eyes were a bit watery, and he rubbed a finger against his bushy grey-black moustache. 'The light and the water. They *can't* be the same, can they, when you think about? Ever. Gorgeous.'

'Superb,' said Archie, who turned to face Jack. 'And I can say with utter authority that I would rather view that every day than that!' With this he pointed to Jack's face.

Jack grinned. 'Or your mirror, right, Baird?' He winked at me.

'Oh, dear,' said Douglas quietly. 'Here we go.'

Surprisingly, Archie did not respond immediately, but seemed to descend into a kind of mental root cellar, a sub-compartment of his concentration which he perhaps kept locked until the contents were required in times of exceptional need. Jack laughed, hitched up his pants like a batter waiting for a pitch. 'I'm afraid to hear what he's going to say now.'

Archie screwed up his face into his satisfied-to-have-remembered-a-good-one expression, his eyes partly lidded, his mouth holding down a big grin. 'I believe it's appropriate at this point to quote the poetry of Bishop Heber on the topic,' he said, using a slow, heavy brogue, aspirating with great violence on the hard consonants of his last word. He lifted a hand, but during his recitation let his wrist go slightly limp as he indicated the glory of nature before him.

> *What tho' the spicy breezes*
> *Blow soft o'er nature's isle*
> *Every prospect pleases* (He turned to face Jack.)
> *And only man is vile!*

He finished, angled his head, and nodded, as if to say Game, Set and Match. Jack raised his eyebrows, sighed, and pointed at the tee. 'Go on then, you. Stop orating, and play a shot. You're holding us back.'

Archie had noticed something on the ground, and moved forward to pick it up. It was a gnarled old plastic golf tee, the kind which no real golfer would be caught dead using in North America, but which Scots seem to love. Archie ceremoniously presented the tee to Jack. 'I want you to have this, Mr Marston, in apology and also as a token of my deepest regard.'

Jack broke out in a grin. 'Archie, you shouldn't have.'

'. . . you're right.'

Archie and I won the match that day when I birdied the last for our one-up victory. 'Gillespie!' he shouted as I holed out. 'What a hero!' He'd played nicely enough, but to my surprise I had played very well indeed. ('You played some beautiful golf today, son,' Jack had said mournfully as we walked off the 18th green. This was his way whenever we were squaring off against one another, and it was so much more fun, in fact made me feel closer to him, than when we were partners, because as opponents we were both easier to tease, both looser. As partners we worried too much about letting the other down. On the 10th hole, I had hit a long straight drive on the difficult 450-yard par-four. 'Well struck, Cartiss,' Archie had said. But Jack leaned on his driver, eyed me disgustedly, and said, 'That's the end of a beautiful friendship.')

It was gratifying to hit the ball well and to score well. The two didn't always coincide. Adding it up later in my head (because, as usual, we didn't keep a medal card), I found I'd shot 69. I couldn't quite believe it. A score in the 60s. But the numbers weren't lying. It was one of those things that I had always wondered: just how good could I be at the game, if I ever genuinely applied myself? Or rather, if I had ever been able to approach the game in a proper mindset. Sure, I'd played some good golf here and there, but the truth was that I considered myself a woeful underperformer. I had always harboured, perhaps unreasonably, the belief that I could actually be a good golfer some day, if only I could cure a few small things: namely, lack of money, time, dedication and focus. But still, I always thought, the *talent* is there. If only the conditions were swung my way, maybe the talent would emerge.

And so any score in the 60s, even on the short No. 3, was a good sign. My swing was feeling tight and strong, my short game had improved dramatically since arriving in Gullane, and my putting had always been reliable. All I needed to do now was learn how to think on the golf course. This was problematic.

'Golf keeps the mind from being quite vacant; but the mind must be quite vacant for golf.' So wrote the golf correspondent of the *Edinburgh Evening Dispatch* in May 1891. No truer words were ever said, for golf is the most unusual of sports in that it requires a fierce application of one's mental powers simply in order to get one's mind out of the way. Rare is the person of contemplative or poetic temperament who excels at golf – though, with great irony, golf is unlike nearly every other sport in that it lends itself naturally to a literature, a philosophy, precisely *because* it is such a contemplative game. After all, you've got lots of time out there. But the cruel twist is that it is nearly impossible to be, for lack of a better word, philosophical *and* good at golf. One thing I most certainly am not is a philosopher, but my mind is so comfortable on the golf course, so generally at ease in its own company, that it roams across the width and breadth of my consciousness. The task at hand, golf, is rarely on the screen. This makes for extremely pleasant and rewarding rounds of golf; it's just that the pleasure and rewards are only occasionally, and never systematically, related to golf.

The game's best players are not its greatest philosophers. The difference between Tom Weiskopf and Jack Nicklaus was not physical talent (except in that Weiskopf perhaps had more). No, the difference was that Nicklaus was not cursed with introspection. Each shot was a unique moment in time to Nicklaus. To Weiskopf, each shot was fraught with history and import, with a significance he understood and recognised in the present moment. Tiger Woods' greatest strength as a golfer is that, besides his great physical gifts, he genuinely does not seem to care about the meaning or history of the game or his place in it *while* he is engaged in the struggle to carve out his place therein. While engaged in the physical action of striking a stationary object, the attempt to hold competing ideas in one's head simultaneously (that is, a golf shot made in the present moment versus a golf shot made both in the present moment and as a brick in the construction of one's myth – and we all do this) is nearly impossible. There have been times when I have hit a golf shot, usually a bad one, and realised immediately afterwards that I cannot even recollect swinging the club, so immersed was I in thinking about something else (a stalk of unusual grass, a plane on the horizon, the sandwich I had for lunch, the sound Grace made eating cereal that morning . . . you get the idea). When I hit good shots, and play great stretches of golf, I tend not to notice my surroundings or playing partners as much. This is a loss of another kind, and often induces a sense of mild depression, because I know at that point (on the verge of a great round) that I've been too blinkered to the world. At some point, hunched over a four-footer to keep a good round going, I'll inevitably hear a whisper from the far corners of my head, a voice muttering, *Does it really matter? Does any of this really matter? What does matter?*

I wonder often if golf is a game for the solitary soul. I love playing alone, and I do it often. But is it good for me? Or is it just a chance to be alone, and to let my thoughts and emotions spill all over the place simply because there are no boundaries to speak of? One thing I do believe is that golf is a trivial game somehow connected to the world's depths. Maybe not even connected, so much as golf being a kind of portal one might step through to get to this other, more meaningful place. I feel at ease going to the golf course, this open ground with no ceiling and no walls, on my own, to ask certain questions, though neither the questions nor the answers, if there are any, have anything to do with golf. The answers are always elsewhere. Home. Love. The meaningful application of our talents towards the benefit of others. Who cares about a four-footer? How could that possibly matter?

Where the middle ground is, I do not know. There is, however, only one sure cure for the golf-course blues, only one thing that provides momentary relief from the depression, and that is a properly struck golf shot. Robert Marshall, who wrote the very funny 1902 classic *The Haunted Major*, recognised this feeling, and had his protagonist, the insufferably pompous Major the Honourable John William Wentworth Gore, 1st Royal Light Hussars, experience it. The Major has ill-advisedly embroiled himself in a challenge match against the reigning Open champion; ill-advisedly because, although the Major considers himself the 'finest sportsman living', he does not golf. He therefore takes himself off to St

Andrews (called St Magnus in the book) and hires the
caddie/teacher Kirkintulloch to teach him the game. The first
session does not go well.

> I went steadily on, ball after ball. They took many and
> devious routes, and entirely different methods of reaching
> their destinations. Some leapt into the air with half-hearted
> and affrighted purpose; others shot along the ground with
> strange irregularity of direction and distance; a number
> went off at right or left angles with the pleasing uncertainty
> that only a beginner can command; whilst not a few merely
> trickled off the tee in sickly obedience to my misdirected
> energy. At length I struck one magnificent shot. The ball
> soared straight and sure from the club just as Kirkintulloch's
> had, and I felt for the first time the delicious thrill that tingles
> through the arms right to the very brain, as the clean-struck
> ball leaves the driver's head. I looked to Kirkintulloch with
> a proud and gleaming eye.
> 'No' bad,' said he, 'but ye'll no' do that again in a hurry.
> It was guy like an accident.'
> 'Look here, Kirkincountry,' I said, nettled at last, 'it's
> your business to encourage me, not to throw cold water;
> and you ought to know it.'
> 'Ma name's Kirkintulloch,' he answered phlegmatically;
> 'but it doesna' maitter. An' I can tell ye this, that cauld
> watter keeps the heed cool at goalf, and praise is a snare
> and a deloosion.'

You'll have to read the book yourself to uncover the Major's comic
and supernatural fate, but I have always loved that description of
the sensation of the well-struck shot, that 'tingle' that goes through
the arms to the brain. A 2-iron off the middle of the club is so pure

a feeling, such a honeyed sensation, that it's not unlike that first blissful (and not entirely healthy) moment when a drug you've missed pours itself back into every crevice of your body, whether that drug is alcohol, nicotine, cocaine, whatever. You crave it. You want it. The sensation of hitting that 2-iron dead-pure is like a melting through your limbs, a warm waxy softness that leads to a sensation of utter pliancy throughout your body. You coil, release, finish in balance, watch the flight of the ball, stare at your creation. It leaves the earth, rises, peaks . . . then falls and come to rest. It's over. And then you only want to do it again.

There was no sense upon waking that mid-December morning that something quite extraordinary was going to happen that day. It seemed like any other day. Grace started complaining at 6am, demanding to be released from her crib, that miserable cage we'd so inhumanely placed her in the night before. Cathy and I both pretended not to hear it for as long as possible, just to see if the other would get out of bed. Jessica got up, rubbed her eyes, said she'd dreamed about a unicorn, and then complained about having to dress and brush her hair before we let her have breakfast (a school promptness issue). I made coffee, went to Mr Rasool's to get the papers ('The weather,' he'd sighed, looking dolefully out the window. 'The weather is the weather. What can we do about it? It's just the weather, and that's what it is'). Cathy and I had toast with our coffee. Jessica had three bowls of cereal. Grace smeared pureed apricots all over her face, and then used it as hair gel. In short, it began much like any other day.

Except that this morning, there was a difference right away, a difference that I'm sure was related to what was to happen later on that day. There was a different feel to the house, a fine feel, but a different feel. First, Charlotte staggered into the kitchen, smiled wearily, then went to the bathroom. A few minutes later, Rich stumbled in. Both had jet lag, having arrived late the night before from somewhere in Eastern Europe.

'How are you feeling?'

'Good,' said Rich, sounding haggard. 'Great. Can't wait to play some golf.' He cast a sceptical glance out the back window, where the normally dramatic line of the Lammermuir Hills was obscured by mist, the sky a heavy broth that seemed to have both the colour and specific gravity of mercury. I had told Rich of my 69 the week before with Jack, Archie and Douglas, but also had to tell him that neither Jack nor Archie was going to be able to join us, which had been quite disappointing to me. I'd told him a lot about both men, and had told him how much Jack reminded me of my father.

'Maybe we can meet up with him later,' said Rich. 'Or maybe tomorrow. I'd sure like to meet anyone that reminds you of Ghost.' He shifted his gaze back to the window. 'It doesn't look all that promising out there. But then I guess it is December.'

I smiled, now a local when it came to understanding the inner life of the weather. 'Let's just wait and see.'

An hour later the mist rose and dispersed, though it did so only over Gullane. This was not such an uncommon meteorological event along our stretch of coastline. It was the hills of Fife and the Lammermuir Hills, Archie always said. They were like weather magnets, drawing bad weather away from Gullane. It was true. There were countless days when I stood on top of Gullane Hill with the sun on my face, looking at bad weather both ten kilometres to the north and ten kilometres to the south. I once asked Archie to explain this phenomenon in more precise scientific terms (since, being a retired veterinarian, I assumed science was second nature to him). He looked at me as if I were unable to see the very ground we were standing on. 'Because this is Paradise,' he said.

On the 1st tee of Gullane No. 2 I waved my driver at the hill and then to the Lammermuirs to the south. 'Like I said this morning. Perfect.'

'It's actually sunny,' said Rich, as we teed off into a stout breeze. There was nothing so unusual about pushing my drive right on the opening 366-yard par-four, but I drew a bad lie, pulled a 6-iron left, chunked my chip shot from some evil greenside rough, fluffed my next chip shot, and then two-putted for a clumsy six. Double bogey.

'I thought you said you shot 69 last week,' said Rich, grinning.

The next six or seven holes were hardly about golf, but they were all about golf. I was showing Rich my corner of Scotland, my home course, the place where I'd so badly wanted to bring my father. Rich knew all these things, knew the whole story. He exhaled loudly when we got to the top of the hill.

'Ghost would have loved this,' he said, staring, turning his head every way to incorporate the vision. 'And he would have loved the courses, with that stupid little cleek of his. This is amazing.'

All I'd really been concentrating on for the first six or seven holes was pointing out the highlights, the Paps, the Isle of May, the Forth Bridges, Elie and Anstruther on the Fife coast, the Tranter dunescape, the midget subs in the bay. Nevertheless the golf wasn't half bad; well, at least my golf. Rich has always had a good golf swing, but he doesn't play enough to score consistently, and the Gullane rough was not treating him kindly. After my double-bogey on the 1st hole, I'd birdied both the easy par-four 3rd, and the shortish par-five 6th. After scrambling to make a ten-foot putt for par on the 9th hole, Rich, who was keeping our medal card, told me I was even par after the front nine.

I hadn't been keeping track. 'Really?' I said, somewhat surprised.

On the par-four 10th hole, I hit a sand wedge to eight feet and made the putt. I parred the next two holes, and Rich had a double and a quadruple bogey. This took us out to the 12th green, the tip of the course, where the green and the 13th teebox are practically in the Nature Reserve. From that spot, the dunes and the bay are so close, you almost want to toss aside the clubs and go clamming, or strolling through Tranter's world. After a good drive on the 13th, I hit an indifferent second shot into the uphill 400-yard par-four, but for some reason my thirty-foot putt from off the green turned left at the last minute and dived into the hole. At that point, we turned the corner of the golf course, as it were, and started to head for home. We'd played many of the last ten holes into the stiff breeze, but now we could ride the wind all the way into the clubhouse. The 14th hole is 336 yards and my drive left me just short of the green. I pitched on, made the putt. I was now, as the saying goes, unconscious, though I still managed to miss a three-foot putt for par on the next hole.

Uh-oh, I thought. Here we go. *Old reliable is kicking in.*

But I didn't collapse. I can't explain it. I fully expected to choke, and after missing the three-footer had already recited in my head the discussion we would have over dinner that night. *Yeah, I was three under after fourteen holes, but I guess I just lost my concentration or something. Got a couple of bad breaks. Just didn't play that well coming in.*

After birdieing the next hole, the long par-five 16th, I was back to three under for my round, with two downwind par-fours to play. I wasn't even that worried when I hit my tee ball into the chewy, spongy rough to the right of the downhill 17th.

'Wow,' said Rich, as we tromped around looking for my ball. 'This stuff is just *brutal.*'

I laughed, despite the growing concern over my missing ball. Rich had already played his second shot, a nice effort up just beside the deep bunkers that protect the left side of the green. We kept looking for mine. 'We've got to find it,' said Rich. 'It would just be wrong to have such a great round going, and then lose a ball on the second last hole.' As he spoke, he halted as if he'd nearly tripped on something. 'Wait a minute.' He bent over, felt around in the grass. 'Curt, you lucky dog. I stepped on it. Here it is.'

It seemed obvious, given the way my day was going, that all I had to do was swing the club and something good was going to happen, so that's what I did with my next shot, a sand wedge. The ball flew over the scandalous little pot bunker guarding that day's pin placement, and settled down about a foot from the hole. I tapped it in for birdie, walked to the 18th tee in a bit of a daze, and then nearly drove the last hole, a 305-yard par-four. I chipped to about six feet, and missed the putt, which shocked me to the core. It *had* to go in. It was my day. But it didn't; this was still golf, after all. Rich and I shook hands, as we did after every game.

Rich pulled out the scorecard as we walked into the clubhouse. 'You shot sixty-seven. Four under.' He paused for a second. 'What's your best ever?'

'You just saw it.'

He was silent for a moment. 'Ghost would have liked to have seen that.'

'He would've *had* to see it. He wouldn't have believed it otherwise.' We changed our shoes inside and then hoisted our clubs on our shoulders and started for home. We were to meet Cathy and Charlotte and the girls back at the flat, and then get a nice big dinner going; some salmon, rice, asparagus, a couple of bottles of wine. Walking down the High Street I realised how melancholy my round had made me feel, despite my exhilaration. The one person I would have loved to have shared this with wasn't there to share it with. I told this to Rich.

He nodded, stayed silent.

Our short reverie was shattered by the loud intrusive honking of a car horn, followed by a mild screeching of tyres. We looked up to see an old blue Ford swerve off to the wrong side of the street and jam itself into a tight parking spot.

'Oh, you can't be serious,' I said, grinning.

'What?' said Rich. 'What?'

Jack got out of his car, checked both ways for traffic and then ambled across the street. 'Out working, I see, boy,' he chortled, happy as always to have caught me out in yet another of what he was sure was an endless series of work-avoidance schemes.

'Well, I have to show my friends a good time,' I protested. 'You wouldn't want me to leave them on their own, would you? Jack, this is Rich.'

They shook hands. 'I've heard a lot about you,' said Rich.

Jack chuckled. 'Oh dear, oh dear.' He put his hand on my shoulder. 'Don't trust a word this young lad says.'

'I never have,' said Rich, grinning widely.

'Oh, well, we'll get along then! Heh, heh. Shame I couldn't make it out with you boys. Just busy with getting ready for the holidays and all. How'd you play, then?'

Rich dutifully pulled the scorecard from his back pocket, saying nothing as he passed it to Jack. He fiddled with his glasses, pretended to lick a pencil in mid-air, and then inspected the numbers hole by hole, nodding here, nodding there. I could see the change in his face when he saw the 67, but I had no clue what he'd say. He appeared to have finished, and then he turned his attention to Rich.

'Curtis told me, but I've forgotten. Where'd you say you were on your way back from, then?'

'Australia.'

'Right . . . and they count differently down there, do they?'

Rich laughed. 'I'm afraid not.'

Jack nodded, returned his attention to the card, going through the hole-by-hole scores again. 'Oh, yes,' he mumbled. 'Birdie at three, good . . . par at four . . . birdie . . . yes, yes . . . six, seven . . . mmm-hmmm . . . par at twelve, good . . . what iron did you hit in?'

I thought back to the 408-yard par-four. 'Wedge.'

He allowed his jaw to drop slightly. 'Were you playing the front tees?!'

'I can't explain any of it, Jack. I really can't. It was just one of those days. Well, I've never had one of those days. It just happened.'

He returned to the card, scanned the last few holes. 'Sixteen, birdie, seventeen, birdie, very good, very, very good . . . eighteen, what happened on eighteen?'

'Missed a six-footer for a sixty-six.'

'Shame.' He handed the card back to me. 'Fine stuff, boy. You'll be giving me a few more strokes after Christmas, I'll tell you that much.' We stood chatting for a few more minutes about Christmas plans, and the shocking winter weather back in Canada, talk which always delighted him.

'Rich,' he said, finally. 'A pleasure.'

'Likewise.'

Jack turned to me. 'Will I see you before you go back for the holiday?'

'I hope so.'

'Me too. Me too. Love to the girls. Right then. I'm off. Bye, boys.' And with that he danced back across the street, and squeezed himself back into his tiny car. Then he was off, honking and waving. Rich and I stood and stared as he drove away.

'What did I tell you?'

'Unbelievable,' said Rich. '"What happened on eighteen?" That's exactly what Ghost would have said.'

A few days after Rich and Charlotte left for Canada, it was time for us to return to Alberta. Temperatures of 30 below zero celsius awaited us, as did waist-deep snow. I'd played golf just a week before our departure day, shooting the single best score of my life, and now I was going home to a land where exposed flesh would freeze in thirty seconds. Though the difference between the physical landscapes might be a shock, the emotional landscapes were also going to be at odds. Since my father's death Christmas had never been the happy occasion it once was. The first few years after his passing were painful in the extreme, and though they had become less painful over time, major holidays were nevertheless not the happiest of times. There was simply a presence missing, like a phantom limb you keep believing is attached, and are surprised when you go to use it and it's not there. It didn't help that his birthday was 21 December, now just a few days away.

When the phone rang later that night, just as we were packing, Jessica picked it up, and was her usual brisk, informative self. 'Hello, this is Jessica speaking. Who is this speaking, please?' I could almost hear the chuckling coming from the other end. Jess handed me the phone. 'It's Jack, Daddy, and he said he wants to talk to you.'

I took up the receiver. 'Mr Marston,' I said. 'How are you?'

'Good, boy, good. You?'

'Very well,' I said. 'Just packing up here.'

'Right, well, I won't keep you. Just wanted to wish you a good journey.'

'With all this luggage and two little kids, an eight-hour flight isn't always the most fun you can have, but I'm sure it'll be fine.'

'Yes, well, listen . . . I just wanted to say . . . make sure you come back.'

'We will,' I said, laughing. 'We'll be back in early January.'

'Good. Leave all that snow in Canada, and just bring yourselves back here. That'll be good. I'll look forward to that.'

'Me too,' I said. 'I'll see you then, soon after we get back.'

'You will,' he said. 'That you will.'

6

Our first day back in Scotland after Christmas was fogbound, and the lack of light and the low sky combined to intensify the jet lag. None of us carried much energy about. The East Lothian sky was a damp and chilly tarp. There had been quite a bit of snow while we'd been away, though it had melted quickly. Talking with Jack and Stan our first few days back, both assured me this was highly unusual, and that some decent weather would soon return. Grace was fussy that first night, and after both Cathy and I had taken turns rocking her back to sleep, I noticed the light was on in Jessica's room. Before I could step in and shut it off, I heard her voice. 'Daddy?'

'What is it, sweetie?' I said, on my way into the room. I stepped inside and saw that she was fully dressed. She had her blue and white Gullane Primary uniform on. She'd brushed her hair and was holding her new Christmas present from Isla, a Barbie watch. 'Jess,' I half-laughed. 'It's one in the morning.'

'Daddy, I want to be ready. Can you put my watch on? I can't get it on.'

'Jess, you have to go back to bed.'

'I can't. I want to be ready for school. I'm up. I can't sleep.'

'No, you have to sleep, Jess. I haven't even started my sleep yet.'

She began to cry.

'It's okay, sweetie. I'm having a hard time sleeping, too. Don't worry about it. Here, just put your jammies back on, and I'll lie down with you for awhile, okay?'

She nodded. After fifteen minutes, she seemed to be breathing softly and deeply, so I rose from her bed. In a shot she was upright. 'Daddy?'

'Yes, Jess?'

'Sleep tight.'

'Okay, you too.'

'And Daddy?'

'Yes, sweetie.'

'Don't forget to wake me up in the morning, okay. Wake me up in time.'

I smiled at her through the dark, and kissed her on the forehead.

On cold 'grum' January days, when the barometer was going wacky, the mail slot in our door breathed. The windows in the flat were closed. The hallway leading to the stairwell and the door outside was a small wind chamber, and as the air pressure changed, the mail flap opened and shut ever so gently, sighing like the gills of a large fish. The flat was a living creature; we were in its belly. Not trapped, just unwilling to leave the visceral warmth of its guts to venture out into the damp cold. That was how it felt to me when I rose in the hushed silence of the town early the next morning. Making my coffee in the kitchen, looking out over the mixed mist and gloom of East Lothian towards the Lammermuir Hills, I watched the sun peek over the horizon to the east. It rose more quickly than I thought it would, dodging banks of fog, and five minutes later it was just visible over the range of hills and just below a long soft loaf of pewter cloud. The orange ball was now shining and glimmering as if made of liquid ore, its bottom edge a spout about to release a glowering dribble of heat and fire. It lasted only a couple of minutes before rising into the cloud bank.

The mail shot through the slot in the door. A bank statement. A letter for our landlady. And a rather official-looking envelope from Canada for Cathy. She was still in bed, but was sitting up, coming to life, so I passed her the envelope as I sat down at the desk in our bedroom to turn on the computer and check the e-mail. Before I'd even got the machine up and running, Cathy had torn open the envelope and was directing noises of disgust my way.

'What?'

'This!' she said, brandishing the envelope at me, as if it were a glove she was about to throw at my feet. 'Parking tickets. On my car. At Christmas!' She tossed the envelope on the floor at my feet. 'I'm not paying those.'

'These can't all be me,' I said, scanning the notice, which also informed her that if she didn't respond immediately, she would be prosecuted in court. 'Look,' I said, pointing at one. 'I wasn't even in Edmonton that day. See. I was back in Calgary. You came down the next day. That one had to be you.'

She snatched the notice from my hand, her normally deep well of patience now dry and hollow. Pointing at the details listed on the page, she said, 'This one *is* for Calgary.'

Staring mutely at the page, the only mature course of action seemed to be to admit my wrongs and try to rectify them, so I continued to deny they were mine. I claimed it was a genetic irregularity, a fluke of nature it would be wrong to hold me accountable for. I tried to pay for parking, I really did. I plugged coins into meters. I paid attendants. I tried to be honest about it. But it was out of my hands. Sometimes I didn't have the right change. Sometimes I was in a hurry. Sometimes I just, well, I just forgot. This was the genetic part. My father had a shocking memory for some things. One of them was traffic tickets, and though I really remember only one incident from our childhood, how spectacular it was.

We were gathered around the dinner table one night, all eight of us, plus, I think, one or two of my brother Bruce's friends, who always seemed to be around the house when the dinner bell rang. The conversation, as always, was free-flowing and even a little competitive, as might be expected with six kids. I would have been perhaps fifteen at the time. Our dinner table was a large square surface surrounded on three sides with bench seating, like a booth in a restaurant. My father was the only person who occupied the section at the head. I sat to his right, and my mother sat to his left. Everybody else in the booth, the other five kids and any other guests, were essentially trapped, a captive audience, as it were, though the entertainment tended to flow in all directions.

This particular night we had just settled down to dinner. With our plates full, and the conversation picking up, it was turning into a grand and wonderfully quirky hour, as every dinner did. Then the doorbell rang. I bolted from my seat. When I opened the front door I was met by two policemen. I was a short kid, and, granted, these two cops were wearing thick rubber-soled boots, but they were huge. Monsters. We had been told occasionally at school that police officers were our friends, and that they were there to help us. These two didn't look friendly, and I can't recall if I even squeaked out a hello.

'Is Gerald Floyd Gillespie present?' said one of them, I can't remember which; in fact in my mind's eye they are not two persons but one, like the three-headed knights from *Monty Python and the Holy Grail* – one huge body with multiple heads. I retreated instantly and went into the kitchen.

'Who is it, dear?' said my mother.

'Uh . . . it's for Dad.'

My father put his fork down and finished chewing what was in his mouth. 'Who is it?'

I looked at him, said nothing, though I imagined my eyes said much.

He pushed his chair back and padded out to the front hall in stockinged feet. We heard the door creak open again. 'Yes?' said my father.

'Gerald Floyd Gillespie?' They had booming voices, these two, and we could hear every word at the dinner table.

'Yes.'

'I'm afraid you'll have to come with us, Mr Gillespie.'

'It's the cops!' I hissed out to everyone else at the table.

'The cops!' said all my siblings at once. There was a moment of chaos as the six of us tried to leave the booth at once, resulting in spilled cups and coughed up food. My mother got to her feet. 'Sit down. All of you!'

We sat. She marched off to the front hall, and we scampered into the living room to watch through the bay window. My mother was giving them hell. My father was standing there looking sheepish. One of the policemen was holding a pair of handcuffs, but he was just swinging them around, making a show of it to let everyone know that he had them ready, and was in fact demonstrating great benevolence by leaving them off my father's wrists. The policeman not holding the handcuffs was talking calmly to my outraged mother. He was explaining that Dad had not paid a speeding ticket, and had ignored all the notices of failure to pay.

'But I get all the mail!' my mother said angrily. 'I have never seen any notice of anything like that.'

'I'm sorry, ma'am,' said the officer. 'I don't know what to say. We've got to take him downtown and charge him. He'll be released without bail, I'm sure, and then he can pay the ticket and the additional fine tomorrow, but we can't process that in the squad car.'

'This is outrageous,' said my mother. 'This is a father sitting at the dinner table eating with his children.'

The two cops were starting to look embarrassed, but they were intent on fulfilling their duties. My father was looking at his feet, at the cop car, at the houses across the street. Finally, they led him away, stuffed him in the back seat of the car, and drove off. My mother followed the squad car downtown and sprang him. He never did say what he was thinking as the cops led him away, but I can guess. *At least I'm not a murderer or a drug addict. It's just a speeding ticket. I've just got a lot on my mind.* He never said it out loud, and when he got home he absorbed our teasing with as much dignity as he could, smiling along with us when we gleefully told him we'd go visit him in jail, and that maybe he could get us one of the licence plates he was going to be hammering out in the prison metal shop.

I told Cathy the story, and she laughed in all the right places. 'That was a good story,' she said, handing me the parking ticket from Calgary. 'Now don't forget to pay this.'

Perhaps we were all feeling emotional upon our return to Scotland. Leaving home was hard, though we were returning to a place that had welcomed us, to new friends and a new family of sorts. But perhaps we felt vulnerable our first week back, having left the safe harbour of home and family. Jessica had enjoyed her Christmas, and though she now had friends in Gullane, she still missed the friends she'd left behind.

'I wanted to stay with Astrid, Mommy,' she'd told Cathy on the plane when we left Toronto for Edmonton. 'I miss Astrid.' She paused. 'I wonder if my message in a bottle ever got to Astrid's Mormor and Morfor?'

The wind was wheezing and moaning beyond the window of the flat. We put Grace down for the night, and once she'd drifted off to sleep, Jess brushed her teeth, got into her pyjamas and crawled under her covers. Cathy sat on the bed beside her, and picked up the book we'd started before leaving for home, Milne's *The House at Pooh Corner*. We were nearly at the end. Jess sat rapt as Cathy finished off the book, reading from the chapter 'An Enchanted Place', wherein Christopher Robin tries to explain to poor Pooh Bear, he of so little brain, about the ways of the world. He talks about how wonderful it has been to do nothing with his beloved friend and then knights him Sir Pooh de Bear, and tries to tell Pooh what is going to happen. He's trying to tell Pooh that he has to grow up now. Cathy read to Jessica.

Then suddenly again, Christopher Robin, who was still looking at the world with his chin in his hands, called out 'Pooh!'

'Yes?' said Pooh.

'When I'm – when – Pooh!'

'Yes, Christopher Robin?'

'I'm not going to do Nothing any more.'

'Never again?'

'Well, not so much. They don't let you.'

Pooh waited for him to go on, but he was silent again.

'Yes, Christopher Robin?' said Pooh helpfully.

'Pooh, when I'm – you know – when I'm not doing Nothing, will you come up here sometimes?'

'Just Me?'

'Yes, Pooh.'

'Will you be here too?'

'Yes, Pooh, I will be really. I promise I will be, Pooh.'

'That's good,' said Pooh.

'Pooh, promise you won't forget about me, ever. Not even when I'm a hundred.'

Cathy stopped reading. I'd been watching Jessica and she'd been staring at the book, at the picture of Christopher Robin knighting Pooh and doing Nothing in the grass. Now she looked up when the words stopped coming. Cathy put a hand to her face.

'Mum?' said Jessica.

Cathy handed the book to me. 'Daddy has to finish,' she said hoarsely, her eyes glistening. I went to pitch hit, sitting down next to Jessica, but the sight of Cathy made me mist up. She went to the foot of the bed, and tried to stay calm as we finished. Jessica looked up to me, confused, intent on the story.

'Do you know it's sad, Jess?'

'Yes.'

'But it's okay. It's just that they're saying goodbye.'

'I know,' she said, waiting for me to continue. I read on.

Pooh thought for a little.

'How old shall I be then?'

'Ninety-nine.'

Pooh nodded.

'I promise,' he said.

Still with his eyes on the world Christopher Robin put out a hand and felt for Pooh's paw.

'Pooh,' said Christopher Robin earnestly, 'if I – if I'm not quite—' he stopped and tried again – 'Pooh, whatever happens, you will understand, won't you?'

'Understand what?'

'Oh, nothing.' He laughed and jumped to his feet. 'Come on!'

'Where?' said Pooh.

'Anywhere,' said Christopher Robin.

So they went off together. But wherever they go, and whatever happens to them on the way, in that enchanted place on the top of the Forest a little boy and his Bear will always be playing.

I closed the book, and put my shirtsleeve to my eyes. Cathy had bent her head towards her lap. Jessica was silent for a moment, and then said, 'Why is that sad?'

'Because Robin is explaining to Pooh that . . .'

'What?'

'. . . that . . . that he's growing up. Christopher Robin, that is. He's telling Pooh that he's growing up, and that things might not always be the same, that they might not always have what they have right now.'

Jessica thought about that for a minute and looked back to the book. 'But they're going off to play together. Look.'

I closed the book. 'Exactly. And that's the best way to think about it. They'll always be going off to play together.'

We switched off the light and went out to the sitting room, not really saying much to one another. *They grow up, don't they?* was the composition of our silence. We can't stop it. Like it or dislike it, we're helpless. Jess didn't read this last scene the same way as us because she was just five years old, but also because she was identifying with Pooh not Christopher Robin. Cathy and I had more smarts than the Bear of Little Brain, enough to see who was being left behind and who was doing the leaving. The very first time Jess had slept straight through the night, when she was perhaps five months old, we got up in the morning and made some coffee. Jess was still curled up in her crib. Cathy took a sip from her mug and this seemed to induce more emotion than a morning coffee ought to.

'What is it?' I'd said.

'She slept without us, without our comforting her,' she'd said. 'It's the first step. She already doesn't need us in the same way any more.'

She was right. It's all a process, a process of not so much cutting them loose, as coming to terms with the fact that they will, must, cut you loose. That's the hardest thing. Not that you have to cut them loose but accepting that they are going to do it to you. My parents let their children go with ease and good wishes, though I only know now how truly difficult that must have been, especially considering that they'd more or less sacrificed twenty years of their lives to raising six children. The day I left home, as a twenty-year-old, to go to university in a different city, my mother stood at the kitchen window, crying, watching me toss my suitcase into the car. She had her arms folded and couldn't even bring herself to wave goodbye. I was the oldest child, the first to leave home, the first to go to university. I suppose I was the one prying apart the dam. My father came out to the car with me.

'Drive safely,' he said.

'I always do,' was my standard and not wholly accurate reply.

He grinned through his grey and reddish beard, his bad teeth showing. He looked at me above his bifocals, the cheap ones he'd found in between a car seat, which he wore because he thought they suited him (and because he never could afford a proper pair of glasses). We stood there briefly, my car door open, my mother visible in the window, her hand over her mouth. It was a moment ripe for maudlin emotion, for vaguely threatening utterances about obligation and communication, but only now do I understand and truly appreciate the gift of lightness with which he (and my mother, by staying inside) let me go.

'We're around,' he said. 'We might come up to visit at Thanksgiving, otherwise, I guess we'll see you at Christmas.' He shook my hand, and didn't even watch me drive all the way to the end of the alley. In my rear-view mirror, I saw him pass through and close the rear gate without looking back. I can't be sure if this is fact or simply the result of a revisionist memory, but I remember thinking that he wasn't looking at me because he was looking towards the kitchen window, where my mother was probably still standing with her arms wrapped around her torso. With that I was gone, never to move back into my parents' household, but never unwilling or uneager to return to visit.

In mid-January I had to go into Edinburgh to look at some documents at the National Library, though the word 'had' is perhaps not the best choice, since it was, and always is, less an imperative than a willing choice; spending time in that library is as close to a meditative state as I'm capable of reaching. There is perfect light, just the right level of ambient noise (to occupy the levels of conscious and subconscious thought not engaged on the task at hand), and an overall air of study, intelligence and application. Being in that library, any library really, makes me feel as if I'm spending my time – not just my time on that day, but my time on this earth – in a useful and productive way. In the foyer to the Reading Room, there stood a statue of David Hume. There he was, Oswald's dear friend. Standing proud, holding a book. I looked at the face for a moment, acknowledged the irony, and continued on to the library, where I then chose to work for the first hour or so on the first section of this very book, inspired as I was by Hume's stare.

After an enjoyable morning filled mostly with leafing through an original copy of Reverend Kerr's great (and aesthetically beautiful) *Golf Book*, I took a lunch break, heading down towards Edinburgh University and a nearby East Indian restaurant hoping to satisfy my near daily craving for curry. I had my copy of Jonathan Raban's masterful *A Passage to Juneau* with me, as well as my notebook, and after a morning of libraries, I was looking forward to Raban's perfect, evocative prose and a good scorching vindaloo. I'd walked past this restaurant many times, and had often seen patrons inside, enjoying what looked to be a buffet lunch. It was a rainy, misty day, and the thought of a fiery curry at the bottom of my stomach was almost warming in itself. I went inside and found a completely empty restaurant. Granted, it was just after noon, and Edinburghers do tend to be late lunchers, but I still thought I'd find at least a few tables occupied. I pressed on.

'Are you open?' I said to the man who approached me.

'Oh, yes, of course,' he said. 'Of course we are open. Please come in.' He smiled widely.

'Do you have a buffet?' I asked. 'Is that the standard lunch?'

He shook his head. 'No buffet. We have a lunch special. Or you can order *à la carte*.' He stood patiently, waiting for me to decide, now that the buffet proved to be non-existent.

'Can I see the lunch special menu?'

He provided me with a menu. On it, prominently displayed, was a sticker that said all dishes featuring chicken or lamb were subject to a 75-pence surcharge due to the foot-and-mouth outbreak. I found this piece of information somewhat unwelcome, but ignored it. The lunch special menu looked to be reasonable value, and I also found my vindaloo. 'Good,' I said, returning the menu to him. 'That looks good.' I looked around the cavernously empty space of the restaurant. It seemed somewhat fusty with its plush gold and red trimmings and ornate furniture, all of it so completely devoid of human activity. 'Anywhere?' I motioned across the room, smiling broadly so that he understood I was both offering to seat myself and making a bit of a jest.

He did not smile. 'I will seat you.' He picked up the menu I had just finished surveying and motioned for me to follow him. He led me directly to the middle of the room, and gestured towards a table the size of a fold-up dinner tray. He laid the A4-size menu across the table, covering about two-thirds of the available surface area.

'Oh,' I laughed, pointing at my book and notebook. 'I was hoping to spread out a little, do some reading while I eat. That's okay, isn't it?' I pointed to the table right next to the one he'd led me to, a four-seater that was still not much bigger than many deuces I'd found myself at in the past. Still, it was better than the alternative, and so I made overtures to sit down.

'Oh no, sir.'

'Excuse me?'

'That is a table for four, sir.'

I looked around the restaurant. A quick survey indicated at least thirty tables. The door had not opened since I'd come in, and, as far as the visible evidence had revealed, we were the only two people in the place. Our voices reverberated off the distant walls. Smiling, I said, 'Well, I know, but I was hoping to, you know, read, maybe do a little writing. I don't think I could do it at this table.' I pointed to the postage stamp with legs he wanted to seat me at.

'You are one. This is a table for two. That is a table for four.'

'Well, I know, but . . . seriously,' I looked around the room again, purely for effect. 'You don't think it's going to fill up, do you?'

'No,' he admitted straight away.

'Well . . . I mean, if it does I can move. How's that?' I made another motion to sit down at the larger table.

'I'm sorry, sir, that is a table for four.'

'Look, that's absurd! There's no one in this place. It's not going to fill up, you just said so.'

'But that table is for four. I can't waste three seats like that, just to put one person at that table.'

'Waste three seats! You're joking!' I looked around the restaurant again, less now for effect than to try to locate any person in some way connected to the real world.

He smiled. 'I am sorry, sir.' Again, he opened a hand to the table for two.

I almost sat down where he was directing me, but a spasm of anger went through me. 'Oh forget it,' I said, brushing past him. 'You're not getting my business.'

He did not follow me to the door, and I can only imagine he was secretly relieved and overjoyed not to have to rearrange and then clean a table set for four. I also guessed he was not the owner. As I swept through the foyer, the sharp complex scent of a chicken vindaloo filled the air, and it was only through the most strenuous application of willpower that I carried on my way, craving my vindaloo but in possession of my self-respect and devotion to common sense. I vowed to seek Shafqat Rasool's opinion on this piece of absurdity, in case there was some subcontinental custom I had rudely but unknowingly transgressed.

Still muttering with disbelief I went around the corner to the Bookstop Café, sat down and ordered a brie and cranberry sandwich, and a coffee. They accepted my order, took my money, made my sandwich and delivered it to my table, all in an amiable and frictionless manner. *Isn't this the way it's supposed to happen*, I thought. I took a bite of my sandwich, and opened *A Passage to*

Juneau to read what the gifted Raban, an Englishman now living in Seattle, had to say about Canada as he sailed up the Northwest Passage. Newcomers to Canada, he wrote,

> . . . were under relatively little pressure to 'Canadianize', to adapt their styles and manners to those of the host country; more easily than in the United States, they could go on doing things much as they'd done them at home. The English stayed English, the Chinese stayed Chinese. America was a land of immigrants, Canada a country of émigrés.

This blunt distinction fitted nicely with a subtler one made by Russell Brown, a Canadian literary critic. Trawling a broad net through American and Canadian fiction, Brown suggested that one essential difference between the two cultures lay in the characters of Oedipus and Telemachus. In the States, a society founded on revolution, the mythic hero was the runaway son, the patricide; Oedipus as Huckleberry Finn. Escape, rebellion, the cult of the new life at the expense of the old, were the commanding American themes. Up north, in a society founded on the refusal to rise up against its parent, the mythic hero was the loyal son of Odysseus, Telemachus; the voyage in search of the lost father. Americans broke with their ancestral pasts, whereas Canadians honoured theirs.

> . . . after hard-edged America, Canada seemed out of focus. As it resisted ideology and national myth-making, so did it resist definition . . . in America, people were expected to get above themselves. Over the border, it was a social transgression, and people learned to mask their ambitions . . . which made them seem diffuse and evasive by American standards.

It seemed relatively accurate to me, as far as characterisations of national identity went, but the explanation was still somehow unsatisfactory. I felt more than heard the echo of a word somewhere near the bottom of the well of my mind, and it took a minute to winch it back up to the light. *Deferential.* That word had always stuck in my mind. It was the word the American writer Edgar Z. Friedenberg had used to characterise Canadians in his 1980 book on the Canadian psyche, *Deference to Authority*. (One of Canada's 'most significant and distinctive features,' says Friedenberg, 'is its willing acceptance and even celebration of its own colonial status,' and later he continues, saying that Canada would be improved as a nation if 'Canadians could get the message that is already grasped at some level by most Americans: that authority is, in every sense, inherently questionable'.)

But why are Canadians this way? Why, when so many of our ancestors were not deferential, particularly the Scots, who at least in day-to-day life are among the least deferential people on the planet? We've been deeply influenced by the Scots in Canada. I thought of something even as obvious as the place names in my home province of Alberta. There was a Banff, a Canmore, a Cochrane, an Airdrie, and on and on. It's astonishing the number of place names Scottish–Canadian immigrants, in their effort to re-create a sense of home I suppose, simply took from their homeland. But was that all they brought? Perhaps the sheer number of competing early influences (Native Indian, English, Irish, French, Eastern European) kept our forebears from assuming more Scottish cultural characteristics. But then, what is a Scot, anyway? Thrifty, hard-working, and devout? Given to glorious defeat, romantic disappointment, and resentment towards the English? These are gross simplifications, of course, and are but a few of the 'infamous Scottish shibboleths', to use Alexander Linklater's term, writing in the *Glasgow Herald* in 1998. Since the devolution of the Scottish Parliament in 1999 (and the vote for that devolution in 1997), there has been much written about what Scotland is and is not. Carl MacDougall, in his new book on Scottish identity *Painting the Forth Bridge*, spends a great deal of time discussing not just the everyday manifestations of Scottish nationality, but its symbols, symbols he hopes are disappearing in the face of a new Scottish identity.

> There is every indication that the power of our symbols is diminishing, that a new sense of national pride is emerging, with the scattering, if not the abolition, of the disparaging Scottish cringe factor. This is the sense of shame, maybe even humiliation, that comes from the more obviously mawkish representations of the Scot and Scottishness.
>   . . . But to understand the Scottish identity crisis as it appears today, with its conglomerate of symbols and surfeit of symbolism, it is necessary to understand how our most positive characteristics have been repressed and subsumed into a larger identity within which they were often barely accorded any status at all (meaning the English). So-called expressions of Scottish identity are often cruel misrepresentations of actual Scottish life, so that authentic expression has been absent from the cultural life of the nation.

Tom Nairn, in *After Britain*, his recent (and brilliant) deconstruction of New Labour and the problem of Scottish devolution within what he sees as a disintegrating United Kingdom, makes the case that the Scottish elite in some sense capitulated to the English in the 1707 Act of Union. And that this one 'choice' evolved into a pattern, became a kind of habituated self-subjugation.

'Self-colonisation' is like 'self-censorship': a chosen and

pre-emptive suppression, undertaken to avoid something worse. When institutionalised into a sufficiently general habit it of course becomes 'instinctive' and can appear as nature – in this case, the canny, circumspect (etc.) people that Scots are known to be (when not being uncouth, England-hating savages, etc.)

. . . It has nothing to do with 'ethnicity', or with aversion to English people as individuals, still less to suppurating nonsense about blood and descent. The resentment inseparable from it has been hatred of a collective situation, which has always embodied an unhealthy measure of self-hatred, too – since our own ancestors helped to create the situation, and for long eagerly collaborated with it. But it's over.

Oddly enough, in my readings it was an American who perhaps most pithily summed up the problem of Scottish national identity in this very turbulent period of its history. Jonathan Hearn is a cultural anthropologist from the United States lecturing in politics and sociology at the University of Edinburgh, and in 2000 he wrote *Claiming Scotland*. In his rather overly academic prose he suggests that the generations-in-the-making politicisation of the Scottish people (through causes such as their belief that their egalitarian state has constantly been under attack from outside) is what has brought about the desire for independence, or at least meaningful political autonomy. In other words, it's not so much the case that devolution will create a Scottish politics, but that the inherently political nature of the Scottish people through the generations is what brought about devolution (and which will thereby lead to a clearer national identity).

Scots are used to living in the cultural shadow of England,

having their history, language and culture measured against
an English standard. For centuries Scots have been told
that historical progress is a matter of following England's
example. Getting ahead has often meant suppressing the
Scots language and approximating to the norms of middle-
class English speech – and even leaving Scotland all
together. Scottish culture has tended to be crudely stereo-
typed, portrayed as quaint and romantic, a pastiche of kilts,
clans and bagpipes, and somehow suspended in a distant
past, no longer truly relevant. These images and attitudes
have been created as much by the Scots, especially expatri-
ates and the middle class, as by the English. But the result
none the less has been a legacy of resentment, and many
Scots believe that greater control over their own politics
would foster a more confident and self-assured culture.

. . . any argument for any future must do so by recourse
to the past. It must both pose and address the questions:
who are we? what do we want? and why? Moreover, people
must come to believe that the past they know can cause the
future they have chosen.

I wondered what Raban thought of the Scots. He found Canada without focus, diffuse. But he was English (and American).
Not Scottish (or Canadian). English-speaking Canadians (Quebec
would require another book altogether) have always tended to
define themselves via the blunt instrument of contrast, setting
themselves in relief against the brilliant, but sometimes corrosive,
heat and light spilling over the 49th parallel. I felt sure that as
gifted an observer as Raban was, he did not understand what
went on in the heart of a Canadian (or would that of a Scot). His
observations were technically correct, but lacked empathy. He
did not know, *could* not know, what it felt like to be inextricably

connected to, yet culturally overshadowed by a close neighbour; to be, as Pierre Trudeau once said of Canada's relationship with America, a mouse sleeping with an elephant (which is how Scottish nationalists must feel).

After finishing my brie sandwich and coffee at the delightful Bookstop Café (where I was served warmly and efficiently by a dusky Polish woman who might have stepped off the set of a Kieslowski movie), I walked back to the National Library, past the Indian restaurant. I looked in the window. It was still completely empty, though a cheerful sign on the door said OPEN. The waiter who'd disallowed me the table I wanted was still inside, laconically leaning against the check-in dais, reading a magazine. *I'm coming back here tomorrow*, I vowed. *And I'm going to sit where I damn well please.* I didn't, of course. I walked down that street the next day, and twice the following week, and many more times than that in the following months. I never did go in, despite often passing it with the vindaloo shakes, caught in the grip of an addict's craving. And though it wasn't a conscious choice to do so, I even found myself walking on the other side of the street, just in case that waiter happened to be looking out the window. I'd have been horrified to have him recognise me.

7

I have always found it astonishing how quickly one can go from comfort and ease, to embarrassment and anxiety. It takes so little. I'd been playing golf with Liam and a couple of his police officer friends, Callum and Colin. We'd had a fine game across Gullane No. 3, and had retired to the lounge at the Visitor's Clubhouse, where (as seemed to happen with Liam) one quick pint of Guinness had turned into two, then two to three. I knew Cathy and I were scheduled to go out for dinner that evening to Corinna and David Dawson's house for a Burns Supper, but we had teed off before lunch, and had as usual played quickly, and so it was pleasing to think, sitting there with my pint before me, that the pleasures of the afternoon were going to join seamlessly with the pleasures of the evening. It seemed only right and fair, even natural.

Una Kerr, who works as the Assistant Secretary at Gullane Golf Club, appeared at the doorway of the lounge, a large space which was about two-thirds full. Una had thick glasses, and from where I was sitting I could see that she was peering around the lounge, looking for something or someone, I didn't know what. I soon found out. Rather, the whole lounge found out. Her scanning gaze came to rest when she laid eyes on me. Instead of coming over to say what she had to say, she decided that each and every person in attendance might want to know the contents of her message.

'CARTISS?! CARTISS, YOUR WIFE JUST CALLED. SHE SAYS YOU'RE LATE, AND THAT YOU'VE GOT THINGS TO DO BEFORE GOING OUT TONIGHT, AND THAT YOU SHOULD GET HOME RIGHT NOW.'

I don't wear a watch, but I saw that Colin had one on. I told him to stop laughing and tell me what time it was. I was an hour late. After downing my pint, I sprinted home, and blamed Liam for it all.

Cathy nodded. 'Right,' she said. 'Did you remember to get the wine in Edinburgh yesterday? Is it in the car?'

I stood there, arms hanging slack at my sides. I shut my eyes, and pressed the lids together hard.

'Oh, Curtis! Acch! Well, you'd better get down to Mr Rasool's and see what he's got. Hurry up. We have to leave in fifteen minutes.'

I highstepped it down the street to Mr Rasool's. 'Hello, Shafqat,' I said, picking out a couple of bottles of French burgundy from his surprisingly well-stocked wine shelf.

'Ah . . . Mister Curtis,' he drawled, emphasising the hard C. 'And how are you today?'

'Not bad,' I said. 'No complaints.'

He looked up sharply from his till. 'Really? No complaints?'

'Well,' I said hastily. 'None that anyone would listen to.'

He closed the till, surveyed his empty shop, and eyed me

seriously. 'Let me tell you,' he said, leaning his body just slightly over the counter. '. . . I am here to listen.'

There was no hint of a smile or a twinkle in the eye, no sign that he was winding me up, but something told me the moment I betrayed even the slightest earnestness he would slowly release his grin. 'I'll remember that,' I said, deadpan.

Back at the flat, Cathy was ready, and our sitter Caroline had arrived, wearing a T-shirt that had the slogan *www.idontgiveafxck.com* written across it. She was a streetwise sixteen-year-old, who worked part-time in the kitchen at the Old Clubhouse pub. Because she seemed a present-day example of precisely the type of female that had scared me to bits when I was a teenager (meaning any girl that was confident, attractive, oblivious to my earthly existence, and breathing), it seemed safest to keep her happy by paying her well and ignoring her methods. 'Besides,' Cathy had added, 'the girls really like her.' It was true. Jess and Grace adored Caroline, though this was possibly due to the fact that the minute we left the house, she took them down to the Co-op where Jess gorged on sweeties and pop, and Grace got some vinegary crisps to suck on.

'Bye ya,' Caroline sang. Before we'd even shut the door Jessica's voice piped up from the other side; she was innocently assuring Caroline that her Mum and Dad had okayed staying up late to watch a movie with a bowl of popcorn and a jug of apple juice.

We squeezed ourselves into the Egg and set off. The Dawsons lived outside Gullane, about five kilometres away, in the now-sectioned-off garden of an old manor estate. This estate was set in the pine forest near Athelstaneford, a ridiculously quaint village that legend says was the site of a ferocious eighth-century battle, in which King Angus of the Picts was pitted against Athelstan, the Anglian King. At a crucial moment, Angus fell to one knee and resorted to prayer. He was instantly rewarded with a vision of the cross of St Andrew, the familiar white and blue diagonal, unfurled against the sky. Angus was apparently so moved and inspired that he made the assertion that if he were to win the battle he would make this cross the symbol and flag of his people. He won the battle, though you have to wonder if it was for the best, because Bede characterised Angus as 'a slaughtering tyrant' and said that his reign was marked by 'bloody crime' from beginning to end. Nevertheless, St Andrew's cross, or the Saltire Cross, is today the symbol of the Scottish flag. To drive straight through the middle of the single T-intersection linking the two streets of Athelstaneford, however, you wouldn't guess the town had ever been the site of anything other than long naps and the occasional raised voice over the price of potatoes.

It was fully dark when we pulled into the long, fir-lined drive-way leading down to the Dawsons' house. A late January chill had set in, though it was clear we were already on the right side of the calendar as far as daylight was concerned. The sun had gone down that day at around 5pm; this felt like a long day after the mid-afternoon closures of late December. The dark, Batcave drive into the Dawsons' fortunately provided a proverbial light at its conclusion, that being the open door to their cosy home. We stepped inside, exchanged greetings, handed over our coats, and went into the drawing room. The O'Riordans, Lucy and Robert, had already arrived. Both David and Robert were decked out in their kilts, and, Cathy noted, didn't look half bad.

'And where's your kilt?' said Corinna.

I grinned weakly, muttering something about not knowing my tartan. Lucy spluttered. 'I'll make you a kilt,' she said. 'It's so easy.'

I assured her it really wasn't necessary.

'Oh, I don't know,' said Cathy, grinning. 'I might like to see that.'

'A drink,' said David, not as a question but as a confidently made prediction. He grinned his big, wide grin. He and Corinna had only recently moved back to Scotland after years managing tea plantations in Tanzania and Malaysia. He returned with a scotch for me and a glass of red wine for Cathy.

'And so,' said Robert, leaning back in the couch near the log fire David had set in their drawing-room hearth, 'here we are. Burns Supper.' He raised his glass and we raised ours along with him. Robert had been born in Auchtermuchty, near St Andrews, and worked in high finance. He and Lucy and their three children (who had befriended Jessica), lived up on Gullane Hill, in a stunning gentry house that looked straight out over the Firth, and so it came as something of a surprise when Lucy, seated beside me at dinner, turned and said, almost in a half-whisper, as if seeking guidance, 'And how do you say Gullane?'

'Attention, attention!' said Corinna, from the head of the table. 'The haggis is ready, and we'll now have the ceremonial piping-in of the meal.'

I hadn't noticed until that moment, but David was not at the table. Corinna turned her eyes to the kitchen window. With no warning, the sound of bagpipes squealed in through the slightly open window. The mournful yet piercing wail was coming from the Dawsons' garden, and Corinna picked up the steaming haggis and walked out to be with her husband. Together they made the procession back through the front door of the house, through the halls, into the kitchen. All the while the skirling of the pipes was getting louder as they closed in on us. Say what you will about the bagpipes, but close at hand they are hugely thrilling, even when played by someone who claimed, as David did, to be a rank amateur (though I thought he was miraculously good; how stunning life is, I said to Cathy later – you go out for a little dinner party and find that your host learned to play the bagpipes in Tanzania when he wasn't growing tea between tribal civil wars). Though they are thrilling close up, however, the bagpipes are also an instrument capable of inflicting actual physical damage. They are not just loud, but debilitatingly loud, and they've got tasselled ribs poking out from all angles; I nearly took one to the temple in my over-enthusiasm to get a good view as David, Corinna and the haggis paraded by me.

Finally, the wheezing of the bags ceased and Corinna placed the honourable sausage on the table before us. Before going any further we applauded David. 'Bloody good!' said Robert, leaning back in his chair and grinning. 'Can you believe it? The bagpipes!'

David's duties were not yet complete. Smiling broadly, he pulled from his back pocket a sheet of paper. A toast, I thought. Of course, it had to be: Burns' 'Ode to a Haggis'. The dinner would not be complete without it. But David then placed the sheet of paper to the side, and did not look at it as he launched into a fully memorized rendition of the Burns classic, which he delivered with impressive drama and feeling:

> *Fair fa' your honest, sonsie face,*
> *Great chieftain o' the puddin-race!*

After these few words, I lost track of his eloquent and highly felt, but largely unintelligible, rant about the sausage in front of him. About five minutes later, he seemed to become even more overwrought and loudly declared, 'Gie her a Haggis!' With that, he took a dagger-like carving knife and speared the unlucky haggis straight through to the marrow, making noises of savage clannish glee as he did so. A turret of steam erupted from within the gored intestinal sheath.

'Ooh, that looks excellent,' said Lucy. 'That looks great. Let's eat.' She reached for the dishes of neeps and tatties.

'Wait,' said David sternly. He was still standing at the end of the table, and at 6′4″ he looked to be someone you obeyed.

Lucy withdrew her hands.

'There's another toast,' said David. He kept the humourless expression on his face as he reached for the sheet of paper he'd laid by his plate before delivering the 'Ode to a Haggis'. 'I think in honour of our Canadian guests, we should let them share in the spirit of the evening. It's the Scottish way, the way of true Scottish hospitality. I've prepared this for Curtis.' He handed me the page. 'It's in Burns' dialect, so you'd best just leap in and try your accent.' He sat down, and I noticed the slightest of cracks in his serious mask. Honoured, I took the page, cleared my throat, and started reciting my lines, though it took me a moment to cotton on to what I was reading. By then it was too late to stop. 'Tae a Ferty', it was entitled.

> *Oh what a sleekit horrible beastie*
> *Lurks in yer belly efter the feastie*
> *Just as ye sit doon among yer kin*
> *There sterts to stir an enormous wind.*
>
> *The neeps and tatties and mushy peas*
> *Stert werkin like a gentle breeze*
> *But soon the puddin wi the sauncie face*
> *Will have ye blawin' all ower the place.*
>
> *Nae matter whit the hell ye dae*
> *A'bodys gonnae ha tae pay*
> *Even if ye try to stifle*
> *It's like a bullet oot a rifle.*
>
> *Hawd yer bum tight tae the chair*

Tae try and stop the leakin air
Shift yersel frae cheek tae cheek
Prae tae God it does nae reek.

But aw yer efforts go asunder
Oot it comes like a clap a thunder
Ricochets aroon the room
Michty me, a sonic boom!

God almighty it fairly reeks;
Hope I huvnae shit ma breeks
Tae the bog I better scurry
Aw whit the hell, it's no ma worry.

A'body roon about me chokin,
Wan or two are nearly bokin
I'll feel better for a while
Cannae help but raise a smile

Wis him! I shout with accusin glower
Alas too late, he's just keeled ower
Ye dirty bugger they shout and stare
I dinnae feel welcome any mair.

Where ere ye go let yer wind gang free
Sounds like just the job for me
Whit a fuss at Rabbie's perty
Ower the sake o' one wee ferty.

I'd done my best throughout my recital to lay on as thick a Scottish brogue as possible, but the laughter – my own and other's – made it impossible to maintain, and I frequently descended into a spitting, gurgling mixture of accents, as if I were a Parisian trying to imitate an Irishman. Not only was I unable to produce anything like a reliable Scottish accent, I was unable to call forth the kind of sound effects that (it occurred to me about halfway through my ode) would make this a truly memorable reading. I'd contracted my insides and twisted around in my seat, doing everything I could to actually produce a fruity trumpet-blast of flatulence at just the right moment, but it wasn't there; like a good comeback that only comes later, when it's too late.

In the end, the haggis was surprisingly good (and by the end of the year I had, somewhat to my horror, actually developed a taste for the offal odds and ends boiled in a sheep's intestinal bag), and we retired to the drawing room, full and happy, where the conversation briefly switched to Cathy's ill-fated attempts to find work in Scotland. She had decided before coming over that she would like to work part-time, just to get a true sense of life in the country, but also to meet people outside the daily routine of school and children. The search hadn't gone well, despite Cathy's wealth of experience working in a demanding and complicated Industrial Relations position back in Edmonton.

'Did you not have any luck, then?' asked Corinna.

'What a disaster!' laughed Cathy. 'First, I signed on with this temp firm, just to do anything really. They made me take a typing test.'

'Well, that's not too taxing a start, I shouldn't have thought,' said David supportively.

'Except I can't type,' said Cathy, 'or at least, not under pressure. And then I was halfway through the test, and this printer started spewing out all these old typing tests. I didn't know what was going on, and they had to restart the test. It was a nightmare. Then the woman from the agency calls me up a couple of weeks later to set up an interview, and I couldn't make it that day, and she basically just hung up on me, she was so frustrated.'

'I see,' said Robert, sipping his scotch. 'Perhaps there's a sign here, Cathy.'

Indeed, there was. Cathy never did find gainful employment during our time in Gullane, though she had her chances. She managed to all but sign a contract with the Scottish Census, until they mentioned the actual day of the census. 'Oh,' she told them. 'I'm actually away that day.' So determined was she to say she had worked in Scotland, that when an advertisement came out in the *East Lothian Courier* for golf-course labourers she gave it more than a moment's thought. Having worked such positions as a teenager, I told her about the 5am starts and back-breaking labour, work doubly painful for having to perform it alongside people out golfing. In the end, she decided against applying. It seemed like hard work for little pay-off. Besides, the advertisement called for applications to be sent to Mr Stan Owram.

After dissecting Cathy's employment woes, Corinna, a lithe and compact woman, suggested we do some Malaysian Leg Wrestling, which called for the opponents to lie on their backs on the floor parallel to, but head to feet against, their opponent. Robert was Corinna's first, and speedy, victim, whipping him more or less ass-backwards into a stunned fluttering heap of limbs, buttocks and tartan folds. Reaching for a quick fortifying nip of scotch prior to dropping to the floor for my own dose of humiliation, I quietly thanked myself for possessing the judgement to avoid wearing a kilt.

The Comfort of His Own Skin: Although It Wasn't Really His Own Skin

The neighbours across the back alley at home in Calgary, Jean and Otto Silzer, decided to have a party one year. I think it was the autumn, and I think I was about eighteen years old. This was an adults-only party, a party with a theme. It was a 'Come As You Were When We Phoned' party. This was more complicated than it sounded, because the Silzers had a strong cheeky streak to them. Naturally, they called people to invite them to this party at all kinds of different hours. I don't imagine it would have been much of a theme party if they'd called everyone at dinner time. They called around the neighbourhood first thing in the morning, at lunch, directly after they'd seen somebody out for a jog. They happened to call my parents very late at night, well past midnight in the middle of the week. My parents were sound asleep, and it was my mother who got up to answer the phone, grumbling, mumbling, complaining about what kind of person would call at that hour. She was wearing her nightgown and a ratty old pair of slippers. My father was still in bed, asleep, completely nude, as was his habit.

This presented a problem, since this was the uptight prairie Bible belt of Canada in the 1970s, after all, not the eastern seaboard of Updike and Cheever. No one would have said anything if my father had simply shown up in pyjamas. But that would have been too easy. That wasn't my parents' way.

The night of the party a few of us kids were sitting around watching TV, doing nothing in particular, when our parents came through the front room on their way out to the Silzers'. We knew of Ghost's dilemma, but weren't in on the solution, and so when he came into the front room wearing nothing but a long beige trench-coat we naturally sat up to attention. I think we may even have turned off the television. He was barefoot and, it seemed, barelegged. Chest hair poked out of the coat near his neck. My mother was smiling, an anticipatory smile, and Ghost was giving us that little grin he had that almost seemed to sneak out between his beard and moustache. He made sure he had our attention, and then he lewdly demonstrated the solution to the problem, causing us all to howl with delight and disgust.

Since it was an adults' party, I was only able to glean what happened from a few different sources over the next few days, but as best as I can tell, my parents went to the party, and pretty much slipped in unnoticed. It was a bit of an event, this party, for reasons I can't remember, but I do recall looking out of our kitchen window at one point in the evening, a vantage point from which I could see across to the Silzers' back windows. Their house appeared to be stuffed with people. The whole neighbourhood must have been there. At any rate, the evening went on; there was lots of food and drink, some serious suburban socialising. People were dressed in jogging gear, business suits, pyjamas, underwear, golf attire, swimsuits, and so on. At one point during the party, someone asked my father, who was still wearing his long buttoned-up trench-coat, what he had been doing when the Silzers had called, what activity called for the wearing of a trench-coat?

'I was sound asleep,' said Ghost.

'Sleeping! In a trench-coat?'

Soon word had spread that Gerry Gillespie was asleep when the Silzers called, but that he was now wearing a trench-coat. In short order, a movement was started to have him doff the coat. My father was the furthest thing from an exhibitionist, but maybe it was an extra rum and coke that gave him the courage to climb on the stone shelf fronting the Silzers' large room-dominating fireplace, at which point he ripped open his trench-coat for all to see.

There were gasps and howls of shock, followed right away by screams of laughter.

What they saw was a man in a flesh-coloured set of body-length underwear. Sewed to the Y-front was a scrotum the size of a small throw cushion and a two-foot long penis constructed from a wand of foam and half a pair of nylons. The penis had a sailor's knot tied in it. It wasn't long before men and women alike were grabbing him by the member and leading him around like a puppy on a leash. My father never did finish High School, but he was Big Man on Campus that night.

8

When it hit, it hit with the kind of force we hadn't yet seen in East Lothian, a ferocity we couldn't believe existed in this seemingly benign part of the world. Snow fell for two straight days, the 3rd and 4th of February. A stinging sub-zero gale blew in from the North Sea. The power in the village went out, and from our front window the street took on an eerie Victorian shimmer. Only the glow of candles in house windows up and down the street lit the way. I called Jack and Doris to make sure they were okay.

'This is what we get for letting a Canadian into the village,' he chuckled. 'Of course, the worst storm of all was 1947. You know the road round by the old quarry, where it turns near the 5th hole at Luffness New? That road was impassable. Couldn't get through. Eight-foot drifts.'

'Hey, don't forget,' I said. 'Dinner on Saturday night. Is that still okay for you and Doris?'

'Oh, yes,' he said. 'Lovely. Can't wait.'

Before ringing off I made him promise to call right away if they needed anything, any food or blankets or candles. I called Archie and Sheila, two miles down the road in Aberlady. They had full power. 'None in Gullane?' exclaimed Archie. 'Serves you right for living in the sticks.'

This weather seemed so severe, but then it was just a matter of what you were expecting, and we certainly weren't expecting this. Back home, in February, we would have been in the middle of a ten-week stretch of weather where the daily high might reach minus 15 celsius and the nightly lows would dip well into the minus-30s. But that was winter on the Canadian prairies. You expected that, and were always ready for it. This was different. I had played golf just the day before. This was not something that people around here planned for, and it showed over the course of the next two days. It was just three inches of snow but the country pretty much shut down. Whole counties went for days without power. Traffic was utter chaos. There were massive rail delays and cancellations. The schools shut down. It was reported that over a hundred thousand homes in Scotland had some sort of power loss.

It seemed romantic and even nostalgic as the snow was still falling, because it reminded us of home, but we ended up going without power for twenty-four hours. That first night we heard Grace crying at 2am. She'd shrugged off her blanket, and when Cathy picked her up the poor little thing was shivering like an abandoned puppy. She had to cuddle her under her blanket just to get her warm and back to sleep, and then she brought her into our bed.

'It's a bit of a joke,' Cathy said to me the next morning over coffee (we had a gas stove). 'I mean, it's almost as if this is a third-world nation in some ways.'

It felt true. The rail system, after the Hatfield disaster, was officially in a state of crisis. The agricultural industry was just getting over mad-cow disease, and then was plunged into chaos again with the foot-and-mouth epidemic (which led to nightly pictures on the news of burning pyres of hoof-in-the-air carcasses). A petrol war had brought the country nearly to a standstill in the autumn. The Millennium Dome was a billion-dollar-boondoggle. The Scottish Parliament couldn't build itself a home for even double the forecast budget. The London mayor was predicting disaster on the Underground. The east-coast fishermen were threatening violence unless the government did something to make up for the collapse of fish stocks. The worldwide press had been taking it to Great Britain all year, but it was the foot-and-mouth crisis that pushed journalists from criticism to predictions of the apocalypse. The German paper *Suddeutsche Zeitung* wrote in an editorial that, 'England is an island of sick animals.' Hugh Byrne, the Irish Minister for marine and natural resources, was quoted in the *Independent* as saying, 'Britain is now the leper of Europe.' Patrice Claude of *Le Monde* wrote, 'You never hear debates about ethics or morals here [in Britain], just about saving money. It's no wonder the place is falling apart.' And to go even further, Marc Champion, writing in the *Wall Street Journal*, said, 'One in five adults in the land of Shakespeare . . . is functionally illiterate . . . The public services on which the country depends for its long-term economic health are in a state of extreme decay. The health-care system belongs on life support.'

'And yet we love it here!' laughed Cathy.

'I know. Why is that?'

She shrugged. We didn't have the logic, just the feelings. We cleaned up the kitchen, gathered the girls, bundled them up as best we could, and went outside to build a snowman. Two days later, the sun returned and within an hour all that was left of him was the carrot nose and raisin eyes, laying in a puddle on the grass.

Walk to School Week seemed a good idea in principle. The reasoning was that by having children walk to school all week without their parents, it would encourage self-reliance and self-esteem. It succeeded, all too well. Gullane being a small village, the logistics of setting up Walk to School Week were not overly complicated. Normally, there was just one Lollipop Man in Gullane, Bill Telford. But during Walk to School Week there were to be volunteers, wearing bright yellow jackets, at every visual checkpoint throughout the entire village, so that a child, any child, could simply leave his or her front door and start walking down the street. At the corner of every street there would be a yellow-jacketed volunteer. Each yellow jacket would have visual contact with the yellow jacket at the next corner. This way every child would move from station to station, as it were, eventually making their way to Gullane Primary with adult visual accompaniment. Simple, effective.

We were nervous the first day. After all, Jessica was just five years old. We stood outside the front of the house, watching her amble down the street towards the volunteer standing at the walkway that led down to the school. It was hard to believe. She was five. She was walking to school. Didn't she need us? When she reached the checkpoint, she said Hi to the volunteer, turned the corner and kept on going. She didn't wave, didn't turn and smile, just got on with business. Cathy and I walked back upstairs a little unsettled, feeling, not for the first time, that on our daughter's planet we were already more moon than sun.

By the end of the week, however, we were pretty much

mumbling goodbye from the kitchen table as she headed out for school. The whole enterprise had worked its magic, and, never lacking confidence in the first place, Jessica became openly problematic. Or rather, in her world view, we had become the problem. The next week came and Cathy insisted she walk Jess to school again.

'But I know how to walk to school. I did it all last week. I don't need you.'

Then we went to draw her a bath one evening. 'I'll do that,' she said, marching naked into the bathroom.

Making a cheese sandwich, she made the case that if she could walk to school on her own, then surely she could take that huge carving knife and slice her own cheese. A monster had been created, and it took great parental control to foster the independence while not breaking out laughing. The kitchen was the real problem. She had now decided she could cook, as if a decision was all it took. One Saturday afternoon, she decided to 'make a recipe', something she intended to be edible, which did not bode well for the person she chose as her taster (and as her kitchen helper Jessica took my advice that Cathy would be quite honoured to eat what she made). 'I'm making you something, Mum,' she shouted out from the kitchen. Cathy was playing with Grace in the living room, and there was silence as a reply.

Each item was carefully considered, as was the order of insertion into the mixture. First came a spoonful of sugar, then a handful of Cheerios, followed by an application of bran flakes. So far, so good. A cup of water was next. Then came the vinegar, then a teaspoon of espresso, a handful of flour, and, to firm things up, a piece of wholegrain bread lustily broken into pieces. Next came the honey, the baking powder and, to turn the whole thing into a foaming cauldron, baking soda. After the mixture had stopped bubbling, Jessica dipped her head into the bowl, her nose nearly to the level of the mixture. She reappeared, turned to me.

'It needs more water.'

After another cup of water – and some more baking soda I added just for fun – she pronounced it ready, and we poured (if that's the word for an action involving soggy lumps and the use of a spoon) a cupful for Cathy, who was reading the paper after having put Grace down for a nap. Jess presented her recipe to Cathy in a clear wine glass. It looked like the kind of thing a prisoner might be lucky to get during a long spell of medieval solitary confinement.

Cathy put her nose to it. 'Smells interesting.'

Jess smiled. 'Isn't it good, Mum?'

Cathy handed it back.

'Aren't you going to drink it?' I said. 'I mean, she made it just for you. Didn't you, Jess? It was special for Mum, wasn't it. A mother ought to at least try something her daughter had made especially for her. At least, that's what I think. Don't you think, Jess?'

'Yeah.'

Cathy glanced briefly at the cup, gave it a swirl. Lumps of engorged bread, flecked with espresso, squidged against the glass. 'No thanks,' she said.

The problem after that was how to dispose of it. We couldn't really pour it down the sink, since it had taken on the consistency of a loaf of bread dropped in a mud puddle, and we couldn't really put it in the garbage, since the ooze would leak out the bottom. The answer, naturally enough, was to leave it to dry out. We put it on the windowsill, but that took longer than we thought it would, because it kept raining just as the mixture looked to be drying out. Eventually, after a couple of weeks, the weather did allow it to dry out, giving it the appearance of an abandoned, blackened yet somehow cemented wasps' nest. It came time to pull it off the windowsill and clean it, and Cathy suggested that as much as she'd like to do it, it was a good chance for further father/daughter bonding, a way to break down the stereotypes that only mothers spend time in the kitchen with their daughters.

The Face: Run!

Ghost had a fairly large nose, which looked even bigger than it was because he was not a tall man. At 5'8" his nose was long and beakish, though it was not a nose of Roman aquilinity. It had been broken while playing hockey as a youngster growing up in Wetaskiwin, and his skin colouring was rather florid, so that his nose always had the appearance of being a pressurised chamber, a tube pointing at something, ready for action.

My father had a sneezing problem. I don't mean he sneezed a lot, but rather that he was, so he said, physically incapable of controlling himself when seized by the need to sneeze. It was a violent act, but was preceded by no warning, no foreknowledge other than past experience. Usually, why I don't know, the need to sneeze would come over him while walking. He'd be passing from one area of the house to another, often from the basement upstairs, through the kitchen. Maybe he just planned it that way, to have it happen in the kitchen so that he could impact as many people as possible. Whatever the reason, he always seemed to sneeze at just those moments when there happened to be a lot of people around. We never heard it echo from a distant, private corner of the house. It was always the main show, under the big top.

The tickle would emerge, and from the moment that look came

over his face, we knew what was coming. His eyelids would close together, his lips would part slightly, and the angle of his head would change in relation to whatever he'd been doing, so that he always raised his face not so much to the ceiling as to a point just a few degrees above his previous point of concentration. Then his dramatic side would kick in. If sitting at the kitchen table, he'd jerk his chair out from underneath and spring to his feet, as if he were seriously trying to make it to the hallway or the bathroom. If watching TV, he'd leap to his feet. Walking somewhere, he'd abruptly change his pace to a staggering lurch. Inevitably, the next movement was a half-blind grope to his back pocket to reach for his hankie, a move that was successful only about 5 per cent of the time.

Witnessing any one of these predictors, those around him, our mother included, would disperse.

Run! one of us would shout. *It's Ghost!*

And then he would sneeze, his whole body building to it, a nearly peristaltic process that seemed to start at his toes and end at his nose. It was a violent noise that seemed to come from his mouth as much as his nose, and which always ended with his face oriented towards the floor. The comparison to peristalsis was not inaccurate, because there was a major product to his sneezes, namely swinging ropes of snot that swayed like jungle vines from the canopy of his beard and moustache. The dénouement found him locating his hankie and wiping up the mess.

'Oh, Gerry, honestly,' my mother would say. 'Why can't you just make it to the bathroom?'

He'd stand there, wiping his nose, refolding his hankie and putting it back in his pocket (which, when you think about it, was almost as disgusting as the sneeze itself). 'I would if I could,' he'd claim, his face and voice passive. 'It's not like I plan it.'

But I sometimes wondered. Not that he meant to specifically

subject his family and friends to these revolting discharges. But I wondered if he hadn't decided, or at least recognised, somewhere along the way that this was just part and parcel of who he was, and that it might be just one support beam among many in his frame-work, each necessarily connected and co-dependent; to compromise one would be to compromise them all. Maybe it was just an issue of structural integrity. Perhaps he thought sneezing differently – in effect, bottling himself – would affect the way he would act in all areas, even if only subtly. After all, his words were like his sneezes; they didn't come along that often, but were always delivered with full commitment. No trifling sniffles, no corked-up little squeaks, just the direct release of what had to be released. No waffling, no platitudes, just the plain saying of what he meant to say.

It seemed a fair bargain.

They came in, both of them laughing. Jack said, 'I've been doing everything wrong for fifty-five years. Can you believe it? Fifty-five years, and it's always wrong. Now, I can't even park the car right. Just now,' he jerked a thumb towards the street. 'I couldn't park the car right.'

'Well, really, Jack,' said Doris with exasperation, turning to face Cathy and I. 'There was enough room to park a double-decker bus in that spot, and there he was going backwards and forwards, backwards and forwards.'

Jack laughed and looked at me. 'See what I mean, boy?'

Ushering them inside, I noticed how formally dressed they were. We'd invited them round for dinner, but had neglected to mention that it was supposed to be a casual affair. I answered the door in my golf shirt and jeans, and there was Jack in a suit and Doris in an evening gown.

'Wow! Look at you two. What a couple!'

'Oh, look, Jack,' said Doris. 'I told you we'd be overdressed.'

'Well,' he said. 'I wanted to look good. It's not every night you get a dinner out at our age, you know!'

We were all seated in our living room, listening to Handel's *Water Music*, each with our drinks, Doris with white wine, Cathy with a beer (I'd asked her what she wanted and she said she'd have a beer. Jack practically burst from his seat. 'That's my girl!' he enthused), and Jack and I with a pint of darker ale to wash down a little nip of single malt. We'd put some bread and pâté out as an hors-d'oeuvre and had deputised Jess to ensure that everybody was properly served. She made one round with the pâté plate, sneezed on it, and then sat in the corner and proceeded to eat most of it herself.

'Jess?'

She looked up, her face like a squirrel's stuffed with nuts.

'Have you asked everybody else if they'd like some?'

Jack came to her support. 'She's been very good,' he said. 'She brought them around right away.'

Jess choked down the wad of bread and pâté in her mouth, and then took the plate around again. I checked on drinks and offered Jack another. 'Beer, wine, I could even do a gin and tonic, if you like.'

'Oh, that might be nice. A gin and tonic. See if Doris would like one of those, too.'

I did check, but Doris was still nursing her wine (she was the designated driver, so Jack was free to have as wild a night as an 83-year-old can have), and when I came back with Jack's drink, he said, 'Now, Curtis, did I ever tell you the story of my gin and tonic in the tropics?'

Grinning, I said no. Doris broke off from her conversation with Cathy. 'Oh, Jack,' she said. 'You're not going to bore poor old Curtis and Cathy with that story, are you?'

'Heh, heh, why not? Or do you want to tell it?'

'No, no, on you go then, if you have to.'

'Well,' said Jack, holding his gin and tonic before him as if it were a prop. 'Some years ago, what, I don't know, maybe six, seven years ago, Doris and I decided to have a nice warm holiday somewhere, so we packed ourselves off to one of these islands, you know, warm weather, nice beaches, that sort of thing.' He stopped and chuckled to himself, then turned and looked at Doris, who raised her eyes to the ceiling.

'Oh, just get on with it, then,' she said.

'Right, so, anyway, there we were. We got there our first day, got all unpacked, and it was just so lovely, so beautiful. We went for a stroll right along the beach, came back to the hotel, had a lovely dinner, just the two of us. It was almost like a honeymoon or something. Of course, our kids had grown up and left home, and it really was the first holiday like that we'd had in a long time. Maybe ever. After we had this delicious dinner . . . it was . . . oh, now what was it . . . I can't quite recall . . .' He peered over at Doris through his bifocals.

'Acch!'

'Right, right. Anyhow, we had this lovely dinner, and then we went back up to our room, and sat out on our balcony. The sun was going down, we had our gin and tonics with us.' He held up his gin and tonic, the mnemonic point of the story. 'And we just sat there in the warm evening, sipping our drinks. And I thought to myself, *What a lucky old bugger I am.* And so I raised my glass and looked over to Doris, and said, "What a wonderful life we've had, Doris." She turned to me and said, "Yes, Jack, you have." Ho! Ha, ha. Oh, let me tell you, that made me laugh.' Jack pointed both crooked forefingers at me and laughed out loud.

Cathy and I laughed along with Jack, and we looked over to Doris who was sitting still cradling her white wine. She let out a small grin.

'Did you say that, Doris. Really?'

She nodded at me. 'Well, he has had a great life, hasn't he?'

Jack kept laughing.

'Well, there you go, Jack,' I chuckled. 'She's just telling you the way things are.'

He stopped laughing at once, and pointed just one forefinger at me. 'That's it. That's exactly right. It's the way things are. Mind you,' he paused, 'I don't think it's been all bad for her either.'

'No, it hasn't, Jack,' said Doris.

Jack grinned and changed gears. 'Now, 'ow's it goin', then?' he said to Cathy. 'Still enjoying Scotland?'

'Oh, yes,' smiled Cathy. 'Loving it.'

'Are you not even a bit homesick?' said Doris.

'A bit,' said Cathy. 'But my parents are coming for a visit, and that will be good.'

'Ah, yes,' said Doris. 'That'll be lovely.'

After we got the kids off to bed, we went into the kitchen to eat. Halfway through the pork tenderloin and broiled potatoes, I asked Jack more about the war.

'Can you imagine?' he said, his eyes wide behind his glasses. 'Ten thousand men aboard one ship, three ships in all, a huge convoy. Off we went to the Middle East.'

Doris had been aboard an earlier convoy. She and Jack had yet to meet, but that moment wasn't too far away. 'It took a month for the convoy to get there, you see,' said Doris, 'because the Strait of Gibraltar was closed off. We had to sail around South Africa. And then back up the Red Sea. Oh, I was sick for ages on that boat.'

Jack turned back to Cathy and I. 'These were massive ships. And we had destroyers accompanying us, right? To the left and right, way off, on the perimeter. And it took for ever because we had to zig and zag on the trip.'

'Zig and zag?' I said. 'Why?'

'Aha, you don't know that one, do you? Because there wasn't the equipment then they have now, you see, so we had to zig and zag, so that we couldn't be tracked as easily, especially by U-boats.'

I glanced over at Doris. She nodded at this.

'And there we were, thousands of us, all the enlisted men down in the bottom of the boat, right. So if a torpedo hits, they close off all the doors inside to stop the ship from sinking, so they close off just the compartment that's hit. And if you're inside that compartment, you're trapped inside. We lay there all the time, just waiting for it. Waiting for a torpedo to hit us. But we all had our drills. The way we were supposed to get up top, get on deck, get overboard and get on to our life rafts.'

'Life rafts!' added Doris. 'They were wooden pallets, was all.'

'Right,' said Jack, pointing at Doris. 'But then, it happened. We were all laying there one night, supposed to be asleep, but you never really slept that well, laying in the pitch black. And then, suddenly, just like that, BOOM! And oh, did we jump. We knew right then. Torpedoed. Just what we'd been fearing. And it was still dark. But you know, I don't know why or how it happened. Everybody was in a panic, but I just said to the boys around me, to our outfit, "Right lads, take it calm." Just like that. "Right lads, take it calm." I don't know why, but I just said that, and we got up top in all the noise and confusion, and then the lights came back on. We were up top on deck and then we saw that it hadn't been a torpedo at all. The whole ship had shaken like we'd been torpedoed, and we were so sure it was, but what had happened was that another one of the convoy ships, one of our ships,' Jack halted briefly and used his hands on the kitchen table to illustrate, 'one of our own ships had zigged when they were supposed to zag. Bang! Right into us. They didn't zig when they were supposed to.'

We were silent for a couple of seconds before Doris spoke. 'Oh, that's such rubbish, Jack! For heaven's sake. Where are you getting that from?'

'It's true!' he half-cried, turning to Doris.

'Oh, Jack, I've been married to you for fifty-five years, and I've never once yet heard that story!'

We all burst out laughing, and turned to Jack, who had adopted a slightly hurt look. 'That's true, Doris. That is a true story.'

Doris reached over, laughing hard, and put her hand on Cathy's arm. 'Oh, it's just such rubbish. He's telling stories. He's just telling stories! Jack, you're terrible!'

'I swear that's a true story. Don't believe me. That's fine. But we had to go into port in Freetown for repairs.'

We sat and talked about their early days, about golf, about the way of life around Gullane as it was then. Doris was born at their home near the smithy, in one of a tiny row of flats along the High Street that no longer exist; they were long ago torn down to make way for the Bank of Scotland building.

'I remember what it was like in the Thirties, between the wars. You know, just on Middleshot Road, up there, there were sixty-eight children living along that street. It was like that. Gullane was a very busy place in the summers back then. There were no cars or anything, but it was the place to come. Visitors used to come from all over, for the beach, I suppose, though quite a few for the golf, too. Back then, there were two different tea rooms set up down at the beach, that's a sign of how active a place it once was. There was Mrs Town's Tea Room and Mrs Oliver's Tea Room. They did very well, but you know, I think it was all the traffic that actually broke down a lot of the higher dunes.'

'You mean they used to be higher?'

'Oh, yes,' said Doris, putting a hand to her cheek. 'Oh, they used to be much higher. Of course, the war didn't help, either, because our army and navy used Gullane and the dunes to practise landing-craft things. I'm sure that broke down a lot of the dunes, as well. Gullane was a closed town during the war. No one allowed in or out without special permission.'

Jack had joined up and was stationed in Glasgow until being sent to Khartoum in June 1941, and he was there briefly before being transferred to Port Sudan. Doris arrived his second year there. Earlier, I'd seen a picture of Jack as a man in his early twenties, in full uniform. He would have been hard to resist. Tall, jaunty, impeccably turned out. In 1940, Doris volunteered for the Wrens and was trained to work in coding and ciphering. She went to London to do college training, then volunteered for abroad. She was stationed at Port Sudan on the Red Sea in 1942, and it was there that she met Jack. There were only nine Wrens in all of Port Sudan and thousands of troops.

Jack had referred to this story when we'd first met, that day Lorne and I had played with him and Archie. Jack and his friend Ken Hall who won the raffle for their unit. Jack had been dancing with some other lady, saw Doris, and mentioned in passing to Ken, 'Oh, I'd like to meet her.' Amazingly, Ken (who must have had a few moves of his own), had already set up a date later that week with a woman at the dance, a woman who knew Doris. The double date was arranged for the Pelican Club, and now here they were sixty years later in Gullane after a lifetime of companionship. Jack's eyes as he told the story were dreamy, a little eggy, and he ran a finger across his moustache as he finished talking.

'Yes,' said Doris, 'but has he ever told you what he said to me that first date at the Pelican Club?'

Cathy and I shook our heads.

'Oh, Doris, now don't go ruining a good story.'

She laughed. 'Well, it's the truth, it is. We met up at the Pelican, and he came up to me and the first thing he said to me was, "Hello, Jean." Can you believe it?'

'Well, Doris, how was I to know? I didn't know your name!'

'Well, you could have asked someone. Like me!'

I had also seen pictures of Doris as a young woman. 'Maybe he was just taking notice of other things,' I said.

Jack turned to me and grinned. 'You're right there, boy.'

After the war, they returned to Gullane and were married in the town church, and had the reception in Dirleton. They lived in a side wing of the Church of Scotland Recreation Hall until 1951, when they moved into the house in which they still live. Jack had started working after the war with the Lothian Structural Development Company, and worked there until 1974–75, when they opened Marston's Fruit & Veg shop right on the High Street, not thirty metres from Lammerview Terrace. They ran the shop for ten years before retiring.

'Oh, the potatoes we used to get through,' said Jack. 'Astonishing. We had five staff there at times, and oh what a challenge that was sometimes to run that shop. Just the number of different things we had to think about. And the rebagging! We used to get in fifty-pound bags of potatoes twenty bags at a time. And then we had to divvy those down to three-and-a-half-pound bags. Oh, what a lot of work that was. Every week. But it was wonderful, having that shop. Wonderful.'

'Oh, Jack, who wants to hear about potatoes,' said Doris, putting her hand on Cathy's arm again, laughing.

I smiled, and let a kind of indulgent nostalgia wash through my system as I thought of Jack and Doris operating their own shop, of the rapport they would have had with the townsfolk, and the satisfaction they must have derived from creating something out of nothing and making it work. I could hear the pride in his voice as he talked about it. No, it wasn't nuclear physics, and he sometimes seemed almost apologetic talking about the Fruit & Veg shop, getting animated and then stopping, as if he thought for some reason that he was overemphasising something that didn't warrant the enthusiasm. But I never felt that way, nor did Cathy. I never felt burdened for one second hearing Jack tell stories about how many bags of potatoes they went through in a week, or how many employees they'd needed, or what a challenge it was to try to get fresh fruit out of season. It was, after all, a story about self-determination, autonomy, even a search for a legacy of sorts, even if this search was defined with humble words. I remembered (and looked up later) some words I'd written in my journal just after Ghost had died, when I was asking myself what his legacy was.

> So what did Dad leave behind? No poems. No chain of retail stores. No corporation. No sons following him in his business. In other words, nothing really measurable. We can't say, 'His books are selling more than ever now,' or 'His business is still rock solid,' or 'His research redefined psychoanalysis.' What he left behind was himself, things that were him, that can only continue as his legacy through cherishing his manner, which I have no doubt we will all do. So much of what he left us was intangible, an example: How to treat people. How to treat your spouse. How to believe in other people. But we'll never hear him laugh again, crack sarcastic jokes, force us to listen to some obscure singer. He'll never BBQ or make breakfast on Sunday mornings again. These are the things, it seems to me, that might be the biggest loss. The day-to-day things are gone. Sure, we'll have the example of his honesty and integrity. These things did not die with him, and we'll strive after those. But it's the small stuff, the pocket change, not the large bills, that I already miss the most.

Listening to Jack and Doris talk about the Fruit & Veg shop the words, and the tools of the trade, may have been slightly different from the ones I'd heard growing up. But they were no less powerful, no less symbolic. The fundamentals were the same. We finished dinner and then settled into the big chairs in the living room. I poured coffee and Cathy served up dessert. We listened to Jack and Doris, conscious of, but quiet in, our privilege, acknowledging the large bills, but taking simple pleasure in the pocket change.

9

The phone rang, and Jessica picked it up. 'Hello, this is Jessica,' she shouted into the phone. There was a muttering sound from the receiver. Jessica moved the phone away from her mouth by the width of her pinkie finger and then bawled out to the kitchen where I was seated no more than ten feet away. 'Daddy, it's for you!' She dropped the receiver on the table, clattering it against the wood. I went over and picked up the phone.

'Hello.'

'Curtis, Mark Rigg here. How goes it?'

I was delighted, as always, to hear from Mark. He runs a highly successful golf tour firm called Links Golf St Andrews, and has become a friend over the years. We had a lot in common: married, two kids, similar ages . . . golf. Enough, in other words, to become fast friends.

'Listen,' he continued on. 'I've got a free time for tomorrow on the Old Course. It's all paid for and someone backed out. Can you make it?'

We teed it up the next day around 10am, and I was back in the world of my memories. The Old Course is the one place above all else in golf that has true totemic power. The Road Hole. Hell Bunker. The Swilken Bridge. The Valley of Sin. The Royal and Ancient. It's a place of such history, such depth, and such familiarity to golf-lovers around the world, that often they can't quite believe it when they step on to the 1st tee for the first time. Through my days with the Varsity Golf Team, I'd played it a hundred times anyway, but each and every time remained something special. The Old Course isn't the most beautiful golf spot on the planet, but it's certainly one of the most powerful.

Not that any of this made me play better. My round was summed up at the 14th hole, the long par-five, which I nearly reached in two shots, only to find myself presented with the classic links golf problem. The green was no more than fifteen feet away, but a massive hump the size of a rhino stood between myself and the flag. The rhino's back was perhaps two feet wide. The green was sloping away from me, and the flag was just ten paces on. Essentially, I was twenty-five feet from the cup, but had an almost impossible shot, a shot that could come up short, kick left, warp to the right, scoot long, or, if something incredible happened, might even stop within ten feet of the flag. Mark came over and stood by my ball, grinning.

'What are you going to do with that, then?'

'You tell me.'

He laughed. 'Forget it. You're on your own with that one, mate.' He stood aside as I tried to figure out a shot. Eventually I settled on a pitch-and-run straight along the rhino's back, hoping that if I ran the ridge, I could nestle the ball nearly to a stop at the edge, where gravity would then take it down to the pin.

'Just watch,' I said to Mark. 'A little bump and run, I think.'

'Right, on you go.'

I lined up, waggled, visualised the shot, and then bladed the ball dead across its equator, sending it skidding across the huge double green. It came to rest at the feet of a group playing the 4th hole. After my deft shot from twenty-five feet away, I now had a putt of one hundred and forty feet.

'Nice,' said Mark.

'Thanks.'

Walking down the next hole, Mark said to me, 'When was the last time you played the Old Course, anyhow?'

I actually had to think about that, because I knew it couldn't have been as long ago as my days at the University. Then I remembered. It was on my honeymoon. Cathy and I were on our way to France but we stopped to visit some friends living in Aberdeen, who'd come down to meet us at St Andrews. When I say 'our honeymoon', however, that's not quite accurate, since it was two years after our wedding. We had to cancel the honeymoon we had originally planned to take.

Cathy and I were married on 6 June 1992, a Saturday. That morning, about seven hours before the ceremony, my father had a stroke. He remained conscious so we went ahead with the wedding, but he slipped into a coma two days later. The day after that, 9 June, he was dead. As I gave the eulogy at his funeral, I looked out at the same crowd of faces that had been at my wedding exactly seven days earlier, almost to the hour. Every face the same, yet never the same again.

The last time my father and I played golf together was two days before my wedding, at a function arranged by my friends and brothers. Ghost and I were paired with his old friend Ludy, and Bob, my father-in-law to be. Though Ghost had said he'd been working too hard as of late, he wasn't using this as an excuse for his poor play that day. We had a fine time, teasing one another about our bad shots, boasting that we could repeat the good ones. On the 3rd or 4th hole I started to notice he was limping. His feet looked heavy, like he was having trouble getting his spikes out of the ground. He was squinting, too.

On the 4th hole he made a thirty-foot putt for a par. 'Not bad for an old guy with one eye,' he said, smiling.

I looked at him. 'What do you mean, one eye?'

He made a face. 'My right eye,' he said. 'It's this goddamn headache.'

'Are you okay?' I said.

'Oh yeah,' he said. 'I took a couple of aspirin before we teed off.'

We kept playing and he still didn't look right, though he seemed to be enjoying himself, bantering back and forth with all of us. After we'd finished playing, he sat on the deck of the clubhouse, slumped in a chair, looking deeply tired. My brother Keith was the first to come out and say how bad he looked, and he took him to the hospital, where the doctors pronounced it a severe migraine.

The next night we had a rehearsal dinner at the home of my aunt and uncle. After dinner and dessert, I went to use the bathroom and found the room occupied but the door ajar. I pushed it open slightly. Ghost was standing in front of the mirror, looking at himself, as if he was meeting a person for the first time. He seemed slightly stunned, and I wondered if he'd slipped and hit his head. I said, 'Oh, sorry,' and was about to back out and wait for him, but I stopped because he turned towards me. I was confronted with the most curious and now forever poignant sight. My father had chocolate icing all over his left hand and running down the left side of his face. It looked as though he'd deliberately smeared himself with the brown sticky goop.

'Dad,' I said. 'What's going on?' I almost started to laugh, assuming he'd had a run-in with a grandchild at the cake table. But he didn't laugh, didn't smile.

'It's my face,' he said, looking at himself in the mirror.

'Your face?'

'I can't feel it,' he said. 'At least my left side. And I've got this damn headache.'

'Well, you've got icing on your face.'

He rotated his head slightly, as if inspecting the recovery of a fresh scar. 'I can't feel it,' he said. He put his left hand to his face, and touched the icing, actually applying more of it via brown clots stuck to his fingers.

'And it's all over your hand. Here.' I stepped forward and helped him get cleaned off. 'Dad, are you feeling okay? I mean, what's with the numbness?'

'I'm fine,' he said. 'It's just that same damn migraine I had the other day. I'm just tired. That last big job earlier this week kept me up till all hours.'

'Are you sure? I mean, maybe we ought to go back to the hospital and have them look at you again.'

'No, no,' he said quickly, a little dismissively, as if I was somehow trying to spoil his own fun, not my own wedding weekend. 'I'm okay. I'm just going to rest up next week.'

I nodded. And then I let him go back to the party.

I was up early the next morning. The sixth of June. My wedding day. Rich and Charlotte were staying with me, and they were still in bed when I left the apartment at about 7am to go do some work at my local café. I had a short story I wanted to complete and post, before heading off to get married and then jetting off to France with Cathy for three weeks. This wasn't an urgent task, but it was in my head and I wanted to go through that day and our trip with a clear head. My plan was to spend a couple of hours finishing off the story, be back home by about 9, spend the morning getting ready with some friends, and then head off to the church.

I sat at Café La Gare for what seemed longer than two hours. The sun was gushing in the floor-to-ceiling windows, and it was a warm, bright and expansive day. My life, I thought, is blessed. I'd just completed a story I was happy with. I was surrounded by friends and family. And today I was marrying a woman I loved. Those two hours I spent by myself that morning at Café La Gare were so full of happiness and joy, that I can recall the picture in my mind's eye with utter ease. One of Bach's cello suites was being played over the sound system, and as I left the café the world seemed to me a place of such utter plenitude and grace I wanted to tell every person on the street to never give up hope, that no matter what their circumstance there was a well of joy and generosity in the world that we all deserved to dip our toes into during our lives. It was a peaceful and clear moment.

Ten minutes later I was back in my apartment. Rich and Charlotte were up, and met me in the hallway, their voices hoarse, quiet. The telephone had woken them.

He was still alive, still conscious, in his bed at the University of Alberta Hospital. I went straight there. The doctors told us that strokes could go one way or the other, depending on the swelling in the brain. The next seventy-two hours would tell.

At the hospital, my mother apologised, as if his stroke were someone's fault. 'I'm so sorry,' she said. 'Your father is so sorry this happened today. But we both want you to go through with it. Don't even think of postponing it.'

There was nothing to apologise for and I told her so, but something else touched me then, another angle of what was taking place, and I was going to tell my mother what I thought, but doctors bustled in. Tests. Prodding. They tried to crack his big-toe joints, for reasons still unknown to me. There were tubes, gowns. An MRI. It was decided that I ought to go to the church and get married. As I left, my mother walked out with me, and apologised again for ruining my wedding day.

'No,' I said, able now to tell her what I'd been thinking earlier. 'He's reminded me how much I love him. That's his gift to me today.'

My mother looked at me and nodded half-heartedly, lit a cigarette, and started to cry. I went home to put on my tux, and made it through my wedding day without my parents. Cathy and I cancelled our trip to France, because though my father was conscious we just couldn't know what might happen. That day, my brother Keith made a videotape of the wedding and the reception. I have never been able to watch it.

There was one night in the hospital I had a chance to be alone with him. I convinced my mother to go home and get some sleep, to take a break from her vigil. I sat with my father and described my wedding to him. I told him I was going to describe it to him in such detail that he would feel as though he'd been sitting at the head table.

'Good,' he said softly. 'I want to hear it.'

He couldn't talk much as he was partially paralysed and in a fair bit of pain. I told him about the meal at the wedding, about all the guests, and about how beautiful Cathy looked. I told him about the Toast to the Groom, which Rich had done, and which had been very funny, touching, and even a little bit of a toast to him, as Rich loved him very much, too. My father nodded and sometimes laughed softly as I told him these things. Most of the time I was with him we held hands and occasionally he put his palm against my cheek. 'It sounds like it was a very nice time,' he said quietly, lisping a little through the one side of his mouth that wasn't paralysed.

I told him we had lots of pictures and that I would get them developed right away so he could see them. I talked to him for two hours and would have talked to him all night, but he got tired and wanted to sleep. Before I left he looked at me and, for the first time since my early teens, said in a plain sentence that he loved me. Leaving the hospital, I told myself he would not die, because he was too good a person and too many people loved him. I wept on the way home as I convinced myself of this. He went into a coma later that night.

Two days later, at 8:45am on the 9th of June, his breathing stopped. Holding him, I whispered the names of his family and grandchildren in his ear: Pat, Curtis, Bruce, Keith, Conor, Janine, Matthew, Evan, Eric, Mark. My mother and sister were also in the room, but my mother couldn't bear the awfulness of it and went out into the hallway. My sister went to be with her. After he stopped breathing, my father's heart continued to beat for a few more minutes. But his pulse rippled away until my lightest touch was unable to find it. I removed my hands from his already-cooling cheeks, and stood for a moment, leaning over him with my cheek and ear on his breastbone, wishing only that I could go with him. Eventually, I forced myself to stand up, and went to find my mother and sister.

Seven days after making a speech at my wedding in Edmonton, I was delivering Ghost's eulogy in Calgary. Hundreds of people showed up, filling the cavernous space of St Luke's Church, not far from the home in which I grew up. It was a warmish, overcast day, and near the end of the hour-long ceremony I rose to deliver words that my siblings and I had written together. Looking out over the crowd, I saw many of the same faces I'd seen staring up at me the week before at my wedding. They were all wearing the same clothes, but different expressions.

Loss is universal to mankind. We all go through some kind of loss at some point or another in our lives, and often that loss is so great, so unspeakable, that words just will not adequately describe it. The death of my father is that kind of loss. I do not want to stand up here and spend my time remarking upon the things that we all knew about my father – I'm sure that each and every one of you who knew him have already written personal eulogies in your own hearts and all those remembrances will no doubt include the things he shared with all of us. His kindness, his generosity, his wisdom, his humour.

But what I would like to do is to share with you some of the recollections of my brothers and sister and I. We wrote this together and I am up here representing Matt, Janine, Conor, Keith, Bruce and of course, our mother. And since the tragedy of our father's passing is too unbearable for words I would like instead to tell you about the past love and joy, rather than focus on the present sadness and grief.

Our father was an extremely funny man. Even as he was dying, he kept his sense of humour. My mother asked him to laugh when he was in the hospital because she had not heard him laugh in a few days, which was very unusual for him. She said, 'Are you going to laugh for me, Hon?' He looked at us with that sly look he had and said 'I will if I hear something funny.' His sense of humour was perhaps his most lovable feature. He had that devilish grin and an incredibly sharp wit and around the dinner table none of us could ever top him for jokes no matter how hard we tried. He would crack one of his jokes and my mother would break into laughter and we would always say, 'Mum, don't laugh at him, you're only encouraging him.' But the truth was that we all thought that he was the funniest man we knew. He gave us laughter almost every time we talked to him.

Dinner time was a special time in our house, as you can imagine with six kids. Invariably one or all of us would proudly uncork a loud burp and he would say, 'That's disgusting!' Then he would show us how to do it politely and discreetly. 'You don't have to make a show out of it,' he would say.

Our father was also a man who seemed capable of any-thing – everything he did he was good at. We bought a big school bus to travel in as a family – like a Partridge family bus – and it seemed like the day after we got it, he was wheeling it around the alley, parking it into an incredibly tight spot. We were all so impressed one trip when some camper watched Dad back the thing into a spot that didn't seem big enough for a station wagon and then stated that he obviously drove these things for a living.

Or it would be playing floor hockey in the basement as kids. He would stand fifteen feet from the net, with one of us as goalie, and he would say, 'Okay, I'm going to put this one in the top right corner, just so you know.' And we would swear in disbelief as he did it every time just like he called it.

He was also a skilled golfer. For a guy who played five times a year, he still went out and shot 85 if he was on his game. He loved the game and most of us have inherited that love. And then there was his mythic skill as a card player. All of our friends still shake their heads in awe about some of his exploits with us at the poker table, back when a quarter bet was huge.

Our father was a man who inspired loyalty. Even our dog, Tommy, was devoted to Dad. Tommy would follow Dad around the house. He would stand at the door and whine if Dad went out. And he would leap at him in ecstasy the moment Dad came through the door. I can honestly say that Tommy had a greater purpose than just being a dog because he did for all of us what we were too embarrassed to do ourselves.

Our house was a place of friendship and openness. All our friends spent as much time as they could at our house because our parents made it such a welcome place. They never failed to greet our friends with open arms and generosity. If a friend happened to be around at meal time, it was understood that an invitation was not even necessary. The friend simply picked up a plate and took a place at the table. I remember that two friends of Matt's gave Dad a lighter for his sixtieth birthday and on it they inscribed – 'To Gerry. Our Friend.' It was like that with all our friends. Dad was not just the father of a friend of theirs. He was their friend, too. No matter what it was that we as kids were planning, our friends always wanted to know if Ghost was going to be involved. Card games, baseball, street hockey, especially rounds of golf – our friends wanted him there and we were proud that we had a father our friends sought out.

My parents through their generosity sacrificed almost every scrap of privacy that they otherwise might have had, but it was important to them that our friends wanted to come to our house. All of us kids want to thank our father and mother for that. We had a childhood that, as we become adults ourselves, we realise more and more was a great, great gift. Thank you Dad and thank you Mum.

Our father was also a wonderful grandfather. 'Papa' was always reading to his grandsons and carting around the 'second wave' of children. His grandchildren were extremely special to him and to see him with them reminded us of what it must have been like to be so loved as little children. This was the kind of love that we saw every day in our house. Dad would come home from work and the first thing he would do would be to find Mum and give her a kiss, which was usually no ordinary peck on the cheek, but a good hugging smooch. I even remember that sometimes he would still be holding something in his hand, as if he simply had to have that kiss before he could do anything else.

One recollection that we have, most of us kids and I'm certain, Mum, too, is the vivid memory of driving around – he was always taking us somewhere – and having to listen to *As It Happens* on the radio. My brother Bruce said that the musical theme always takes him back to the backseat of Dad's car. It does me, too, and now that programme and that theme music are always played in our cars. Another thing he shared with us as kids was his work. He had his own business for most of his life, and he would always let us come down to the shop and play around in his repair shop, fool around amongst the seemingly endless rolls of fabric at the back of the shop, shooting the staple gun at one another. He always kept an eye on us but never stopped us as long as we weren't setting fire to the place. Sometimes, as will happen with six kids, we got some discipline, but we remember him as a man with a store of patience that seemed inexhaustible.

It's important, I think, to recognise that our father was not Catholic in the religious sense of the word. He believed in God but wasn't particularly interested in associating with a particular denomination. However, he had a very sympathetic view towards other's beliefs, especially my mother's. He agreed to, and fully supported all of us through our baptisms and first communions. He liked to tease occasionally but at heart he was open-minded to anyone as long as they did whatever they did honestly. He did go along with Mum on not practising birth control, which of course, led to five kids in five years. Many years later I asked him just why he and Mum had had so many kids, and with typical tongue in cheek he replied, 'It wasn't me. It was your Mum and the Pope.'

Our father was a man of wisdom and goodness, and I think that we will each always remember the little things about him that spoke of that wisdom and goodness. Once, as adolescents, my brother Bruce and I were trying to decide who was closer to manhood by comparing the amount of hair we had under our arms. He pulled us aside after hearing this and said quietly, 'You don't become a man under your arms, you become a man in your head.'

Finally, I want to remember him for his greatest yet most fundamental characteristic – his honesty. To be honest is rarely the easiest course, and over the course of his life, especially his business life, he had to make some difficult choices. A few times he could have made the easy choice for more money, less hassle. But he always made the choice that was the honest choice, the choice that he could sleep with. He has always and will always have the respect of his children who through him know the meaning and the price of honesty.

In the end I would like you to take one more look at the poem in the pamphlet that we have made for Dad today. I doubt that the question asked in that poem is the kind of question that our father would ever have asked himself. But I want to tell you Dad that today I am going to ask that question for you and I am also going to answer it.

Did you get what you wanted from this life? Did you feel beloved on this earth? Yes, Dad. Your friends, your family, your grateful sons and daughter, and your wife, the person who you made whole. To all of us, you were the most beloved man on earth. Thank you for everything that you have given us.

I stepped down from the podium, sat in my seat, looked again at the small pamphlet we'd created for the ceremony, and the words reprinted inside, 'Late Fragment', the wondrously brief and moving Raymond Carver poem I'd been referring to in the eulogy.

> *And did you get what*
> *you wanted from this life, even so?*
> *I did.*
> *And what did you want?*
> *To call myself beloved, to feel myself*
> *beloved on the earth.*

The rest of the ceremony and the reception afterwards passed slowly, stolidly, stuck in a molasses-filled tank of rictus half-smiles meant to indicate a mixture of love, pain and the courage to carry on, but which really indicated nothing more than utter exhaustion and the fear of what life would be like without my father.

In the weeks following my father's death we were dumb with grief, stunned that our lives were suddenly so different. It was a heavy and eerily muted time, though there were also moments of great love and caring. Of the many things my family had difficulty with during that time, one of the most awkward, was deciding what to do with the ashes from his cremation. Eventually I suggested we divide them seven ways for my mother and the six children, so that we might each find a personal expression for my father's remains. This was agreed on, and it was left to me to divide the ashes. I went to an empty room in my parents' house and closed the door behind me. Never will I lose the image of opening the box containing my father, a box about the size of an aluminium coffee tin anyone might have sitting on their kitchen counter. I don't know what I was expecting to find when I looked inside, but it wasn't five pounds of what seemed to be road gravel. Never would I have guessed I'd be able to hold him in one hand. I divided him up, carefully, and put him into seven separate containers, trying to make it equal and fair. But how could that be done? One person does not go seven ways.

Once I'd completed the task, however, I knew what I wanted to do with his ashes. Wolf Creek Golf Course, about an hour south of Edmonton, mixes the dunescape aesthetic of Scottish links golf with the gullies, creeks and hummocks of the Canadian prairie belt. There are many holes at Wolf Creek that could easily be set at Gullane, or Muirfield, or North Berwick. The 3rd, the 5th through 8th, the 13th through the 15th. Any of these holes would not look out of place on the windswept east coast of Scotland, particularly down around the duneland and marsh flats at the outer reaches of Gullane Nos 2 and 3. The turf, the sandy base, the waving fescues and purpling heathers; it's no wonder Wolf Creek is my favourite course when I'm back in the countryside where I grew up. All that's missing is the ocean. The closest Ghost ever got to playing golf in Scotland was Wolf Creek. We played there often, and this was where I played my first round of golf after his death.

I went with my close friend Murray. We talked on the way

there about my plans for Dad's ashes, and Murray knew I was waiting for the 4th hole, a par-four walled by eighty-foot fir trees, its small green protected by water left and back. I wanted to release Dad's ashes into the hazard on that hole because one or both of us was always dumping a shot into that greenside pond. Call it black humour, but I knew he'd appreciate the logic in part of him being consigned there for ever.

There were the first three holes to get through. By the time I got to the 3rd hole, a difficult par-three, the least of my earthly concerns was golf. One-seventh of my father, who I'd played golf with a month before, was now in a charmless Rubbermaid container in my golf bag. Standing on the tee it didn't seem to matter that there was a stiff prairie breeze coming from the south-west, or that the pin was tucked back left behind a mound, or even that I hadn't parred this hole the last few times I'd played it. Who cared? My only thought was this: *On the next hole I'm scattering my father's ashes. He is gone. This is what's left of him. I'm saying goodbye for ever.*

I pulled a club from my bag. I made a waggle or two and pulled the trigger. The ball landed on a nice spot and disappeared over a mound protecting the pin.

'Good shot,' said Murray. 'That'll be close.'

I picked up my tee and looked around. A stillness erupted out of a hollow in the windscape. The sky was cloudy, but it was warm. I gazed at the pin, 197 yards distant. Though the wind seemed to have abruptly died, the flag was fluttering, waving at me.

'Murray,' I said. 'It's in.'

'In? The hole?'

I nodded, said nothing else. We left the tee and walked to the green. I didn't even need to look in the hole, though I did, of course. My ball was nestling in the bottom like an egg hidden from a fox. I looked to Murray who was short right in the scrub.

I raised my arms. 'Murray!' I said, overcome but unable to shout. 'Murray!' I thought I would cry. I did cry.

'No!' he shouted back. 'Oh my God!'

The wind came up, snapping the flag like a pillowcase on a line. I picked the ball out of the hole. The smell of grass and earth came up off the ground. My father.

On the next tee Murray kept staring at me. Neither of us was able to speak. We made our way through the 4th hole in a state of shock. I got to the green and walked to the water hazard. Murray left me to my task and stood on the other side of the green. I knelt on the embankment and took the container with my father's ashes out of my golf bag. Grey chips, black bone shards, wispy oven dust. I fought back the notion I was about to drown him, and poured the contents into the water. The heavier pebbles sank instantly. The dust sat on the surface, then gradually went under. I put the empty container back in my golf bag, zipped the pouch shut. He'd said goodbye to me the hole before, and now I said goodbye to him. As we walked off the green, Murray put a hand to my shoulder, said nothing, just left his hand there for a few seconds. Then we played on.

When I got home I phoned my mother and told her what had happened. First she wept and then she said, 'I wish he would talk to me like that.'

'I guess he was talking to me, wasn't he?'

She was quiet for a minute. 'I guess you made the right decision, didn't you?'

'Yes,' I said, smiling even before I said it. 'Six-iron.'

Mark and I finished off our half-pints in the New Club, his home club, which borders the 18th hole of the Old Course. I said goodbye, and thanked him for the round (and throughout the year we would play many more times). Though we'd finished, and I still had to make the drive back to Gullane, I'd actually told Cathy that I'd be home around dinner time. It was only just mid-afternoon, and so I had a couple of hours to myself and decided they'd be well spent just wandering around town. First I passed by the History Department. I stopped and stared up into the second-floor office window of Professor Crabnook. For a brief second, I actually considered going in and knocking on his door, but the feeling passed through me almost as soon as I'd had it. What would that achieve, after all? Rich fantasies swirled quickly through my head, but knowing Crabnook, it was likely he'd forgotten me, which would render any real-life abuse much less enjoyable than the film of it in my head. I turned back and headed towards the golf courses and the Royal and Ancient.

I stopped behind the 17th green of the Old Course to watch some of the golfers come through the final stretch of holes. From where I stood I could see down the length of the infamously difficult 17th hole, the Road Hole, as well as the shared fairways of the 1st and 18th holes, all of which are pretty much part of the town, squeezed as they are alongside ranks of granite and sandstone architectural treasures. These are perhaps some of the most revered, most photographed, and most butchered holes in golf. For every visitor through here, you can be sure it's close to a peak moment in their golfing lives. Golfers come to St Andrews, and Gullane, and Dornoch, and Muirfield, to pay homage. They wait for years, decades even, for just this moment and when it arrives it's sometimes just too much. If you watch enough play around the 1st and 18th holes of the Old Course, you see pilgrims standing over their ball, practically genuflecting, trying to find enough game to not make fools of themselves in front of both the game's history and its custodians. I know these travellers are frozen in awe, stuck between thought and action; yet who knows exactly what is passing through their heads. Standing there, I had a kind of bittersweet, somewhat melancholic reaction, and remembered the term 'swing thoughts', that phrase people use to describe what you should be thinking about as you swing.

I have a personal swing thought, and I am quite sure it will never change. This swing thought doesn't help my grip or my balance. It doesn't calm me down or pick me up. Neither my tempo nor my confidence are stabilised by it. My own swing thought is not a mantra, a mechanical reminder, or a Pavlovian trigger. It's all about perspective; in this case, a perspective on the things I love, one of which happens to be golf, another of which happened to be my father.

In preparation for every shot I hit I check my yardage, pick out a club, stand over the ball, waggle. I may be about to hit a great shot or a lousy shot. But I know there will be two words running through my head under any and all golfing conditions, two words that bracket the sum of what I have been given through knowing my father. *Thank you.*

Looking at the imposing sandstone fortress that houses the Royal and Ancient, I whispered those words under my breath. I watched strangers swing, and decided to make a clubless motion of my own. I shifted my weight back, then through, and held my finish as I imagined my ball going . . . where? I don't know. The golf swing is like every other act of optimism, in that it values the possible over the probable. Anything could happen, but I learned from my father to accept the result with humour and dignity. *Who else can I blame?* So simple, but is there a better lesson a parent can teach a child? I wondered what lessons Jack and Archie had taught their children, or, more to the point, what lessons I was now teaching my own daughters. I did not doubt the value of my father's example to me, and I could be quite certain of the high quality of the information passed on by Jack and Archie, but I was, as ever, less than comforted by the conclusions I reached about myself. *Keep trying*, I told myself. *Just keep trying.*

I heard a bombastic North American voice. On the 18th tee was a tall and very heavy man in an iridescent plaid outfit. He looked nervous. I wandered slightly closer. He was staring at the Royal and Ancient, and I could hear his caddy tell him in a gnarled Dundee brogue to take his 3-wood and aim for the famous R&A clock. The man nodded dumbly (the Dundee accent might as well be Swahili for the uninitiated), stood forever at an address position, made a gruesome pass at the ball, and then watched, horrified, as the ball sailed right, out of bounds, and went crashing into the car park at Rusack's Hotel. He turned and scowled at the caddy, genuinely upset, fully engaged in transference. The caddy stared into the distance with a kind of pained forbearance.

I smiled.

Thank you.

My car was parked over by the Whey Pat Tavern near South Street, not far from where I'd lived as a student. Before leaving to head back to Gullane, I stopped in at the Whey Pat for a quick beverage. It had been my pub as a student, and as I sat there, nearly fifteen years later, it looked much the same. The stools, the dart board, the people. I suspected even the small pink and green packets of prawn and onion crisps hanging from pins on the wall were the same ones that no one had dared touch those many years ago. The barman was an old gent, bearded, ruddy-nosed.

'Sir?'

'Guinness, please.'

He set the pint in front of me, took my money. 'Out golfing were ya?'

'Earlier, yes, but I was only watching for a bit just now.' I took a sip. 'It's so much easier than playing.'

His expression might have been a smile, but such gratuitous emotion is rare in Scotland, so I assumed it was some kind of nervous tic. 'I'm the same as you,' he said flatly.

'How do you mean?'

'That game,' he said, wiping the bar with a rag so grimy it could only make things worse. 'Too much for my dear old heart.' This time I was certain it was a smile; pinched and embarrassed, but a smile, nevertheless.

I raised my glass to him. 'Mine, too,' I said. 'Today, anyway.'

10

I saw Jack in the car park and shouted out, 'Hey, handsome!' He looked up right away. I went over to him, and the first thing he said, as he always did when he saw me golfing during the week, was: 'Now just when exactly do you work, boy? I don't know. What a life. Dear oh dear.'

'You asked me to play!' I protested.

'Ah, yes, but you could've said no. You could've said you had to work.'

I decided to change the topic. 'You know, Jack, I'm a bit worried that you're starting to get egotistical as your years progress.'

'Why's that?'

'I shouted out, "Hey, handsome" and you looked up in a shot. Were you assuming I was talking to you?'

He grinned, paused for effect. 'Is that a Canadian compliment, then?'

I nodded. 'Take it for what it's worth.'

'Actually, I didn't really even hear you.'

'Oh, come on! Of course you did!'

'My boy, I couldn't hear you shouting at me if you were stand-ing right next to me, let alone from across the car park. I'm as deaf as a stone, you know that.'

Perhaps ten minutes later, as we were walking down the 1st fair-way of Gullane No. 1, he said, apropos of nothing, 'I just can't figure us out.'

'How do you mean?'

'Us. We've . . . well, now, how would you say it? We've clicked.' Jack made a sort of snapping motion with his forefinger and thumb. 'I can't explain it, you and me. Sure,' he held out a hand as if offering me a seat; his signature gesture, 'we can golf and that's good. We share that. But you, you're a writer, you've got an edu-cation, you're young. I'm not educated, old. But Doris is always saying, *You've got something, you two.* She's right. But what is it? I can't quite figure it out.'

We kept on down the fairway, walking together towards where our drives had come to rest, both in the middle of the fairway. It was the end of March. There was still a shimmer of moisture on the ground from an overnight squall, and the wetness mixed with the coltish midday light had brought all of East Lothian tem-porarily leaping into colour, the normally dull olive winter grass now emerald, the usually ochre clay roofs now the colour of split pomegranates. Even the greys of the Garlton Hills and the Traprain Law seemed somehow more vibrant than on other days, taking on a bluish sheen in the distance. We finished the 1st hole and moved to the tough uphill par-four 2nd.

'I think I know why it is we get along.'

He was wearing his Hogan cap, a woollen lid that gave him a distinguished air. He adjusted it, then turned to me, attentive. 'Why's that?'

'You've got good taste.'

'Oh, very good, yes! Now you're starting to sound like Bairdy.'
He laughed, teed off, and I followed him.

'I remember telling you once before, though.'

'What's that?' he said.

'About one of the reasons why we get along, or at least why I get along with you. I told you a long time ago. You may not remember. I said it the first time we met, when we played with Archie and Lorne. I said you reminded me a bit of my father.' I smiled. 'That's a compliment, by the way. He was like you in a lot of ways. Ran his own business, not highly educated but really smart, and just, well, what's the best way to put this . . . he didn't put on airs. He was who he was, and he was comfortable with that. It was enough. Like you.'

Jack pointed a knobbly finger my way. 'That's important,' he said. 'People that have the highest opinions of themselves . . . well, they usually have the least reason to hold that opinion, if you see what I mean.'

I smiled, nodded to indicate that I did see what he meant.

'That's nice . . . what you said about your father. Thank you.'

He walked on ahead of me for a few paces while I fished something out of my golf bag, and when I looked up again I had a vision of him set almost perfectly against the lip of the hill just four hundred yards ahead of and above us. It was as if he were perched on the horizon, a cutout almost, and it was a picture that came back to my mind's eye some time later when my friend, the poet Tim Bowling, sent me a poem he'd come across written by one of the greatest of Canadian poets, Irving Layton, who is now nearly ninety. What might have compelled Irving Layton to write about golfers is beyond me; I can't imagine that this brilliant and confrontational man ever had the time (or the patience) to play golf given the amount of writing, drinking, partying and womanising he got up to in his long and mythic life. In any case, the poem, entitled 'Golfers', sparked in my head that vision of Jack in relief against the hilltop.

> *Like Sieur Montaigne's distinction*
> *between virtue and innocence*
> *what gets you is their unbewilderment*
>
> *They come into the picture suddenly*
> *like unfinished houses, gapes and planed wood,*
> *dominating a landscape*
>
> *And you see at a glance*
> *among sportsmen they are the metaphysicians,*
> *intent, untalkative, pursuing Unity*
>
> *(What finally gets you is their chastity)*
>
> *And that no theory of pessimism is complete*
> *which altogether ignores them.*

I suppose I should have added that the poem reminded me of Jack except for the untalkative part. But on we played, making our way up the 2nd hole, up Gullane Hill. We played through the next few holes exchanging easy banter, talking about not much in particular, the weather, the girls, how his daughter was doing (still very well). As usual, we were having a match, and, as usual, he was already throttling me. I'd given him eleven strokes, and after six holes, I was three down.

We made our way to the 7th tee, the highest point on Gullane Hill and, with the exception of the North Berwick Law, the highest point along the East Lothian coastline. The promontory of this tee was so famous, so extolled, and rightly so, that I always stood there wondering what I'd done to deserve such riches. The view flushed me to the core with light and space and colour. The world was below us; it was a spot of such majesty that time and again I tried to find adequate words for it and could not, happy in the face of my writerly failure.

'Almost makes you believe in God,' I said, looking oceanward.

'Are you not religious, son?'

I shook my head. 'I was an altar boy, if you can believe it. At St Dominic's Church in north-east Calgary. I was about six years old.'

We teed off down the hill, heading off the pinnacle. The course was not crowded, but there were still quite a few groups to be seen as we looked out across the hill, a good portion of the three golf courses visible from where we were.

'What about you?' I said. 'You've never really talked much about religion.'

He shook his head. 'No, not at all, I'm afraid.'

'No? How come?'

'It was the war, really, that's what made me go off religion.'

'How so?'

'Well, here we were. Us. The Allies. And we were told, all the time – and we believed it, mind you, for a while – that God was on our side. That the Lord was in our corner, you see what I mean?'

I nodded.

He looked across the hill, over Churchill's anti-tank traps, out towards the Firth, west towards the shipyards of Kirkcaldy, Burntisland and Grangemouth, where warships had been made. 'But they did, too, you see. It only hit me later, you know, later in the war. When I was still overseas. They believed it, too. All of them. The Germans, the Italians, the Japanese.' He stopped and looked at me. 'Isn't it silly? How could it be possible, I remember thinking. How could a God, the God they were telling us all was on our side anyway, how could that God be on everybody's side?

It couldn't be.' We kept on walking. 'And now, well, now I don't have a religious bone in my body.'

'I like to think there's something out there, though,' I said, looking at my feet as we walked. 'It's not so much that I believe in God. It's just that, well, I guess, I just hope that there's something else out there. I don't know what that is. But I think it would be, I don't know, a little depressing, if this, this world, great as it is, was it? You know what I mean? My dad used to say things like that. You know, that you shouldn't blame faith for religion.'

Jack smiled. 'That's good. Quite right.'

'Having kids changes things, too, of course. I've certainly felt that.'

He peered at me through his glasses, nodded in agreement. 'Wonderful, isn't it?'

We got to where our drives had come to rest. He hit his next shot about thirty feet left of the pin; enough probably to win this hole, as well, since he had a stroke in hand. He gave me a sly grin on the side, trying as hard as he could not to rub in the fact that he was thrashing me, again. But somehow, I managed to stem the tide, at least on that, the 7th, hole. I hit a 6-iron to about ten feet. He three-putted for a bogey, net par, and I drained my putt for a birdie. I'd won the hole. When my putt hit the bottom of the cup, he looked at me with his best imitation of comprehensive ill-will. Like the old hand he was, he held off for that crucial extra half-beat, and then said, 'That's it. I've gone off you, boy . . . when are you going back to Canada, anyway? Not bloody soon enough!'

But this was my last moment of glory, and we ended up shaking hands on the 15th green, Jack the victor 5 and 3. (Later, in the clubhouse bar, I dutifully handed over the £1 wager to him. He held it up like a communion wafer, as he always did, and said, 'That's not leaving my pocket, I'll tell you that.')

It was a brightish day, and I'd been wearing a baseball cap for most of the round. On the 14th tee, I took it off. It was feeling tight, and the sun seemed to have turned its wattage down enough that the cap wasn't necessary any longer. Jack was about to tee off, but when I took the cap off, he stopped practically in mid-waggle and looked at me. 'Can I say something?' he said. 'Something a bit personal?'

'Yes, of course,' I said, somewhat surprised to hear him speak so directly. I couldn't imagine what it was that required such a formal request.

'Well, it's just that I fancy you more without the hat.'

'Eh?'

'The hat. You look better without the hat. It doesn't suit you.'

I grinned. 'Have you been thinking that for the last thirteen holes?'

'I don't fancy it at all. I suspect Cathy wouldn't have married you if she'd run across you for the first time while you were wearing one of those hats.'

'Well, I guess I'll just have to get myself one of those,' I said, pointing to his Hogan cap. It was stitched across the front flap with the Gullane Golf Club logo. He looked just then like a figure from the '40s, and it was only too easy to picture him, a tall, good-looking man, fresh out of the army, well-scrubbed, impeccable manners. What a figure he'd have cut. 'But if I wear one of those someone might think I'm Scottish, or English!'

'Oh, well we don't want that, do we!'

Jack often took flak in the clubhouse for being a pseudo-Scot, an Englishman by birth, who had nevertheless lived in Gullane longer than 90 per cent of the village's population. He always handled it with humour, and, anyhow, the others through teasing him were merely expressing their affection for him. Archie, in particular, when he was trying to goad Jack, liked to twist his mouth up and mutter, 'English!' as if that was explanation enough for whatever crime Jack had committed.

'No, no,' Jack said. 'You don't need one of these hats. But, it's true, for a long time when I was young it never occurred to me that everybody hated the English. Never. Ho, ho, what a shock that was!'

'How'd you find out?'

'Well, there I was, this silly young 22-year-old, right? Stationed in Port Sudan in the war. And one day, when there wasn't much going on, I went for a walk out on to the pier with a friend, a little Sudanese fellow stationed where we were. He was a nice chap, and we just went and sat out at the end of the pier one day, and we got to talking, and I said something about England, and how wonderful it was, and how lucky I felt to be English – and that's what we were taught, mind you, in school; that to be born an Englishman was God's gift to us as human beings, and that everyone else was less fortunate.'

'You're joking.'

'I'm not joking. Anyway, my Sudanese friend enlightened me on the subject. I must have been going on about some such rubbish like that, and, heh, heh, I'll never forget this, he stopped me and told me I was wrong. I said, "Do you mean there are people who don't like the English?" He said very slowly in his little Sudanese accent, "Don't you realise how much the rest of the world hate the English?" Oh! I'll never forget that. Wonderful, wonderful. Opened my eyes, that did. Amazing, sometimes, what it takes to open your eyes.'

The Golfer: That Damn Chipper

Ghost was a very good golfer when he was a younger man, though he was never an exceptional player. Once or twice he might have shot around par on easier courses, but at his peak, he was probably closer to a six-handicap, meaning he would often shoot in the mid to high 70s. This kind of form left him, however, once he married and began having kids. During this early phase of starting his relationship and family, he also started his own business. It was to be the road he would follow the rest of his life; putting his energy and emotion into things other than himself. From the age of twenty-eight to the age of forty I don't imagine my father played a total of fifty rounds of golf, despite the fact that the game was the one true sporting love of his life (though he played baseball and hockey as a youth). There wasn't the time or the money for golf. My parents were married in 1959. By 1965, they had five preschoolers.

Still, despite Ghost's almost complete hibernation from the game, when he returned to it he could still play, in the way that only naturals can maintain their form, the kind of form that could allow him to shoot in the mid-80s after a layoff of a year. And when I say form, I don't mean that he was ever able to go out and shoot 68, even at his peak. He was never that good. I mean by form that he *looked* like a golfer. He stood like a golfer, walked like a golfer, swung like a golfer; every action fluid, connected, forward-moving. Real players pull their club from the bag a certain way, tee the ball a certain way, pick the ball out of the hole a certain way. You can see it. He did those things, no matter how often he played. He'd walk to the tee, drag his driver from the bag, tee his ball up, all in that laconic, athletic way of his. He'd stand, give his club a waggle, remember he had a cigarette in his mouth, toss it on the ground just inches from his teed ball, then he'd swing his short, compact swing. Usually the ball was in the fairway, a shorter hit rather than longer, a draw rather than a fade.

In the midst of what I would consider his natural well of golf ability, there was nevertheless one club, one shot, that stood out above all others, both for its ability to perform and to infuriate me. This was his chipper.

I suppose there was a formal name for the club, but the implement was so old, so rusted, that any markings were probably worn off anyway. It was putter-shaped in length and appearance, but was angled at the face, to the tune of about 10 degrees. I didn't know it then, but I know now that it was very similar to putters of centuries past (which were often given a few extra degrees of loft to help counteract both rough patchy greens and the stymie rule). Perhaps his chipper even *was* one of those ancient clubs. I don't know. All I do know is that my father used this club relentlessly, and often from astonishing distances. Sometimes it was from just a few yards off the green, but at other times, when the fairway was flat and there were no bunkers impeding his access to the flag, he would pull out that chipper from a hundred yards away and lay it stone dead, a tap in.

I'd look over to him, scowl, call it a fluke. He'd shrug, ignore me, laugh. Sometimes he'd say, 'Not bad for an old guy.'

Yet another thing I didn't know at the time, but do now, was that this shot was played all the time on the hard, fast-running links turf of Scotland. At the 2000 Open Championship at St Andrews, Tiger Woods hit putter from 60 yards off the green every day on the 6th hole, because there was simply no other intelligent shot to be had. No one else I ever played with in Canada during my youth hit this shot or used such a club, but once I came to Scotland to go to university I saw people everywhere playing the shot my father played. I couldn't believe my own eyes. He belonged in Scotland. It was self-evident.

11

On a warmish, indifferent sort of day in late April, a day that never did make up its mind, I met my past, or at least what I wish my past had looked like, in the shape of two young students. It was on the occasion of an annual match between the Scottish Universities Golfing Society (SUGS), of which, as a golfing alumni of a Scottish university, I was a member, and a team of performers chosen from the active Varsity Golf squads of various Scottish universities. In other words, it was pupil against master, youth versus experience, strength versus guile, student loan against mortgage.

I met my partner on the 1st tee, a man named Mike Reid, who had once played for the University of Edinburgh. Mike, like me, was married with two small children, and he lived across the Firth, in Dalgetty Bay, just about under the structural shadow of the Forth bridges. Later on, when we reached the top of Gullane Hill, he was able to point to a speck of town against the far shore in the north-west.

The plan for the day was this: in our six teams of two players each we would play against their six teams of two players, over Gullane No. 2, with morning foursomes and afternoon fourballs. There was to be a formal break for lunch at Gullane Golf Club, during which, in our suits and ties, we the older set would apply our strategy (after inevitably losing the morning matches) of plying the students with a debilitating amount of alcohol prior to ingesting any food, so that they would become inebriated and therefore incapable of sustaining their play throughout the afternoon, thereby giving us a chance.

There were obvious flaws to this plan.

The major flaw was that we were going to have to drink *with* them before eating, and even if we did manage to get them to drink more than us, I knew for my own part that even one pint on an empty stomach was going to make swinging a golf club comic.

The second flaw was that as students they could, by definition, drink heavily in any and all circumstances. And if playing golf for a Scottish university had remained even remotely like it was when I played, that meant that most of the younger set had probably already played many rounds of golf while under the influence. This was admitted to be the case during discussions after the matches.

The third flaw in the plan was that we actually thought we needed a plan extramural to the golf course. These guys were better than us. We knew it from the start.

Mike and I met our opponents. Gary was a medical student from the University of St Andrews, and young Mike a civil engineering student from Edinburgh University. Both were placed right about the middle of their college's respective playing orders, meaning they were not their team's best players, but not the worst, either. Both were tall. Strong. Confident. This was going to be trouble. It seemed clear that it might be a long day, particularly after I chunked an easy chip shot on the 1st hole (with Archie spectating). Mike then hit a ball out of bounds on the 2nd hole. We were two down after two holes. I silently wondered just how humiliating it would be to return to the clubhouse after losing as badly as we were obviously going to lose. Young Mike, the engineering student, was a gangly fellow with a scruffy unshaven slacker look and a sleepy expression that belied his ability to hit the ball distances that seemed grotesque to me. I'm not a short hitter, but he was sometimes fifty yards beyond me. Soon, I began looking through my golf bag for a ball that might have some compression left in it, because obviously I was using substandard equipment.

It was a deeply instructive day. Yes, I'd shot a 67 earlier in the season when Rich had visited, and, yes, I'd been in the 60s a few times round Gullane No. 3. These were my peak moments as a golfer during the year (and there had been many lows, as well), but there was a difference between Young Mike and I, a serious, real, unbridgeable difference. He was a golfer, a golfer with actual talent, not just a golfer who claws his way around a course. He hit long, straight drives with a hint of a draw. He followed those up with crisp, tight iron shots that went where he aimed them. And when he got to the green, he made his share of long putts and was deadly from ten feet in. My game, in contrast, seemed embarrassingly scrappy. I'd hit longish but crooked drives, and sometimes not find them. When I found them, I would try to gouge an iron out somewhere near the green. When I got greenside, I relied on my short game and putting to get up and down as often as possible, hoping to stay in touch on the scorecard. Only my chipping and putting kept me close. Our scorecards might not have looked so different at the end of the day (he would probably average two or three shots better than me per medal round, and would have beaten me seven out of ten times in matchplay), but it was a different league altogether. I would have hated him if he hadn't been so likeable.

Gary, the medical student from St Andrews, was no slouch, either, though he wasn't nearly as freakishly long as Young Mike. He was, however, even harder to take as a person than Young Mike. Just the sight of Gary made me blanch. He had a squeaky clean, scrubbed, brush-cut, big smile look to him that suggested either extraordinary genetic composition (and impressive personal hygiene), or he was an alien. There wasn't even anything about him to despise, because on top of being a good-looking athletic medical student from a rich English family, he was also a nice and straightforward kid with a sense of humour. Three down after four holes, and I was feeling rather sorry for Old Mike and myself, though he still seemed in good enough spirits. He was a SUGS veteran, and so perhaps was used to this kind of thrashing.

The biggest mistake, of course, was asking Young Mike and Gary how old they were. Their combined ages totalled less than the one number I had to confess to when they asked me the same question in return. Yet (and again, with what seemed tremendous unfairness) both of them seemed somehow quite a bit more mature than me. Not for the first time in my life, I meditated (as Old Mike and I lost the 6th hole in a blaze of ineptitude) on the fact that my life seemed to be digressing rather than progressing. During my supposed physical prime as a late teen I was never a particularly confident or mature person, but I was possessed, for no logical reason, with a misanthropic sort of wit and a bit of self-knowledge; these things (on top of the fact that my parents loved me) saw me through the worst of my adolescence. And I always told myself (or at least believed my mother when she lied to me) that when I grew up, things would be okay, that I'd grow out of myself, that these feelings of awkwardness and insecurity would pass. I'm now physically over the hill (though in truth, I have pretty much the same physique I had when I was twenty; which is not much of a compliment), yet I have somehow managed to retain, and may have even amplified, my inner feelings of awkwardness and insecurity. Confronted with the specimens that were Young Mike the Engineer and Gary the Med Student, my question to the gods was this: if you are, in fact, never blessed with great physical prowess or beauty, should you not be compensated with, at the very least, some kind of insight or maturity?

What would it be like, I wondered, as I watched Mike and Gary pelt out frozen-rope drive after frozen-rope drive, what would it be like to be young, and smart, and happy, and athletic, and good-looking? Not just one of these (any of which I'd have happily settled for as a twenty-year-old), but all of them? It was just so unfair. They were wiping the floor with us, and yet we had no compensating pearls of wisdom or anecdotes laced with the fruits of experience to offer them on their journey. The great P. G. Wodehouse understood how unfair life can sometimes seem on the golf course, as he wrote in *The Heart of a Goof.*

> Golf is the Great Mystery. Like some capricious goddess, it bestows its favours with what would appear an almost fatheaded lack of method and discrimination. On every side we see big two-fisted he-men floundering round in three figures, stopping every few minutes to let through little shrimps with knock-knees and hollow cheeks, who are tearing off seventy-fours. Giants of finance have to accept a stroke per from their junior clerks. Men capable of governing empires fail to control a small, white ball, which presents no difficulties whatever to others with one ounce more brain than a cuckoo-clock. Mysterious, but there it is.

But then a miracle. On the 8th hole, Gary knocked his approach long and the dreaded Gullane rough swallowed up his ball. They took three to get out. We won the hole. On the next hole, Young

Mike missed a four-foot putt and Old Mike holed a twenty-footer. For the first time a scowl creased Young Mike's scruffy happy-go-lucky face. On the 11th, he bladed a pitch from the bunker, and now we were just two down with eight holes to play. Old Mike and I were inspired, we had thoughts of glory, and thought that we might actually get something out of this match. Young blood flowed through our veins. We halved the 12th, halved the 13th, halved the 14th, and then Old Mike stiffed a 3-iron to about two feet on the par-three 15th to win us the hole. We were now just one down. I cast an eye towards fresh-faced Gary on the 16th tee, and I swore he had a tiny pimple on his forehead that hadn't been there ten holes ago. I laced a drive down the long par-five, and Young Mike put it only about twenty yards past me. We both made the green with our next shots and both two-putted for birdie. Still one down. Old Mike, showing some serious steel, made a tremendous par on 17, holing a fifteen-footer for par after the other three of us had hacked our way down the hill. All square going to the 18th hole. We teed off first. Both Old Mike and I hit good drives on the short par-four, each ball coming to rest within about twenty yards of the green, but I was worried. Gary was a long hitter and might reach the green, but Young Mike wouldn't have any trouble reaching the green if he caught one. Gary did hit it long, but a bit crooked, into the humps and rough right of the green. Young Mike straightened up his slouch and addressed his ball. He looked to take something off his swing, as if he knew he could blow it over the green if he wasn't careful. The ball came off straight, and long. It bounded past our balls, and stopped on the apron of the green.

The pressure was on. Young Mike was going to make birdie at worst. Old Mike and I had good lies when we got to our balls, and we both hit bump-and-run shots to about eight feet, acceptable under the moment's excruciating crucible of pressure (namely, some guy watching from the window of the Visitor's Clubhouse; he was munching peanuts and sipping on a pint). Gary hacked his ball out of the rough to about ten feet, and then Young Mike did what none of us expected. He decided to chip rather than putt, since he was still about five feet off the green. What was he doing? This was an offence to the ancient Scottish codes, to rules that had been handed down over the centuries. Thou shalt never allow thy ball to become airborne when thou can keep thine ball upon the Holy Turf.

He fluffed his chip, then scrutinised his club, as if it were responsible. He now had a fifty-foot putt for birdie, his partner had ten feet and Old Mike and I both had eight feet. All Young Mike did next was can his fifty-footer, drilling it straight up the slope to the back pin placement, dropping his ball in the cup with perfect speed and line, as if Archie himself had been instructing him. The peanut man in the window put down his pint and clapped from behind the glass, a silent figure mocking Old Mike and I.

Gary picked up his ball, since his team already had a birdie. He and Young Mike high-fived. Old Mike and I decided that he should attempt his putt first, since it looked the more difficult of the two. He missed. That left me. I surveyed my putt from all angles, stood over the ball, and stroked it in the hole. The match was halved. We all shook hands, and Young Mike laughed as we did. 'Anyways,' he said. 'I'm glad you made that. It was only fair.'

We plied them with drink during lunch, and maybe the SUGS veterans did know a thing or two, because in our afternoon match Old Mike and I managed to get another half against Gary and Young Mike. It was satisfying, but only partly so, because although a half on the scorecard was honourable enough, they were better than us, and all four of us knew it. It didn't say so on the scorecard, but in Young Mike I had now seen up close a level of play I knew

I would never get to. It was on the far side of a river I would never
be equipped to cross.

The Comfort of His Own Skin: The Staple Gun

Perhaps it's not the single greatest commendation I'll ever make
about my father's parenting skills, but I want to thank him for letting us play with his staple gun. As an upholsterer and a glass
man, my father's shop was a place of great fascination for us kids.
He took us there often, gave us odd jobs, let us play around. The
initial and eternal sensation upon entering his shop was always the
smell: glue. There was a peculiar and unmistakable kind of incense
swirling off the industrial-strength glue my father used every day
on both glass and fabric. In its various states of freshness and
application, the glue had many different shades of scent, but was
always recognisable for what it was. Glue. Even the saying of the
word mimicked its function. The smell was thick, fuel-sweetish; at
the end of a drying period nearly like the incense I used to dispense as an altar boy years earlier. It's not a particularly pleasant
odour, but even today that smell makes me happy and nostalgic.

At his shop, you would enter and hit the switch by the door. The
hot arid darkness inside the hangar-like space would implode as the
massed ranks of gargling fluorescent tubes thirty feet overhead
burst into light. Invariably, there were one or two vehicles parked
on the floor of the shop, which was about fifty paces by thirty. He
had long work tables lining both walls, usually with bolts of fabric
splayed across them. Jutting from the flat end of one tabletop, like
an anvil emerging from the floor, was the old heavy-duty Pfaff
sewing machine. Spools of thread of many colours and thicknesses

were arranged beside the machine; there was always a spool on the spindle, black usually, with its thick thread fed through the eye of the needle. Above the work benches were peg hooks rigged into a 20′ × 6′ piece of peg board mounted to the wall. There were hundreds of tools hanging from these pegs: different-sized pairs of scissors (some of them alarmingly long and pointy), screwdrivers, glue applicators, exacto knives, tack hammers, nail hammers, pliers. As one looked from the bottom to the top of the wallboard the tools progressively decreased in size, so that the brute force of a hammer, for instance, acted as one in a line of anchors along the lowest row, whereas a minute pair of pincers or a staple remover or some other tiny precise tool sat floating imperiously above the harder work below. It was a hierarchy of tools.

(After he died I went into the garage at home and looked at some of his tools. I stood there for hours, unable to produce words by which to name them or to signify their purpose. There was a kind of vice grip with a cupped press at the end of one arm and a rimless wheel on the other, the spokes of which ended in different thicknesses. Only after gazing at it for many minutes did I realise it was for punching belt holes, though I still could not recall the name of the implement. There was a pair of pliers with pincers like a lobster's claw. This tool defied me completely. There were so many tools, and so many for which I could imagine no possible application, that I began to wonder if, in fact, Ghost's attitude towards tools was somehow like my own towards books, in that he sometimes bought them just to admire them, to be near them, even though he knew they'd never get off his shelf. As comforting a link as this would have been, I admitted it just wasn't the kind of thing my father would do. It was nothing more than my own lack of knowledge about my father's trade that led me to theorise this way. I thought sadly: if I were to stand in this shop for a month I wouldn't parse out the function of half these tools.)

In the left front corner of his shop, rafts of seating foam were piled like shipping pallets. And along the east wall were large rubber-covered racks that held glass and windshields of different sizes and convexities, in front of which were a variety of drawers and containers arranged on portable wheeled units. There were small labels attached to each drawer signifying the contents: hog rings, thumb tacks, upholstery tacks, finishing nails, glue strips, velcro tabs, loops of piping to section off upholstery and cushioning.

Occupying the rear third of the shop was the fabric stock. This section was divided into upper and lower tiers, so that the lower tier had a seven-foot ceiling and the upper tier was gained by a short set of steps running up either wall. Set into both tiers were shelving units not unlike book stacks, but on these sturdy racks were perhaps two hundred rolls of fabric of an astounding diversity of colours, textures and thicknesses. It was a bi-level library of fabric, a tight catacomb of geometrically aligned paths and hiding places. And yet if you stood amongst the stacks you could peer through the seams and slits to see out into the main space of the shop. My brothers and sister and I spent countless hours in these stacks as children – building fortresses, escaping criminals, tunnelling out of prisons after being captured in a war.

But it was the staple gun – that was what proved he wanted us there, that he loved that place, and wanted his children to love it, too, that place where he partially defined who he was. He wanted us to see him work. And surely only a secure parent would let their children run around with a staple gun, would actively participate in practical jokes with a loaded staple gun? Well . . . at least we all had a great time with him. I suspect that was all he cared about.

Archie showed me to a seat at the front window, which looked out on a serene May day and acres of grass, damp, gleaming like dark jade where it was cut to fairway length. We were at a long table at which four other men were seated. 'This'll do nicely,' he said, pulling a chair out for me. 'Now then, Cartiss. Wine, I think. Red, okay?'

'Absolutely, Archie. This is pretty impressive.'

'Yes,' he said, looking around. 'Not bad.'

'And the mess-hall style? Has it always been like that?'

He nodded. 'The purpose is to force the members to emulsify.'

Archie went off to the bar to get us a bottle of wine to have with our lunch, and I took the chance to have a good look around the grand dining room inside Muirfield. A long, high, church-like space, it was decorated in a masculine, oaky manner, and the walls were positively festooned with historic paraphernalia, from pictures of past Captains to numerous old medals. It was also busier than I'd seen it in past visits; today it was perhaps a third full, meaning about forty men, all in suit and tie, all grey-haired, all looking deeply satisfied to be sitting down to the world-famous Muirfield lunch, as, I have to admit, was I. The lunch experience at Muirfield is unique. It is formal in that suits and ties must be worn throughout the building, with the exception of the locker room. And yet it is, well, the best word might be rowdy. This is no doubt due to the level of alcohol intake. Most men play a morning round of golf, and then come into the clubhouse to change into their monkey suits, at which point the drinking begins. There are the gin and tonics before lunch, in the smoking room that looks straight out on to the 18th green. Then there is the wine with the meal. Following that groups return to the smoking room with large glasses and a bottle of Kummel, the liquorice-flavoured and highly alcoholic digestive that is traditionally downed in great quantities before going out to play golf again. It's no wonder that

Muirfield has within its membership few players with low handicaps.

Archie came back to the table with our wine, poured it out, and we toasted one another's health. Archie then toasted my narrow victory in our match, when I'd holed a long putt on the 18th green to win one-up.

'Well done, Gillespie,' he grumbled, sipping his wine.

'It's your own fault,' I teased.

'How's that?'

I reminded him of his advice on the final green, as I was looking over the putt, and he was tending the flag. *I see no impediment*, he'd said regarding my forty-foot putt. *Simply aim the ball properly, strike it firmly so that it loses its speed exactly over the aperture in the turf, and then allow gravity to complete the task.*

'Ah, yes,' he said, narrowing his eyes, remembering.

I did feel badly, though, because at one point in the match, early on, perhaps as early as the 6th hole (a left-turning dog's leg par-four of 443 yards featuring an undulating fairway and an ancient stone wall, a hole Archie thinks may be the course's best), I had actually not conceded a putt that I could have. It was borderline, maybe four feet long, a putt that I would have conceded had I seen him make one that length, which I hadn't yet. After all, it was now May and the greens were superb and horrifyingly fast. He'd lagged his first putt up to the four foot distance, and then stood over it, thinking that I might concede it. I said nothing, grinned a bit. 'Am I to assume,' he said in his gravelly voice, 'that that is not within the Circle of Canadian Generosity?'

I said nothing. He bent over and made the putt, and proceeded to win the next two holes, spurred on no doubt by the mean radius of the Canadian Circle.

We got up and went to the buffet, and were met by an astonishing array of foods. Two kinds of soup. Three choices of salad.

Prime beef, grilled haddock, roast pork. A haddock casserole. Carrots garnished with parsley, roast and mashed potatoes, brussels sprouts, grilled courgettes with tomato. A groaning dessert table. Three different cheese trays. It was all too much.

'Take all you like,' said Archie, waving a hand at the spread.

'You could become a blimp eating around here.'

'Correct. That's why I don't come to many lunches any more. Too much food. Excellent quality, however.'

'I can see that.'

The spread certainly made me think back to the rather plain dinner we'd served Sheila and Archie just a few nights before, when we had them over for dinner. It was a very nice meal, a chicken casserole, broiled potatoes, peas. (Worried about diets and allergies, Cathy had phoned the day before. 'Not to fear,' said Archie. 'We're omnivorous and omnibibulous.' *Omnibibulous?* Cathy said. 'Exactly,' said Archie. 'We drink anything.') It had been an enjoyable evening, and both Cathy and I appreciated the chance to get to know Sheila better, who is a living link to the history of golf in East Lothian. I knew from prior visits with Archie and Sheila all about Sheila's ancestry, but we learned that night that, despite the incredible impact the Park family, and particularly Willie Park Jr, has had on the history of golf, there is no Park of any sort in the World Golf Hall of Fame, an astonishing omission. Archie and Sheila discovered this fact on a recent visit to the Florida museum. Upon returning to Scotland, Archie wrote them a letter, saying, 'A World Golf Hall of Fame that includes Bob Hope and Bing Crosby, but no Parks, is a disgrace.' He never heard back.

Sheila's ancestry is also closely linked to what must be the most heart-rending story in the history of the game, that being the infamous, oft-referred to, match between the Parks (Mungo and Willie Sr) and the Morrises (Old Tom and Young Tom), played just a few minutes down the road from us at the North Berwick West Links on a pleasant September day in 1875. In these early days of competitive golf, a Challenge or Brag match such as this, played between the day's leading professionals, could sometimes attract as many as 8,000 spectators to the West Links.

The match was hotly contested, but almost the moment the Morrises defeated the Parks on the final hole, a telegram arrived to the links informing Young Tom that his wife had fallen seriously ill during early and unexpected onset of labour with their first child. The Morrises quickly made arrangements to use a yacht put at their disposal by a gallery member, so that they could sail straight across the Firth of Forth to St Andrews, but before they could do so, a second telegram arrived. Old Tom Morris accepted the telegram, and did not disclose its contents to his son until they'd arrived on the far shore. We can only presume he did so because he did not want his son to leap off board. The second telegram stated that both mother and child had died in childbirth. The effect was so devastating on Young Tom, who at twenty-four already had four Open championships, that he never recovered, and died just a few months later, on Christmas Day, apparently of a lung haemorrhage, though Old Tom would say for ever after that it was death by broken heart.

We had discussed this and many other stories during our dinner with Sheila and Archie, but it ended with great abruptness. Without warning, Archie stood up in the middle of the living room and announced to Sheila that it was time to go. We three looked to Archie, only two of us surprised.

'HBT,' he said.

'HBT?'

'Home By Ten. Rule number one.'

I assumed it had something to do with wanting to keep a regular and healthy lifestyle after his surgery of the year before. I looked at my digital watch, which I'd set that day. 9:54:14. Just enough time to get out the door and back to Aberlady for ten.

Sheila looked up from her coffee cup with a rather forlorn expression. 'But I've not finished my coffee.'

Archie said nothing, just stood legs splayed, hands busily jingling the keys in his pocket.

'Oh, all right,' she'd sighed. With this as his signal, Archie marched to the front door, dispensing with all pleasantries. 'Delightful,' he said, reaching for the door. Sheila scrambled to put her coat on. 'We'll do it again soon,' he said, his voice echoing down the stairwell.

Archie and I finished off our grand Muirfield lunch, and he drove me the few blocks back to our house. I thanked him for the great game, and for his generosity. It's not everyday you play Muirfield. But, as is always the case when I play Muirfield, I was left uneasy about the club, about its pre-eminence in golf as a model. The only two people I know who are members (Archie and a friend named David, who I played with on the golf team at the University of St Andrews) are generous, open and intelligent people, men who wouldn't put on airs if the Queen herself anointed them Ruler of the Realm, but it nevertheless must be said that there are serious problems with Muirfield.

We must continue to celebrate everything about Muirfield that so justly deserves our admiration. These things are not inconsequential: an attention to the history of the game (though this is often through the efforts of individual members, rather than as formal club policy); an air of camaraderie amongst members (the emulsification that Archie talked about) which is indeed a model for other clubs; a high level of public accessibility that, if not quite open-armed, is at least clearly stated and fair for all. And, obviously, we must celebrate the golf course itself, one of the world's finest, but not only that, a golf course which represents so much of what golf ought to be about – unadorned, straightforward, difficult golf holes that are artfully designed, well but minimally maintained, and which can also be played by all levels of golfers (as is demonstrated by the somewhat advanced average age of the membership). For all these things, Muirfield deserves commendation. It is, in so many ways, a magical, elect spot.

On the other hand, the world must begin to put pressure on clubs like Muirfield to erase their ugly side. Certainly, there is a kind of arrogance that goes along with being *Muirfield* but that doesn't have anything to do with golf *per se*; that's just the expected outcome when you create any narrow, member-based congregation of people who are in possession of money or influence or both. It's hard to imagine that ever changing. (Muirfield makes no attempt to hide its arrogance. It has two club histories, the most recent of which was written by Norman Mair in 1994. In this book, the author summarises the membership application procedure: 'A would-be new member, having been proposed and seconded and the relevant form filled in and lodged, is considered initially by the secretary and captain who check for what is termed "gross error". If, in other words, he is obviously totally unsuitable then, in order to spare all concerned unnecessary embarrassment, those who have put him up are quietly advised that it would be unwise to proceed further.')

Perhaps not unsurprisingly, there was something of a sense even among locals at the time that the introduction of this elite club to the area might not be the blessing it would at first seem to be. Reverend Kerr, who for all his love of golf and history (and, it's true, a taste for socialising with the gentry), nevertheless often took up arms against the self-declared overlords of what he considered to be the people's game. In his *Golf Book*, he duly recorded the words of a Gullane local just as Muirfield was under construction. This local had been interviewed by a correspondent from the *Edinburgh Evening Dispatch*, a conversation printed on 1 May 1891. It wasn't until 1895, after The Honourable Company, having moved from its Musselburgh home, had fully taken up residence at Muirfield, that Kerr reprinted the article (a bit of a confrontational act in itself).

The 'oldest inhabitant' is how the correspondent refers to the old gent he's interviewing. The oldtimer has heard there's a new course being built, and that it's got a fancy name.

What's a' the fuss aboot this new gowff club an' this new links at The Howes [the location set aside to build Muirfield]? They're a gran' set, they tell me – raill gentry the haill o' them, an' a' spankin' players, an' they ca' themsel's The Honourable Company. An' what for are they honourable mair than ither gowffers, wad ye tell me? Wha' are they refleckin' on wi' their big title? Dae they mean that the weavers o' Aberlady and Dirleton, when they foregathered wi' their clubs on Hansel Monday, as Dawwit Pringle used to tell me, werena honourable, an' Laird Tamson wi' tae cronies o' his i' the Farmers' Club, or the 'Castle' chaps [meaning Dirleton Castle] wi' Happy Chairlie at their heid – are they no as honourable as any Embro' gents? But it's an ill win' that blaws naebody guid.

The translation is: *Who do these bigshots think they are, anyway? What's with all the airs and titles? Who needs them!*

A point of greater consequence than any snobbery or arrogance is Muirfield's attitude towards women. The membership policy towards women (no female members, period) must change. It's misogyny, plain and simple, and to call it by any other name is to insult the intelligence of anyone who cares to listen. Having said that, there are those, many of them otherwise fine and caring people, who would argue something along these lines, 'Well, it's a private club. Aren't private clubs allowed to have who they like as members? Can't I form a gin rummy club and just have my friends as members? Why do I have to let in anyone who wants to get in?'

The answer is obvious. Clearly, private clubs can set their own regulations, and they must necessarily set limits on size. Muirfield can most certainly restrict its membership in any way it sees fit, but this must be the case only as long as no personal freedoms or rights are compromised (the freedoms and rights Western industrialised societies like Scotland claim to believe in). And if women are prevented from joining a club *because they are women*, then their rights are being compromised. Muirfield, as any Edinburgher will tell you, is a club whose membership contains a hugely disproportionate percentage of Scotland's judiciary, business elite, and legal and medical communities. One person even went so far as to tell me that Scottish law is, in large part, formed at Muirfield. Taking into account the exaggeration factor, there still can be no doubt that the Muirfield membership has a significant influence on the workings of many segments of Scottish society. And it contains not one single woman.

Another way to answer the hypothetical question posed above ('Can't a private club have who it wants as members?') is this: if for one reason or another such clubs persist in discriminatory policies, they must not be given positions of recognition in the game. In other words, if clubs like Muirfield (and Royal Troon) continue their discriminatory policies they must not be allowed to hold tournaments sanctioned by the golf world's governing bodies. To be more blunt, the Open Championship, the world's most important golf tournament, must not be played at clubs that have yet to formally recognise the twentieth century, let alone the twenty-first. Golf and golf's history must be put in the hands of forward-thinkers of both genders and all races, not men whose approach to the game is taxidermical.

And here's my final point: it's just more fun to have women around. That's what I cannot, will not, ever understand. I like the company of men, but I also like the company of women. I prefer the company of Cathy to anyone else on the planet. That's why I married her. Presumably, most of the Muirfield membership are married. What is it all these men are so afraid of?

About a week after my game with Archie, I had a friend from Canada come to visit, a friend who is a keen and very good golfer. We didn't have the time or the opportunity to arrange a game at Muirfield, but he wanted to see it anyway, wanted to get close to it, near enough to palpably feel its historical weight. If the Old Course is the Mecca of golf, then Muirfield might be its Vatican City; quiet, influential, business done behind closed doors, forever sending out a pulse even when not on the front page.

'Let's go,' I said to Peter. 'We'll go over and just have a look at the front gate. You can practically see the whole course from the little turnaround space there anyway. They won't mind.'

And so, because we were driving somewhere else anyway, we took the Egg over. After going about three blocks, I signalled left, pulled in along the road to Greywalls Hotel and drove to the end, stopping along the side and switching off the engine. The whole journey had taken less than thirty seconds.

'What are you doing?' said Peter.

'I thought you wanted to have a quick peek at Muirfield?'

'Yeah . . .'

'Well, here we are.'

'What? This is it . . . I mean, we're here? That was just a few blocks.'

I smiled. 'I told you we lived near Muirfield. Didn't you believe me?'

We walked up to the seven-foot-high ornate black gate with its thistle logo on the front and to the side the words *The Honourable Company of Edinburgh Golfers 1744*. We stood at the gate briefly, looking through the widely-spaced grilling. The course appeared to be very busy. Then I remembered; it was a tournament day, the annual Members' Wives tournament. Once a year, the ladies were allowed in numbers on to the golf course and into the clubhouse for the famous lunch.

'Wow,' I said. 'This is the busiest I've ever seen it by at least a hundred times. Normally you stand here and you wouldn't see more than a couple of groups on the course.' We peered through the gate for a moment, and then I said, 'C'mon, let's just step inside, right on to that tarmac part there. We won't get in anyone's way, and that way you can see the actual golf course a bit better. We'll just look for a few minutes.'

We stepped through the gate, and walked perhaps five paces further on. Where we stood there were no cars, no golfers, no golf holes. It was just a small tarmac area perhaps fifty feet in diameter that members use to come in and drop their clubs off before heading back out to the car park proper. I pointed out the far end of the course, which was quite visible. There are few trees at Muirfield, and from where we were standing, virtually every hole on the course could be seen, if not fully, then at least partially.

'If you look, there, that far flag, that would be either the 5th flag, or maybe the 11th, it's hard to tell from here. But that's the farthest corner of the course. And then if you look that way,' I pointed west, towards the looming Gullane Hill, which through the morning's sea haze shimmered as if it had been painted on to an operatic scrim, '. . . over there would be the second green.

Right in front of us here, just to the left, that's the first tee, and just to the right there, that's the eighteenth green.'

Peter nodded in appreciation, almost awe. 'So this is Muirfield. It does look amazing.'

'It is. It's a work of art, really.'

'Old Tom Morris design?'

'Originally. But the real course, the one we're looking at today, was done by Harry Colt in 1925. He pretty much re-did the whole thing.'

We were interrupted by a man in a rumpled blue suit who came bustling over to us from the starter's hut. 'Can I help you gents?'

'Oh, hi,' I said, smiling. 'I've played here quite a bit in the past, and I live here in the village now. My friend is passing through, and we didn't have time to arrange a game, so I thought I'd just quickly show him the course.'

'This is a private club, gentlemen.'

'I understand that,' I said, looking at our immediate surroundings. We were five paces from the gate, and weren't within forty paces of a member, a teebox, green, a practice green, the clubhouse, or anything, in fact, that would have brought us in contact with any member other than one dropping off his clubs before parking. 'We won't interrupt or disturb anyone. In fact, we were just going to stand right here for another minute or so, and then we'll be on our way.'

'I'll have to ask you to leave right now please, gents. This is a private club, and I've been instructed by the Secretary to ensure that anyone who is not a member or a guest does not come on to the premises.'

'We respect that, which is why we're just standing a few feet inside the gate. And as I said, we're not here for any reason other than to take a quick look. Then we'll be on our way.'

'I'm afraid I'm going to have to ask you to leave right now.'

I sighed. Why? I wondered sadly. What made this necessary? 'Excuse me, but isn't it the case that there is actually no provision in Scottish law for trespassing? As long as no other laws are being broken?'

He quietly fumed for ten seconds, buttoning up his jacket. 'This is a private club. There is a tournament going on today. This is Muirfield. If you gentlemen knew anything about golf you would respect that and leave at once.'

I can't recall if I actually pointed my finger at him or not because my vision had coned to a bloodshot pinprick. 'We came here to look at your golf course precisely *because* we know something about golf.'

He must not have heard that one before, because he drew his lips into a tight scraggle. The veins of his temples throbbed. He turned around and walked away, back to his starter's hut, from where he no doubt kept an eye on us. We stood for another couple of minutes, more for symbolic purposes than because there was anything left to point out, although I did direct Peter's gaze straight north, all the way across the course to its far edge, where it was closest to the Firth of Forth.

'There's a public path out there,' I said. 'It borders up against the fifth fairway of this *Honourable Company*, and there are no fences, no ropes, no nothing. We've taken lots of walks down that way. You and I could just as easily have gone that way, and had an even better view of what the actual course looks like. You can walk on to the course from the public paths near the second hole, and you can even get on to it easy as pie over by the sixth and eighth greens if you happened to be passing through the Archerfield estate. So then what's that all about,' I paused and pointed at the starter, 'if we could get in from any other side?'

We shook our heads, and left, neglecting to wave *so long* to the starter. Further provocation didn't seem necessary.

I decided later that it had been, of course, purely about symbols. Symbols of power and influence and demarcation. That's why the starter tried to get us to leave. Not because he needed to or had to, but because he could, and because he felt it was important that we understand this. After all, his honourable lairds must reason, what's the point of owning a line if you don't make outsiders stand on the other side of it? Golfers, I decided, are not always worthy of the game they claim to love.

12

I woke shivering, curled fetally on the edge of the bed. A rich light had already fully occupied our bedroom, though when I looked at the clock, the numbers said 5:20. Turning to face the other side of the bed, I saw that Cathy was still sound asleep, and had the whole of the duvet wrapped around her so tightly she might have been mummified with it. This was normal. On any other day, I would have made the effort to reach over and unravel her like a roll of toilet paper, so that I could get a little bit of blanket for myself. But I was awake, and sleep was no haven. Not on this day, anyway.

It was our anniversary, the 6th of June. A day of memories, obviously, but also one of such strangely unsettled, contradictory feelings. It had been, and always will be, a day of such compromised emotions, that to celebrate it in any overt way has always seemed slightly crass. Grace started to complain about being crib-ridden at about 6am, as usual. The noise must have woken Cathy up, because she was in Grace's room almost right away. Together, they came into the kitchen. Cathy kissed me on the cheek. 'Happy anniversary,' she said.

'You, too.'

Grace immediately began performing her latest trick, the one she'd been obsessed with for the last week or so. She put her fist well up into the sleeve of her jammies, and then displayed the empty hole at the end of the sleeve for us to see. Her grin was so huge, she was sure she was about to pull off the world's greatest display of magic. We pretended to be horrified that she had no hand, at which point she popped her fist forward from within her sleeve, giggling and grinning. Our role was to then express relief and astonishment, which we did so satisfactorily the process was repeated another dozen times or so.

There wasn't much else to our anniversary day in Gullane. It passed as that day almost always did, in the way we'd chosen through a sort of natural emotional evolution over the nine years we'd been married; with very little fanfare, a card, or perhaps a small clink of glasses at dinner over our home table. Later that night, I was writing in my notebook, just bottling a few scattered thoughts, when I came across something I'd copied down a couple of months before. It was a quote by Günter Grass taken from an essay he'd written for the publication *Index on Censorship*. The essay was entitled 'I Remember'.

Recently, the Hungarian writer Gyorgy Konrad wrote about Europe: 'To remember is human, we could even say that it is the essence of humanity.' While nature treats history with indifference, it is, he insists, a specific human characteristic to be able to remember in two ways, as if this ability were both a benefit and a curse. It is a curse because it will not leave us in peace and a benefit because it over-comes death. Thus, in recollection, we may speak with both the living and the dead. As long as we are remembered, we live on. Forgetting puts the seal on death.

I won't forget, I wrote in my journal. *I promise.*

Three days later, I followed what has become my personal tradition on the anniversary of my father's death, that being to do absolutely nothing of any consequence, to just give myself a day free of any kind of obligation or task, a day to let my mind and heart go where they may (though I can see the smile on Jack's face as he suggests that perhaps this isn't so different from any other day). It was a majestic day, though not particularly warm. On the subject of June days, I thought of a passage I'd read earlier that week from the Appendices of Reverend Kerr's *Golf Book* (which, to my great sadness, I'd now finished). Kerr had quoted a man named John Harrison, writing in the *Scotsman* on 6 July 1885. The piece was entitled, simply, 'Gullane Hill'.

> June days are long and sometimes warm and bright, and when a man has toiled, even at golf, all day in the hot sun on a bare hillside, as sundown approaches, and the sheep have come down from the hill, and the cows gone home for milking, and the regiments of geese have waddled past, with that stately solemnity which becomes all empty-headed bipeds, then a man's mind gets chastened for a quiet smoke. He naturally turns from hard work or hard thinking to gaze on the glorious world he lives in, and to drink in its beauties. Let us go up the Hill . . .

And so I did. (Too) easily impersonating an empty-headed biped, I let my feet take me up and across Gullane Hill, making to head straight across the golf courses, as was my habit, to the rocks at Jovey's Neuk and Gullane Point. I went first up the path just to the

right of the 2nd hole of Gullane No. 1, through a small copse of
buckthorn behind the green. I'd never noticed it before, because I'd
never walked through that particular stand of bushes, but the
opening, cut like a portico in a hedge, perfectly framed the outline
of Arthur's Seat in the distant Edinburgh skyline. I came out of the
trees pretty much on to the top of the hill, and the sunshine was
suddenly so strong it felt as if I'd been placed on a high-chair close
to the orb itself. There wasn't much golfer traffic as I went straight
across the course to the far edge of the property, out past the 13th
tee of No. 1. I passed the Churchill anti-tank traps, looking like so
many cubist Easter Island statues. As I got down into the thorny
brush, heading off the hill, I tried to find the path that would take
me most directly to the headland at Jovey's Neuk. It was here, in
this short stretch of utter wilderness between the golf courses and
the sea, that one could easily imagine getting lost and never being
found, it was that dense. Of course, it couldn't have been more
than half a kilometre wide, this stretch of wilderness, but it was
still wild enough that I wasn't shocked to turn a corner in the
bushes and come nose-to-nose with a red deer. I wasn't shocked,
but it was, and it sprang terrified into a tangle of buckthorn.

I got to Jovey's Neuk and found myself a private spot on the
rocks. Though it was June, there was still just enough of a chill in
the air to make you shudder when you took your sweater off, and
the coolness mixed with the sunshine lent the air an almost corn-
flower glow. The waters of the Firth were white, flat, so calm in the
centre channels the surface might have been gossamer. Though the
Firth was quiet, it was still the ocean, and the tide eddied hypnot-
ically in and out against the sharp rocks perhaps only ten feet
directly below where I was sitting. The sea continually folded in on
itself, gently kneading one shoulder of water over another against
the rock. Gulls, scoater ducks, red-throated divers, cormorants,
gannets: all drifted by, stopped, bobbed, dove for fish, perched on

the rock, moved on. I became aware, as if it was something I might never have known without going down there that day, that this, *this*, all this activity and motion, actually took place every minute of every day. It was a revelation. It felt like a once-in-a-lifetime event to be there, by myself, on these rocks, watching the tide, the birds, the wind. Did it really look like this every day?

Though I had my notebook with me in case of any emergencies of thought, I knew, after a few years of expecting profundities on this day, that none were likely to arise. The book stayed closed, though in rhythm with the ocean's mood fond thoughts of days gone by eddied in and out of my head, never staying long, never asking for mediation. After an hour or so of mesmeric peace, I got up to make my way back. Rather than go straight across the golf courses again, I decided to take the long way, back along the shoreline, across the craggy rocks of Gullane Point, around to the beach at Gullane Bents, and then back up through town that way. I got halfway back along the Point, and noticed that the sky out towards the mouth of the Firth at the Isle of May had changed colour. It had been blue when I left but it was now the colour of solder, the tin/lead alloy Ghost had so often used with an electric gun to join metal surfaces. But the most curious thing was that there was a clear separation between the blue and the grey, about 500 feet off the ground. It was a haar.

It didn't look to be advancing at any speed. I kept on my leisurely pace across Gullane Point, and when passing through some of the lower, well-travelled dunes, I saw some lumber in a hollow. This was not such an odd occurrence on its own, given what the tide could wash up, but it looked to be arranged towards some purpose. I went for a closer look, and found when I got there that someone had taken about half a dozen bits of lumber – a piece of 2″ × 6″ about six feet long, on top of a few other bits of stump and driftwood – and had created their own private little meditation chair. Either that or an altar. It certainly wasn't a chair to take the view in, since it was deep in the hollow and would only provide a vista to the marram grass of the nearest dune, which was about twenty feet away.

I smiled, sat down. It was comforting for some reason to think that there was a person living in Gullane who would take the time and the trouble to come all the way out to this empty spot, away from everything, even the ocean, and create his or her own private place of contemplation. As I sat there, a pair of fat black and yellow bumblebees buzzed lazily around my head. *Summer*, I thought. *A sure sign that summer is here.* I got up and almost left the chair's owner a note saying, *Thanks for the use of your chair*, but I didn't. If it was my chair, I'd be happier without complicating thoughts.

I crossed the last of the dunes, scrambled over the rocky headland of Gullane Point, and was then on the long, crescent beach. The tide was as far out as it got, and in retreat it had inscribed on the sand a sensual, braided pattern, so clean it might have been done by human hand, though nearer the water line the sand had been stippled by the wind. There were a couple of other walkers on the beach, but it was not crowded, which I found surprising for such a pleasant day. I felt hot from the exertion of climbing over the dunes and the rock, and looked skyward. The haar was still over North Berwick, and from Gullane it looked like a wall at the edge of the world. They were supposed to be fast-moving systems but this one seemed to be taking its time. I climbed the path off the beach, and headed back up to the Gullane Bents car park, cutting through another short stretch of duneland.

This was a path I'd taken often, and, not for the first time, I looked at the hollows and passes and tight little fescue-ridden valleys cutting through the dunes, and realised how logical it was that golf evolved here. Even just behind the main beach off the Bents, there was an avenue of short grass cutting through the buckthorn and dunes. It looks to be a few hundred yards long and maybe forty yards wide. It had probably been there for centuries, and had certainly never been used for anything other than as a path from one part of the beach to another. But it looked exactly as if it had been carved out of the earth to be a golf hole. The ground was sandy but firm, the grass already short and hardy, and there were plenty of natural hazards; all you would have to do was stick a can in the ground at one end and find a flat place to tee off at the other, and you'd have a glorious little golf hole. ('That's just so sacrilegious!' said Cathy when I pointed this out to her on a future walk. 'Can't you leave nature alone? Aren't there enough golf courses?' I don't blame her for this attitude; she just doesn't understand.) The surprise, I've often thought, is not how many links golf courses there are along the east coast of Scotland, but that there aren't more.

And then, almost suddenly, it was upon me. The haar. I hadn't been paying close attention as I'd walked the hill to the car park, and by the time I got up to the level of the village, the haar was all around me. Five minutes earlier the sun had been on my face, and now I was in a Sherlock Holmes movie. Like a fog, the haar was dense and thick, but it wasn't cold, and there was something almost sentient to it. Creepy isn't quite the right word, but visions of gothic novels and doomed Victorian love began to fill my head. The wind seemed to have picked up, but the mist in front of my face didn't seem to be moving at all. I could wave a hand through it, and it would churn briefly before settling back into place. By the time I got to the High Street the haar had fully coagulated, settling squarely on Gullane. The village, at four in the afternoon, was dark, brooding, murky, lodged in the centre of a giant grey yolk. The thick suspension appeared to be waiting for something. But what?

'Good walk?' Cathy said when I came in. 'Any deep thoughts?'

'Not really,' I said, smiling. 'Thank goodness.'

X

Jessica's school year came to a close, and during the final week of classes Gullane Primary had their final assembly. It had been an important year for Jessica, her first year of full-time schooling, and during that time Mrs Inglis had managed to take on a group of almost thirty five-year-olds, and teach them some of the fundamentals of mathematics, reading and writing, and on top of that to actually inculcate in them the desire to keep on attending school. It was deeply impressive. That she was able to maintain tight discipline as well made her a figure of awe amongst some of us parents. Cathy normally walked with Jess to school, but I went along every now and then. One day I dropped her off and happened to be standing with Robert O'Riordan. Mrs Inglis came to the door leading into the Primary 1 area, and the moment she appeared a skein of five-year-olds that fifteen seconds before had been loud and active instantly went quiet and started lining up to go inside.

'Good morning, P1,' she said.

'Good morning, Mrs Inglis,' they said in one unified docile voice.

Robert and I watched with awe and admiration.

'Amazing,' I said.

'It is astonishing,' said Robert, adjusting his glasses slightly, as if that might help him focus on what Mrs Inglis was doing. 'I'd bloody well like to know how she does it, though. Must be mind control. Let's find out. It could come in awfully handy.'

But the school year had now come to a close and the final event was the assembly. Jessica had been practising hard for the P1 segment of the show, in which her class was to sing a song to the P7 class, who were departing Gullane Primary to attend North Berwick High. We sat near Cathy's friend Pam (who, due to her brilliant smile and infectious laugh I had nicknamed Vivacious Pam), who also had a son in Jessica's class, and we watched as the various classes performed. The P3s performed a song about all the things that make a tree. The P5s each stood up and said one thing that each appreciated about the other throughout the year. At last came the P1s. They dutifully marched to the front of the hall, all twenty-eight of them. In their crackling little sopranos, they began singing to the P7s.

> *So long, farewell*
> *We enjoyed the toys*
> *That you supplied*
>
> *Au revoir, so long*
> *Auf Wiedersehen, goodbye*
>
> *The time has come*
> *For you to go*
> *To North Berwick High*
>
> *Goodbye, goodbye, goodbye . . .*

Ours was a row of weepy basket-cases by the end of the song, which was the last presentation of the afternoon. The crowd applauded, and as we stood up I looked at Vivacious Pam, who was dabbing a tissue to her eyes. Corinna Dawson and Lucy O'Riordan were there, as were many of the friends we'd made during the year.

'It's sad,' said Lucy to Cathy and I. 'It's almost like they were singing for you, too.'

Cathy and I went into the classroom afterwards, and had a moment with Mrs Inglis. We thanked her for what she'd done for Jessica throughout the year.

'Oh, it was wonderful having her,' said Mrs Inglis. 'She's a very impressive little girl. She brought a lot to the class.'

This brought another tissue application for Cathy.

'Stop that now,' said Mrs Inglis. She was smiling, but she also meant that we should stop it. I obeyed, instantly, as if my will had been amputated. I went out for a pint with Robert a couple of nights later and told him about this surrender, the way one was helpless to resist.

'It really is quite extraordinary,' he said, sipping his Guinness. 'That woman could run the country if she wanted to.'

13

'Shocking.'

'What's that?'

'That you're leaving like this. It's shocking, that's what it is.'

I nodded sadly. 'I know. It's hard to believe we're leaving. We're not sure we're really looking forward to it.'

Katriona shook her head. 'That's not what I mean. I mean, it's shocking that you're not taking me with you. I canna believe it.'

Yvonne chimed in from the back. 'Where's he gonna put you? In his suitcase?'

'Hey. You. None of that.' She turned back to face me. 'You come in here before you go, to say a proper goodbye. No slinking off in the middle of the night, understand? I'll not forgive you.'

'I'm not sure he cares about that,' came the voice from the back.

'I told you once, didn't I? I'm not saying it again.'

'Listen, listen,' I said. 'Of course, I'll come in. You know me better than that.'

Katriona went quiet for as long as was possible, and after those few seconds had elapsed she spoke. 'I know. It's just not going to be the same without you here to abuse.'

'I feel the same way . . . I guess.'

We laughed and I stepped next door to Mr Rasool's to get the paper. 'Hello, Shafqat,' I said.

'Ah, Mr Curtis,' he droned. 'And how is Mr Curtis today.'

'Good,' I said, pausing, wondering just what to say. 'You know . . . we're leaving in a few days, Shafqat.'

'Ah, yes, and where are you going?'

'Canada.'

'Oh!' His eyes lit up. It was so unlike him to show this kind of spark that I didn't quite know how to react; it was like putting new batteries in a toy doll that had been low on power for a year. 'I hear Canada is wonderful.'

'Yes, it is.'

'And where are you going?'

'Home.'

He looked momentarily confused. 'Home? But Gullane is home.'

'Not for us,' I said. 'We were only living here for a year.'

He turned his eyes to the stacks of newspapers in front of him as if he was already making calculations about how many papers he needed to order every day, now that we were leaving. 'I'd like to visit Canada some day.'

'You'd like it.'

'I would require a fur coat all year, though, I'm told,' he said.

'Oh no, Shafqat! That's not true.'

He stared at me, and then released a devastating grin, the grin I'd been waiting for all year. His teeth shone under the lights of his store, though his joke still wasn't quite enough to cause him to actually laugh.

'Hey, listen,' I said. 'How do you spell your name, anyway?' The note beside the till said that the proprietor was S. Rasool, and I only knew his name through introducing myself one day. I'd only heard it, had never actually seen it written down.

'Have a guess,' he said.

I gave it a shot, spelling it S H E F Q U T.

'Not bad,' he said slowly. 'Not too bad. It's S H A F Q A T. My name, Shafqat, do you know what it means in Urdu?' He looked at me now using his doleful, permanently sad expression.

'No,' I said. 'Should I try to guess that, too?'

'It means, "Very nice person".' He grinned, as if almost daring me to believe that he was toying with me. But somehow I knew he wasn't winding me up.

'I believe that,' I said. 'It makes sense to me that you have that as your name.'

He nodded, grinned sheepishly, and after that it took all I had merely to be able to reach out and shake his hand, squeaking a goodbye as I did so.

Though I'd only been away from Lammerview Terrace for twenty minutes, Archie had come and gone in my absence, the purpose of his visit to drop off a book, my going-away gift. Archie had known how much I'd loved Rev. Kerr's *Golf Book*, and he wanted me to have another book, a kind of companion volume, a beautifully made little private edition entitled *Rev. John Kerr: The Sporting Padre*. It was written by one of Scotland's most accomplished golf historians, David Hamilton, and only 275 copies have been printed. I was deeply touched by this gift, and told Archie so when I went to say goodbye to him and Sheila later that day.

We spent most of the next few days, our last full week, enjoying the annual Gullane Games, which included a roster of events. There was a long-drive contest (which some brute from Dirleton Castle won with a drive forty yards past my best), there was a putting contest (which we entered with Jack and Doris), there were all kinds of races for the kids, and even races for the adults (Cathy did the sack race, and vowed never to do it again, claiming that it 'jumbled up her insides'). And there was a fancy-dress parade in which it seemed that every person in Gullane got dressed up in some costume or other, and the whole pack went marching up and down the High Street.

I did settle in one night to read *The Sporting Padre*. It was a short monograph, an essay, really, but it revealed the saddest of stories. The great Reverend had not only penned, in the *Golf Book*, what to my mind is the richest book on golf ever written, but he'd also written a history of curling (another of his sporting passions). His *The History of Curling, and Fifty Years of the Caledonian Curling Club* was published in 1889, seven years prior to the publication of the *Golf Book*, but he'd also published two ecclesiastical works prior even to the curling book. These were *Fellowship with the Father* (1878) and *Rich and Poor – a Sermon* (1884). He also contributed regularly to journals throughout his time in East Lothian, and following the publication of the *Golf Book*, in 1896, he managed to produce yet another three books, *The Golf Song Book* (1903), *Curling in Canada and the United States* (1904) and *The Renascence of Worship* (1909). The man was prolific, that is beyond doubt. But a reader has to actually hold and then read a book such as *The Golf Book of East Lothian*, to first feel its weight and then witness the stupefying attention to detail, to fully understand both how much work went into the writing and how passionate Rev. Kerr was about his subjects.

Of course, he was also the minister of Dirleton parish the whole time he was producing these epics. But, as Hamilton points out, that never seemed to get in his way.

Kerr seems to have been successful as a minister and made

many improvements to his church . . . He improved the fabric of the church and churchyard at Dirleton and revived the ancient chapel and parish at Gullane for summer services. He installed a harmonium in the church, and later an organ was purchased when the Church of Scotland was moving from its rather austere service towards a brighter form of worship. Kerr was a progressive at a time of change, and was active in the group within the Church of Scotland who sought a more 'high church' form of service.

Kerr celebrated his twenty-fifth anniversary as a Pastor in 1901, and for a ceremonial presentation people came from all around, including MPs, university Principals, and golfers such as J. H. Taylor and Harry Vardon. However, during this time the Reverend was harbouring a problem, a problem he was clearly unable to seek help with, and that was massive debt. His difficulties came to light early in 1913, though his case was prosecuted privately. No one, Hamilton included, seems sure what brought on this crushing burden, but what was certain was that he was bankrupt.

The reasons for Kerr's excessive and uncontrolled expenditure are not clear. His stipend was a reasonable one, and was supplemented by his earnings from journalism and any profits from his books. Certainly he lost money on *The Golf Book of East Lothian*, but a prudent man would have recovered from this. It is not clear what form [his] extravagance took. It is likely that his circle of golfing, Masonic and curling friends were clubbable men and hearty drinkers who entertained well. It may be that in joining and matching this lifestyle, his expenditure mounted. But he made no effort at control.

Kerr was given a three-month leave of absence, and the public was informed it was due to illness. In November 1914 he resigned from his post as parish minister, though he remained, nominally, the senior minister in the parish. He moved in with his sister in Edinburgh after the meeting of his creditors made his bankruptcy public. He remained there, crushed in spirit, until 1920, when he moved to the spa at Harrogate, hoping this would improve his health. During most of his time at Harrogate, he was confined to a chair. His health did not improve, and he died there that same year, 1920, at the age of sixty-eight. Hamilton writes that Kerr

> had been a substantial figure in Scottish sporting and
> ecclesiastical life. The event of his death would normally
> have been marked in some way and his funeral would have
> been a grand affair, attended by friends and admirers from
> the Church of Scotland, the world of sport, brother
> Freemasons and colleagues from the world of journalism.
> But Kerr's death was hardly noticed. He died far from his
> home and parish of East Lothian . . . He was buried in
> Dirleton churchyard. After his death, a decent interval was
> allowed to elapse before any memorial was proposed. Three
> years later, in 1923, a new oak pulpit and panel were
> installed to his memory and dedicated at Dirleton
> Church . . . These memorials were removed when parts
> of the church were refurbished in the 1940s; a small
> alternative memorial to Kerr was proposed but never
> erected. Nothing now remains.

Hamilton closes his short, sad monograph with a telling figure. In recent years, original copies of *The Golf Book of East Lothian* (and there aren't many) have soared in value, to the point that I have heard astonishing numbers discussed whenever one becomes available, numbers that run into many hundreds of pounds. In fact, notes Hamilton in closing, in 1984, the auction house Phillips sold a copy of the *Golf Book* for £1,300, which was precisely the amount of Kerr's total debt at the time of his bankruptcy in 1914.

I closed *The Sporting Padre* with a great sense of sadness. If there had been one book above all others during our stay in Scotland that had repeatedly given me pleasure, and surprised me, and educated me (not just about golf), it had been *The Golf Book of East Lothian* (though Nigel Tranter's *Footbridge to Enchantment* had come close). Curious, I had a quick scan through my copy of David Dick's book *A Millennium of Fame in East Lothian*, just to see what he had to say about Rev. Kerr. I looked under K for Kerr. Nothing. I looked under R for Reverend Kerr. Nothing! There was no entry. In fact, in the end, there were only two pieces of evidence I could come up with that Reverend Kerr had mattered at all to the people of East Lothian. The first was that Hamilton's *Sporting Padre* had once been reprinted verbatim in a booklet put out by the Gullane and Dirleton History Society. The second was that the *Golf Book* had been reprinted by the East Lothian Council, in an edition of 500 copies, in 1987, a year chosen to coincide with the playing of the Open at Muirfield and (though one year late) the centenary of the original publication date of the *Golf Book*. This reprinted edition of the *Golf Book* has now itself become a highly sought-after collector's item.

It was with astonishment and melancholy that I went into our bedroom to turn in for the night. Cathy had already gone to bed, and was sound asleep. Surely, I thought as I turned off my lamp, the character and work of Reverend Kerr was local history at its apex. Anything beyond even the most cursory of readings of the *Golf Book* would reveal a man so deeply passionate about the fate of his parishioners in particular and mankind in general, that I found myself having to choke back a lump of angry bile that he had now become so neglected. Updike had written of the connection in Scotland between golf and the population's austere Protestant Christianity, a faith that called for modesty and a husbanding of all one's spiritual and corporeal resources. Kerr's transgressions, his larger-than-life persona, must have been acceptable only as long as things seemed to be running smoothly. Once he got into financial trouble he must have been a dreadful embarrassment to his parishioners. They must have shunned him completely. But what was the excuse in the East Lothian of today? It seemed a gift of the highest order to have contained within the history of a region a figure as compelling as the good Reverend. And yet there was nothing. No monument. No plaque. No trophy. Not even a passing entry in a county book of millennial fame. Perhaps in Scotland bankruptcy rendered one ahistorical in local eyes.

I wanted my last game at Gullane to be on No. 3, and I knew it would be with Jack. We were leaving for Canada early Friday morning. He and I agreed to play on the Wednesday, and it seemed as if someone or something had decided that we would have the kind of day I had rarely seen in Gullane. It was sunny, though that wasn't so unusual; what was unusual was the complete lack of wind. The flag on the Gullane Golf Club mast hung folded and slack. There had been many calm days during the year, but they had almost always been accompanied by mist. There had been many sunny and warm days, but they had always come with scalp-tugging breezes.

'Can you believe this?' I said to Jack, as we were about to tee off. 'It's . . . it's actually hot.'

He wrinkled his nose and stared at the sky, as if something about the weather displeased him. 'Lovely,' he said. But I could tell he was so unused to this combination that he simply didn't trust it, in the way of clichéd suspense films. *It's quiet – too quiet.* He reached into his pocket and pulled out three golf balls. They were top-of-the-line balls, with thin balata covers. They looked new. 'I've had these lying around. Don't like those soft balls much.'

'This might give me an advantage, you know.'

'Heh, heh. Well, you'll need it.'

We had our usual game. A £1 match. I gave him twelve strokes, and like most games we'd had that year, he started out turning the screws on me, winning the first two holes. But on the 3rd hole, a shortish par-four, I had about sixty yards left for my second shot, and hit a half sand wedge that landed ten feet past the pin and spun back to about a foot from the hole for a kick-in birdie.

'Hey,' I said. 'You shouldn't have given me those snazzy balls.'

He didn't laugh, and tried his best to look competitive and full of resolve, which only made me laugh even more. Our game stayed close for the next eight or ten holes. Jack was playing well, but so was I, though I'd been paying much more attention to the match score than my medal score, as had become my habit in Scotland. As we walked, we talked easily, openly, about everything and nothing. Politics, family, a stoat that burst startled from the fescue on the side of 9th fairway, our favourite beers, our friendship. 'It's easy,' he said of it, of us. 'That's what it is. It's good, easy, that's the thing.'

By the time we got to the 14th hole, the short par-five, I was actually one-up in the match. Things were getting tight. Bragging rights were at stake, after all, since this was our last match together (though neither of us talked about it in that way, almost as if by mutual unspoken agreement). I hit my second shot to the right of the 14th green, which was almost exactly where Jack hit his third.

There was a huge mound directly between us and the pin. He was about five feet closer and could see the bottom of the pin, but I couldn't. This was yet another of those quintessential links golf moments, where it all came down to choosing correctly from a multitude of options.

There was nobody behind us, nobody in front of us. We were in no rush, and this was my last game at Gullane anyway, and so I decided to stand and think about this one for a minute. There were so many ways to go, so many possible outcomes. It all revolved around simply making the right choice and executing. It deserved a little thought.

I could putt it, but the ground was a bit lumpy. I could hit a little bump-and-run, but the rise was so abrupt it would be hard to judge the speed, and it would be all too easy to leave it short and have it dribble right back to my feet. I could knock a 7-iron straight into the bank, stunning its momentum, hoping it would then pop over the edge and trickle the five feet thereafter to the pin. Or, I could open up my sand wedge, laying it flat like a pancake, and hit a full-swing Tiger Woods lob shot, launching it thirty feet in the air to make it progress just twenty feet forward, hoping then to land it on the very crown of the mound, a space the size of a tyre, after which it might then dribble down to the pin.

I loved it. This was links golf at its greatest. Jack stood watching me, enjoying the fact that I was faced with such a tough shot, but a little worried about what he was going to do with his own. He was closer, and had a slightly easier shot, but was also presented with a complex problem. I decided the best risk/reward shot was the open-blade flop shot, only because I knew I could gauge it well enough to ensure that I at least made the green. It was the least linksy shot, but the best choice. I did a little waggle, made a positive, rhythmic pass through the ball, feathering it straight up in the air. I watched. Jack watched. It landed precisely on the circle of turf I was aiming for and disappeared over the crest of the mound out of my view. I looked to Jack, who was in a position to see the ball all the way to the green. He said nothing, stared at the green for a moment, long after the ball had to have come to rest, and then he closed his eyes and looked straight to the ground. He exhaled heavily, and it was then I knew my ball had gone in the hole. I raised my arms in the air, and burst out laughing. I'd played a hundred rounds of golf in Gullane, and this was my first eagle.

'That's the end of a beautiful friendship,' he said. 'When are you leaving anyway? It's not bloody soon enough. I was standing there thinking that I might hole mine out, and then you go and do it. That's it. I've gone off you.'

I plucked my ball from the hole, laughing the whole time, and then stood waiting for him to play his shot. He now needed to hole his shot for a half, and he nearly did, punching it into the bank, and letting the ball trickle up to the hole. It stopped about a foot short, directly in line with the hole.

'It's a good thing that didn't go in,' I said. 'It would have been very upsetting to have to break my putter over your head.'

He grinned as we walked to the 15th tee. 'Two down, now, am I? Ah, wonderful, wonderful stuff. Well done. You're on today, boy.' He paused as if something had just occurred to him. 'You must have a good medal score going. Exceptional, I'd say.'

It really hadn't occurred to me until that point, but I did a quick mental calculation and realised to my horror that by eagling the previous hole I was now four under par. Immediately, my pulse started pounding in my ears and my stomach contracted.

'I'm four under,' I said.

Jack nodded, as if this news was almost completely without interest to him (which may have been the case). 'Marvellous,' he said flatly. 'Keep it up. You've only got a few holes to go. Just concentrate on it. Don't lose your focus.'

I thought back to my score of 67 with Rich earlier in the year. I was on pace to shatter that. Par at Gullane No. 3 is only 68. If I finished with four pars I'd shoot 64. It seemed scarcely believable. I wasn't that good. But I told myself, on the next tee, *Just par in.* This was a mistake.

I bogeyed the last four holes, and shot 68. Jack shot 80, beating his age by three strokes. Worse, given the strokes Jack had on the holes coming in, I went from being two-up in our match to needing a six-foot putt for bogey on the last hole to halve the match, which I made. It was a stunning collapse. Later, over a pint, I asked Jack if, being the cagey veteran he is, he might have asked me what my medal score was precisely *because* he wanted me to start thinking about it. He hadn't expressed an interest in medal scores the whole round, or for as long as I'd known him, and yet there he was, coming down the stretch of our last match, asking me what my medal score was, telling me to concentrate on it. He sipped his pint, ran a finger over his moustache, let slip a grin. The sly bugger.

Later that night, after we'd put the girls to bed, I went over to Doris and Jack's house to say goodbye. We were leaving not the next day, but the day after. I had a card I wanted to give to him and Doris, a card that said so many of the things I felt about him, and about Doris. I was looking forward to seeing them both that evening . . . but I wasn't. I wasn't sure how I was going to react, or how he would react. We sat in their living room, in the living room they'd been using for fifty years now. He poured us each a beer, poured Doris a glass of wine. 'Cheers, boy,' he said, raising his glass.

I raised my glass to both of them.

'Was it good?' said Jack, peering at me from his easy chair. 'Did your time in Scotland go the way you wanted it to?'

I nodded, not sure how much I was going to be able to say.

'And you achieved what you wanted to achieve?'

I smiled at him, and he smiled back, though he couldn't really have known exactly what I was thinking, exactly how intertwined he'd become in my thoughts and meditations on my father, how he'd guided me in a way, yet how much his friendship had also become a gift to me separate unto itself. I had tried to say some of these things in the card I'd brought, but knew that I hadn't expressed my thoughts that clearly, and knew also that if I tried now I would fail. I had to trust it, had to hope he would, some-how, know what I meant. 'Yes,' I said. 'I achieved what I wanted to achieve. More, even.'

We talked for a couple of hours, about Scotland, Canada, what our lives would be like upon returning, about when we were going to return to Gullane. He asked me this just as I was standing up to go. 'You'd better hurry back here for a visit,' he said as we moved to the front hallway of the house.

'I'll be back . . . why the hurry?'

He laughed, but let his tone betray him. 'Well . . . I'm eighty-three, son. Heh, heh. Eighty-three, you know . . . just hurry back.'

I looked into his eyes. They were clear, perhaps a bit big-look-ing because of his glasses, but their gaze was pure and unblinking. He twitched his nose, wriggled his moustache.

'I will,' I said.

He put his hand on my shoulder, and I thought for a moment there might be a word of wisdom, a dispensation of some sort. But that wasn't him. And looking back it would have surprised me if he had said something meant to be taken as advice. Like someone else I'd loved, the example was sufficient. 'Good,' was all he said. 'Good.'

I gave Jack the card, but told him not to open it until after I'd left. He held out his hand, and I took it, then embraced him.

Doris, standing just a couple of feet away, smiled softly. 'Ah, there, yes,' she said. 'That's right. That's right.'

And then we said goodbye. He stood in the alcove of their porch and waved as I drove off. I couldn't believe I was seeing the last of him. The steering wheel seemed heavy and unresponsive as I turned the corner, as if even the Egg itself was against departing.

Part Three

Who has twisted us like this, so that — no matter what we do — we have the bearing of a man going away? As on the last hill that shows him all his valley, for the last time, he turns, stands still, and lingers, so we live, forever saying farewell.

Duino Elegies, Eighth Elegy
Rainer Maria Rilke

1

The dryness was the most surprising thing. The prairies were so dry, so bright, so hot compared to Gullane, where we'd been just one day before, that the skin around my nose and lips and fingertips was already cracking and breaking open. There simply wasn't any moisture to be found, even inside me. I don't think I could have produced a tear had I wanted or needed to.

We seemed to have arrived back to a very strange world, one that looked familiar, but was unknown to us. After a year away, our house didn't feel like home any more. Perhaps this was partly due to the travel; two different flights, four different airports, nine hours in the air, nine pieces of luggage (weighing 200 kilos), and two tired children (who, luckily but not surprisingly, acted wonderfully on the flights). But we got through that day. The next day we went about the task of trying to set up our home. The people we'd rented our house to had treated it well enough, but we discovered they'd had ferrets for pets, and had actually screwed boards on to the floor between the stove and refrigerator and counters, so as to prevent the little cat-rats from wedging themselves into tight spaces and doing whatever it is that ferrets do. Even worse, it took a couple of weeks to rid the house of a vaguely musky odour. It wasn't quite the fresh sea-tang air of a Gullane morning.

Our second day back, Cathy came downstairs, down to my office, where I was unpacking a box of books. Grace was napping and Jessica was outside in the back yard. She sat down in a chair. 'We're really back, aren't we?'

I nodded.

She looked off, away from me, over to the wall. I followed her gaze. There were plaques, pictures, maps. One of the maps was an old map of the Firth of Forth. One of the pictures was a picture of my father.

'You'll need to write to Jack and Doris fairly soon,' she said. 'And Archie and Stan. Let them know we're back okay.'

We sat there for another fifteen minutes, not saying much, just trying to absorb the change, the shift in worlds. My mind drifted back to what David Dawson had said one April day as we'd been playing Gullane No. 2. It had been a glorious day, and the surf was charging on to Jovey's Neuk as we made our wayward path along the tricky gorgeous holes. 'Look at that,' he'd said, smiling as he did. I turned to look with him. We were atop the hill. To the west the Edinburgh skyline shone like a copper cutout, and the Forth bridges had taken on their normal brilliant late-afternoon skeletal clarity. The fescues and marram grass covering Nigel Tranter's dunescape below us were swaying and waffling amiably in the light breeze. Over our backs, the town itself was sitting nestled comfortably into the shoulder of the hill. The Elie cliffs on the Fife shore were etched in relief against the horizon to the north, and to our south the fields leading to the Lammermuir Hills were arranged so impeccably, were so green and verdant, they might have been a project of Louis XIV.

'I know,' I'd said to David. 'Amazing.'

'It is just *stunning*,' he'd reiterated, before turning a very focused gaze on me. 'You're just pulling our legs, aren't you?'

I half-frowned. 'How do you mean?'

'You're not leaving, are you?' He grinned. 'Just look at this.' He swept a hand in a circular motion, encompassing everything before him. He laughed. 'You're just having us all on, surely? You can't leave this. You'd be crazy to leave.' I joined in his laughter, though I didn't correct or contradict him.

The phone rang as Cathy and I were just about to leave my office and go upstairs. It was Cathy's mother, Marg. She wanted to know how we were set up for dinner, and whether we wanted to come over for a bite to eat, so that we wouldn't have to worry about it ourselves, as we were busy trying to unpack and get re-organised. Marg and Bob were happy to have us back, thrilled to have their only two grandchildren close by again. Jack had taken Cathy's parents out for a game during their visit in the spring, and, of course, they'd been taken with him. Jack felt the same way, and particularly appreciated a story I told him about Marg.

'Marg and I were having a discussion one day about suits and ties,' I'd told Jack, as Marg and Bob listened in, smiling. Jack was smiling, too, anticipating the chance to participate in a joint teasing. His ears were also no doubt tuned in because of the subject matter. He was an impeccable dresser, and had still never quite got over the fact that earlier in the year, when I'd required a blazer for one occasion or another, I'd had to borrow one from him. He just could not believe that a grown adult male wouldn't have at least a couple of suits pressed and waiting in case of emergency.

'Anyway,' I'd continued, as we all sat together in the Gullane Golf Club lounge, 'I finally said to Marg that I didn't like suits and ties primarily because of what they represent.'

Jack leaned forward, grinning.

'And Marg said, "What, you mean like a real job?"'

Jack broke into a spirited laughter, started coughing, and actually tipped some of his 80 Shilling on to his lap. He turned to Marg, and pointed a finger at her. 'Ho, ho! Wonderful. Oh, Marg, well done.' He'd then turned to me, and said, 'She got you there, boy!'

Later that night, I was unpacking from a variety of suitcases, and found the blazer Jack had given me. I had tried to return it before leaving, but he insisted that I take it ('It looks better on you than me, son'). Unfolding it and shaking it out to hang it, I saw a bulge in the pocket and realised I'd left my tie folded inside. As I pulled the tie out, a small piece of paper fell out along with it. It was an old bingo ticket of Jack's, probably from the 1960s (a sign of how old the blazer was), that I had already found hiding in a pocket earlier in the year at a friend's wedding. I had forgotten I'd put the ticket back. On the ticket was a little homily, which I read again. 'Egotism and mumps are very much alike except that the swelling shows in different places.'

I put the note back in the pocket, in a place where I might find it the next time I wore the blazer. I hung up the jacket, and stopped unpacking for the night.

Just the week after we got back there was a reunion at Daysland, Alberta, the provincial seat, as it were, of the Gillespie family. Daysland, a small but prosperous town with a new school and hospital, was where my great-grandfather had first settled after coming from Manitoba and Ontario. It was his grandfather, Dugald Gillespie, born in 1791, who left the island of Islay off Scotland's west coast to come to Canada in the early nineteenth century.

The drive down from Edmonton, about ninety minutes in length, had been a revelation. The prairie sky was monstrously large, and tiny pots of cloud drifted across the skyscape with such utter serenity, such elephantine ponderousness, that the world seemed to be a place of genuine ease and steadiness. There was a stillness to the prairie landscape that was so radically different from the landscape of East Lothian, where there seemed to be movement, always, at every level, in every direction; the sea, the wind, the tall waving fescues, the battalions of cloud. Even the geological cast of the glacier-scarred East Lothian landscape seemed to be in motion, roiling, rocking, moving in waves. We had left this land of constant motion and upheaval, and were now reuniting with my family in a land of vast space and vast silence, of equipoise. The prairie was beautiful, but it quickly began to feel static and untouchable, almost two-dimensional in its composition; a painting.

Cathy, Jess, Grace and I walked straight out of the stinging heat and light of a prairie midday sun into the cool, shaded space of the Daysland Community Hall.

'Curtis!' shouted my uncle Gordon, my father's oldest brother. 'Jesus, look at that! Hey, come on over here, look who's here.' He motioned for me to join a small gathering he was part of at the Welcome Desk just inside the hall. He introduced me to some people I'd never met, some Gillespies from California, distant relatives. 'This is Gus's oldest boy,' Gordon said to them, using the personal nickname for my father that he'd used all his life.

Smiles. Chit-chat. We eventually made our way out to the back lawn of the community hall, where they'd set up games for the kids, and where many more relatives had arranged themselves, beers in hand, in neat rows of deck chairs in the shade; the Gillespie parliament, I thought, laughing, looking forward to joining them. I saw my brother Keith, sister Janine, my mother. We hadn't seen any of them since Christmas, and when my mother saw us she rushed over and warmly acknowledged us, but picked up Jess and held on tight. Eventually, she had absorbed as much of Jessica as she could, and switched her focus and grip on to Grace, who allowed it for a few seconds before wriggling and squirming loose. My mother laughed and let Grace down, then turned to us.

'Welcome home,' she said.

$$ \lambda $$

The Face: Stillness

The last time I saw my father, he was no longer my father. He'd died in Edmonton, at the University Hospital, but the rest of my family had returned to Calgary the day after. And so it was left to me to go to the funeral home to legally identify the body and make arrangements for the cremation. Cathy came with me. My father had been dead two days, we'd been married five.

A junior mortician met us at the entrance, asked us to have a seat, then retreated. We sat, waited, held hands. After a couple of minutes, an older man came out, though he wasn't aged. He looked to be about forty-five, and the impression he gave above all others was of utter cleanliness. His face was antiseptically clear and his fingers were pink, long and nimble. We went into a small office, where he apologised, but suggested that we discuss certain administrative matters prior to identifying the body, since it was often hard to do so afterwards. I nodded, and we quickly settled on such things as finalising that a cremation was to be performed, what manner of container his remains were to be held in, and when we would be free to pick up those remains. There was a legal form to sign, but I couldn't sign that until I had identified the body. You'll be free, he said, to simply sign the form on your way out.

He stood up, indicating that the various pieces of business were done, and he asked me if I wanted to come with him. Cathy returned to the foyer. He led me down a short hallway lined with burgundy velour. There was a door at the end of the hallway. He stopped in front of it.

'You can take as long as you need,' he said softly. 'When you are ready, we'll just be out front, where you came in.'

He opened the door, and motioned for me to go inside. I did.

The smell hit me right away, the thin gassy needle-scent of formaldehyde; it wasn't offensive, just symbolic. It was what I had smelled on the mortician, mistaking it for obsessive hygiene. The room was small, brightly lit, but with muted colourings. It was so silent I could hear the wash of my pulse in my ears, the silence of being buried alive. There was a table like a long narrow desk in the centre of the room, a cover hanging down almost to the floor. My father was on top of the table, laid out flat on his back, another blanket laid over the top of him, up to his chest. The table was high, nearly up to my sternum. He was flat, pale. His cheeks were hollow. He looked incomplete laying there without his bifocals and a cigarette. He was wearing the clothes he'd no doubt been wearing the morning of his stroke, our wedding morning; a plain dress shirt, a brown wool cardigan. He'd have woken up that morning and got dressed thinking he would have to change later to attend his eldest son's wedding.

'Dad.'

I reached out and put a hand to his face, to his beard. I scratched his whiskers lightly. Then I bent over and kissed him, kissed a corpse, rubbed my cheek against his. I smiled, cried. Then I ran a palm across his forehead. It felt then as if all those years, all my thirty-one years, of not hugging and kissing him at every opportunity were such an utter foolish waste. What had I been thinking? Looking at him, or what used to be him, I offered a silent prayer to whatever force happened to be out there to make sure he knew how much I loved him, but perhaps even more importantly how much I *liked* him, how much I enjoyed his simple presence. I couldn't recall ever telling him that. How foolish it was to be standing in front of my father's corpse, unsure if he ever knew the full extent of my love and admiration. I was suddenly so angry with myself that I would have replaced him on that table if I could.

I put my palm back on his cold yellow forehead, ran a finger over his eyebrows, down the length of his nose, across his lips. And then, as I had when his life ran out from under my touch in the hospital, I laid my head across his sternum, left it for a moment, then raised my head and looked at his face, at his eyes, his mouth, his thin lips; I had to fight the urge to roll back his lips just to have one last look at his bad teeth and beautiful smile. *Just smile,* I thought. *Please, just once, then you can go back. I won't tell anyone. Just let me know you're okay.*

He said no with his silence.

Cathy couldn't bear to look directly at me when I came back through to the foyer, though she put her arm around my waist. I signed the form and we left the building together, newlyweds.

I went down to Calgary to visit my mother one weekend a couple of weeks after we'd returned to Canada. When I left to go back to Edmonton, I said goodbye to her and got in the car. I drove northeast along John Laurie Boulevard, the road that cuts across the northern top of the city, high up on the foothills. The massed ranks of modern housing glistened under the elemental Alberta sun, the light reflecting off the polished metallic exteriors and large sparkling windows. Looking down from the high north-western suburbs and the promontory of Nose Hill Park, every-thing cascaded south-easterly, the hills a topographical avalanche off the Rocky Mountains in the west, an avalanche which then slowed, softened and finally ran itself out on to the endless prairie. From this peak high above the bulk of the city, Calgary itself looked to be a kind of foam riding a rampant wave; houses and buildings flecks of spittle to be tossed frittering into insignificance towards the distant horizon in the east.

Having grown up in Calgary, I often used to walk to the top of Nose Hill Park, where I would stare out across the ancient lake bed that now cradled the city's downtown core. Oil and bank towers rose from the flats beside the Bow River like outsized reeds that once might have clustered along the edges of such a lake. The numerous skyscrapers were tall, slender, and accommodated tens of thousands of workers every day, but they remained insignificant under the Alberta sky: the clean blue of it was fundamentally ungraspable, was almost an organism in and of itself that dictated the pace and shade of life beneath. I had always loved the prairie sky; it made me feel small but central, attached to something, a tiny piece of machinery but one on which operations depended. And from high up on the hill, you could see over to Calgary International Airport: almost every day, hundreds of jet aircraft could be seen arriving and departing from that shelf of land in the north-east corner of the city. Sunny, dry and hot was a typical prairie summer day, with the high dome of the sky disturbed only by jet streams hung like laundry lines from one corner to the other. A jet stream could park itself in the atmosphere as if painted there; cottony vapour trails that would lead to Vancouver, Toronto, New York or Edinburgh if you could trace them to their point of origin or destination. The air was so dry, the sky so enormous, that a jet stream from a morning flight might remain visible until finally the light failed in the evening. Only then would the trail disappear from view. On dry, hot summer afternoons when I walked these hills as a child, it sometimes looked to me as if the earth's ceiling, our glazed sky, was also cross-hatched, crazed with cracks, ready to split open from the strain of holding in the world.

I eventually got on to Highway 2, heading north, home to Cathy and Jessica and Grace. Across the immense Alberta sky, a high layer of mixed cloud cover had advanced off the Rocky Mountains and was now over the foothills. From the flat land, looking west to where the stone horizon broke through the earth like a predator's jawbone, I could see five, eight, now ten platinum sun shafts, as clean as torch beams, groping through the elevated cloud, connecting heaven and earth. These shafts appeared, disappeared, silkily shapeshifted as the cloud cover boiled its way eastward. When I was a child, driving with my parents, I would ask my mother and father about those gauzy late-day columns of brilliant white light that appeared to originate on high, prying their way through openings in the cloud cover. 'Sunlight and clouds,' my father would say. 'That's all.' 'No,' my mother would say. 'Those are the souls of people leaving earth and going up to heaven to be with God. Those lights only go to graveyards.' I would stare and wonder how many souls could ride on a single shaft of light. Were they heavy? Or weightless? And did sun shafts truly touch down only at graveyards?

Why I thought it then I don't know, but it occurred to me as I drove north on the straight, wide, prairie highway that the only two things I had ever *created* in my life – my children and my writing – had never been witnessed by my father. I'd not published a word when he died, and had not let him or my mother read anything unpublished because I was too proud for them to see it, in case it wasn't any good (which was stupid and selfish of me). And it wasn't until three years after his death that Jessica was born. 'I wonder if I'll ever meet my other Grandpa,' Jessica had said to me one day in Gullane, 'the one that died before I was me?' 'I don't know,' I had answered then, deciding honesty was the best option. 'I hope you do. You would have liked him.'

The highway was not crowded and I let myself look for longer than I should have at the sun shafts, which had multiplied and taken on an alabaster translucence. They were everywhere, linking earth and heaven all across the long brown plains, over the foothills, all the way to the Rocky Mountains and certainly beyond that, too, to the coast, and the seas, and the lands beyond those seas.

Everywhere, it seemed, souls were on the move.

I arrived in Edmonton just before dinner, and later that night, after the girls were in bed and asleep, I went to the desk in my basement office in our house, feeling, I don't know why, a sense of urgency. It had been a hot day, but my office, with its lack of light and sub-earth level, stayed cool and dark. My desk lamp made me a tent of light as I opened the drawer and found the stationery I was looking for. I pulled it out, arranged it across my desk; two crisp, clean sheets of letter paper, and a matching envelope. The light was strong and clear, but the slightly creamy rinse of the paper's dye softened the glare and lent the pages an elegant air, as if they were two sheets of vellum, though they weren't. A blank page, a pen, and someone dear to write to; a gift. I put the nib on the page, smiled, even chuckled slightly, sensing the pleasure he would get opening his mail. I had much to say, much to tell him, but this and this alone – his pleasure – was reason enough to write, and would be for as long as that lasted.

Dear Jack, I wrote . . .

Acknowledgements

To Doris and Jack Marston, Sheila and Archie Baird, and Julie and Stan Owram I owe so much it's impossible to properly catalogue, so I won't try, except to say thank you, all.

For both seen and unseen contributions to this book, I am grateful to Anne McDermid, Andrew Gordon, John Pearce, Eddie Cobb and the Captain's Committee of Gullane Golf Club, Lucy and Robert O'Riordan, Carol and Liam Maguire, Michael Cox, Douglas Macrae, Audrey Paterson, Corinna and David Dawson, Philip Knowles, Mark Rigg, Tim Bowling, Lorne Rubenstein, Jim Dodson, Sheila Wharton, Tom and Margaret Brazier, and John, Sandra, Alexander and Jennifer Abate. I also want to acknowledge the many parents and families of Gullane Primary 1 who did so much to make our stay in Gullane so wonderful.

Thanks to the Gullane Library, the National Library in Edinburgh, and the Banff Centre for the Arts for information and conducive working environments. Thanks, also, to the various writers whose work I have quoted.

Finally, to Cathy, Jessica and Grace, love and admiration, always.

Detail from 1896
Ordnance Survey Map,
East Lothian